THE LOST BOYS

INSIDE FOOTBALL'S SLAVE TRADE

ED HAWKINS

D1514203

B L O O M S B U R Y

LONDON · OXFORD · NEW YORK · NEW DELHI · SYDNEY

Bloomsbury Sport
An imprint of Bloomsbury Publishing Plc

50 Bedford Square
London
WC1B 3DP
UK

1385 Broadway
New York
NY 10018
USA

www.bloomsbury.com

BLOOMSBURY and the Diana logo are trademarks of
Bloomsbury Publishing Plc

First published 2015
This paperback edition published 2016

British Library Cataloguing-in-Publication Data
A catalogue record for this book is available from the British Library.

Library of Congress Cataloguing-in-Publication data has been applied for.

ISBN: PB: 978-1-4729-1496-5
ePub: 978-1-4729-1495-8

2 4 6 8 10 9 7 5 3 1

Typeset in Adobe Garamond Pro by Deanta Global Publishing Services, Chennai,
India
Printed and bound in Great Britain by CPI Group (UK) Ltd,
Croydon CR0 4YY

MIX
Paper from
responsible sources
FSC® C020471

To find out more about our authors and books visit www.bloomsbury.com. Here
you will find extracts, author interviews, details of forthcoming
events and the option to sign up for our newsletters.

Some names have been changed for security reasons

Contents

Fifa Regulations for International Transfers Involving Minors

Article 19 Protection of Minors

1 International transfers of players are only permitted if they are over 18.

2 The following exceptions to this rule apply:

a) the player's parent moves to the country in which the new club is located for reasons not linked to football.

b) the transfer takes place within the territory of the European Union or European Economic Area and the player is aged between 16 and 18.

c) the player lives no further than 50 kilometres from a national border and the club with which the player wishes to be registered in the neighbouring association is also within 50 kilometres of that border. The maximum distance between the player's domicile and the club's headquarters shall be 100 kilometres. In such cases, the player must continue to live at home and the two associations concerned must give their explicit consent.

Introduction

With only a football shirt on their backs, boots in a bag and hope in their hearts, they come in their thousands. They are football's young dreamers. Inspired by the glamour of Europe's top leagues and cajoled by agents who tell them they can be the next big star, these children leave their families in Africa for the football pitches of France, Spain and England to make their fortune.

But the dream quickly becomes a nightmare. Instead of the metaphorical on-field battle for the likes of Paris Saint-Germain, Real Madrid or Chelsea, they are faced with a literal fight for survival. The challenge is not convincing the manager that they deserve to be in the starting XI, but to find somewhere to sleep, something to eat.

Unwittingly they have become football's dirty little secret. Victims of the sport's version of human trafficking: a slave trade which breaks up families, ships boys to foreign cities and abandons them. All for the pursuit of money.

It is a tale of tragedy and exploitation. In these pages you will read about football's trafficked kids. There's Sulley from Burkina Faso, who went to Portugal at 16 only for his agent to ditch him when he couldn't find him a club. Ben, also 16, paid an unscrupulous agent €3,000 to take him from Cameroon to Paris for trials at clubs. He was told to wait at a hotel. The agent never came back. Didier, another Cameroonian, was traded around the world as young as 13. Then there's Jay-Jay from Guinea. Poor, heartbroken Jay-Jay.

These are not one-off examples. The United Nations Commission on Human Rights released a report in 2009 warning that 'a modern "slave trade" is being created with young African players'. Foot Solidaire, a charity set up by the former Cameroon international Jean-Claude Mbvoumin to counter football trafficking, reported that there were 7,000 cases in France alone in nine years from 2005.

The trade is repeating one of the grimmest periods in human history. The plantation fields have been replaced by football fields. With the majority of boys being brought from Africa because they are considered to be cheaper, stronger, faster, more agile, they are paraded in front of predominantly white masters – managers, coaches, scouts – who pick the most suitable. If they are lucky, they are 'rewarded' with a salary and a place to stay. If they are not, they are cast into the void, ending up in drugs, prostitution and crime.

It is a tragedy on a mass scale and one that football has paid lip service to. In 2003, Sepp Blatter, the president of Fifa, football's governing body, laid the blame firmly at the feet of Europe's clubs. He said they were 'neo-colonialists who don't give a damn about heritage and culture but engage in social and economic rape by robbing the developing world of its best players'. He called the recruitment of children from Africa 'unhealthy if not despicable'. In an effort to curb it, Fifa introduced in 2003 Article 19, a law which made it illegal for players under the age of 18 to be transferred across international borders.

Six years later, in 2009, Fifa revealed that half a million players under the age of 18 were still being sold to clubs. 'It is our duty to the youth of the world to protect young players,' Blatter said. 'We must do it together. Stop the slavery of these young players!' These sentiments were echoed by Michel Platini, the president of Uefa,

European football's governing body, who wanted a complete ban on the transfer of minors.

The slave trade, however, has continued unabated. And each year more boys end up roaming the streets of London or Paris or Madrid. More money finds its way into the pockets of rogue agents. More tears are shed. This increasingly emotive issue has attracted more attention, particularly from those outside football.

At a conference on human trafficking in London in 2014, the Archbishop of Westminster, Cardinal Vincent Nichols, opined: 'There seems to be almost no enticement that isn't being used. They come in search of a dream, but of course don't find it.' He said more needed to be known about football trafficking.

The aim of this book is to do exactly that; to put together the jigsaw puzzle that is football's unedifying trade in kids. At the start, I had just a handful of pieces. There was the greedy football industry desperate for talent which could be turned into points on a Saturday afternoon or millions of pounds in the transfer market. Then there were the sorrowful faces of the victims and their stories. The two 'types' of trafficking that a young footballer could be tricked by were also revealed.

First, the agent who arranged a trial in Europe for the player, only to jettison him without a passport, money or any means to return home when the club was not interested. The second saw an agent ask families to raid their life savings so he could buy the player an airfare for trials with some of Europe's biggest clubs. As soon as the boy left the departure gate, the agent was not seen again.

I would later discover two vital pieces of the puzzle – just who was responsible for the scams and the methods they used.

The real devil would be found in the detail. How were agents and clubs circumnavigating Fifa's Article 19, which was supposed to protect children? How were passports and visas being acquired? How were immigration laws ignored? What was a 'slave contract'?

To find answers to such questions I had to go undercover, to go inside football's slave trade. I spoke to the scouts and agents who revealed exactly how they moved players from Africa to Europe, unwittingly revealing exactly why there were thousands of young boys kicking their heels, instead of a football, in Europe. I discovered why there were almost two football XIs of African hopefuls in a small town in Cyprus. And in the grim criminal underworld of Accra in Ghana, West Africa's footballing hotbed, I was able to negotiate to buy a child and the necessary documents to take him to Europe.

I sought to fathom the football and social culture in Africa, charting the rise of football academies funded by Europe's top clubs, and to understand why families would give up for adoption a child at the merest whiff of a career in football.

The clubs, too, were exposed. It is their insatiable desire for young talent that ensures there is a market for children. Some of football's grandest, and oldest, institutions, like Barcelona and Real Madrid, come under the spotlight. Qatar, the 'new money' in football, were also questioned about the movement of minors. Why was this country, newly obsessed with football, buying 13-year-olds from families and taking them to their academies? Were they using them to build a team for the tainted 2022 World Cup? English clubs were not immune. How had their negligence fuelled the trade? Fifa and its lawmakers, naturally, came under the scanner. Why had they failed to stamp out the problem, instead of effectively stamping passports? Why had they rejected a partnership with Foot Solidaire, football's anti-trafficking charity?

The search for the full picture took me to Paris, Geneva, Cyprus, Belgium, Ghana. And east London. I suffered threats and intimidation along the way. And when the jigsaw was almost complete, it was clear that not all was as it first seemed.

1

Jay-Jay

Somewhere in east London. It was one of the first Saturdays of the new football season; that time when hope is healthiest, no matter what your interest in the game. When every player, manager or supporter, at every level, reckons this could be their season. Through the bars on his kitchen window, Jay-Jay and I watched a couple of kids kick a ragged football around a small yard. They were both wearing new Chelsea shirts, pretending to be Diego Costa with his name on their back. 'Chelsea is my favourite team,' Jay-Jay said. The kettle clicked. The steam rose to the ceiling, a trail to mould and peeling paint. 'It is my dream to play for Chelsea . . . Do you know?'

I knew. I had heard this sort of dream before. So many times over the past two years that I had become blasé – a complacency that would, on this day, prove foolish. This isn't the start of the story. It is somewhere in the middle. The middle of an emotionally draining journey, one where at every stop another wide- and wet-eyed young boy poured out his heart. The agent said I would be a star. We gave him our family savings. He abandoned me. I cannot go home. And Jay-Jay was just another one. Another Lost Boy with a pleading look and tale of woe. Or so I thought.

In fact, Jay-Jay was horribly different. And that is why we start with him. His story was as chaotic and jumbled as the array of muddied football boots in his bleak hallway, as desperate and dark as the fist-wide crack down the loo wall. It had the stench of the drains outside his windows. It matched his forlorn, desperate air as he shimmied with a Nike football in his living room, absent-mindedly watching *Football Focus* on the television. Dreaming of Chelsea again? Or his family thousands of miles away in Guinea? Above all it is testimony to the extraordinary narcotic power of football, of what it can do to a boy and what he will do for just one chance at the big time.

Jay-Jay was trafficked from a village in the east of Guinea to London when he was 17. He was 20 when I met him. He was the only boy I had come across who had been moved to England. And that's about as straightforward as it got.

I was expecting it to be straightforward. Jay-Jay switched off the television and we sat on two faux leather sofas. We could hear the scuffs and thuds of the two Chelsea starlets kicking the ball outside. I began to ask the same reliable questions so to chart the passage from the conformity of home life to a personal hell in a foreign land.

Goals are usually the start of the problem. Too many of them. A passport, supposedly, to the riches of the European leagues. Jay-Jay had scored 'many, many goals for the school team'. His favourite was 'an acrobatic. I went feet over head,' he said. 'A scissor kick. When I was back home, I went to school and I played football. I loved to play football and my father encouraged me to play. My family and siblings loved it when I played. When my father saw me he said I had a talent and that I could progress. When I was back home, I started school when I was ten, but before that I learnt how to be a good Muslim.

'I was playing football for the school team and we played in tournaments against other schools from nearby villages and towns. I did this until I was 16 and I went to play for my village in the second division. They selected me and on my first selection

I scored five goals. Five! But my father was very scared for me – he said, "If you stay to play there you will get injured because they are very strong." They were strong men and I was a boy. I said, "OK." So I trained with them only to gain more experience and I still played for the school team.'

'Exactly how many goals did you score for the school team?'

'Too many goals to remember.'

Jay-Jay spoke with a wistfulness. He had a distant look in his eye befitting the chasm between happier times and his predicament in London. A smile occasionally cracked his face, but it was a sad one. He was, however, anxious to keep talking. To keep telling his story. 'I can tell you what happened next?

'I was playing for the school team again because my father was worried I would get hurt. He said it could be bad for me. We went to the school tournament. The tournament that all the schools play in the region and we won the cup and there was a big party. I was very happy.' He looked at me, as if to check that I understood, that I was still listening. I nodded. 'The village celebrated, a very big party with dancing and everyone was my friend. They shook my hand and said "well done" to me. The school had been in the tournament every year and this was the first win. Everyone was happy. The teachers were very happy.'

He paused and then said, 'This one guy saw me at the tournament and said I was a good player.'

'Enter the agent,' I thought. The rogue. The fake. I reckoned I could complete the story myself from there. It was a plot line I'd heard before. How much money would the agent charge? £1,000 or £2,000? And which clubs would be interested in signing him? Perhaps Chelsea needed Jay-Jay to play up front with Diego Costa? Or maybe Paris Saint-Germain were keen? And would Jay-Jay then be abandoned at the European airport he had flown to or the hotel where he had been told to rendezvous with the agent?

He kept talking, again every so often looking at me to make sure I understood. His English was limited but clear and he didn't search for his words. The only prompting required was for more detail.

'Just after the school tournament, I was training with the men's team. Every day we train, we train. This same guy saw me at the training camp and he said, "You're a good player. I will help you [and] give you the football kit, the football material . . . like the shoes, shorts." I said, "OK, no problem." I was playing bare feet. I had never had boots for football before.

'He was a white man. There are a lot of white people who work in the village because there are lots of companies. He gave me football material, the white man. They were Nike. Yes, Nike. Nike football shoes and shorts. I was a proper footballer, you know? I had never had those before. I don't have those Nike shoes any more.'

'What happened next?'

Jay-Jay did not look at me. He stared at the floor and he fidgeted with his hands. His speech became unclear, he couldn't find the words and there was a hush in his voice. There was one word in particular he seemed to be struggling with, beginning with an s. He could only make a 'sssssh' sound, like twisting the cap off a fizzy-drink bottle.

'Um, after a couple of months . . . the village, there is some kind of um, um, thing, coming in the village. I don't know how to say, rumour? There is something wrong. Gossip? They said, "We've heard something about you and this guy, it's not like . . . it's not like football, he do some kind of thing with you." Sssssh . . . ssssssh . . . I don't say . . . you know? I don't, er, want to say.'

I had been on autopilot up until that point. Jay-Jay looked terrified. He had begun to pull angrily at the flesh between thumb and forefinger. To fill the uncomfortable silence, I asked him: 'What is this word you are trying to say? Beginning with an s?'

'It's like, er, the sssssssh,' he took a deep breath, 'the sex . . . thing.'

My mind had scrambled. He carried on talking.

'Yeah. And I said, "No. Noooo." But they say that to me. This village, their family, and they are saying this and if he do this, "You're a Muslim and we must kill you if that is true." And I say, "No, it's not true." But nobody I can trust. They saw me sometime with this guy, pick me up and we go, take me to my house together. And they see the football kits. These rumours are coming in the village. This thing . . . sh . . . sh . . . sex thing. Nobody want to see me, nobody like me because they think I am like that.'

Then he looked up with pleading eyes. It was not a typical football-trafficking case. Not part of the script. Not straight-forward. Those boys had stopped playing outside. Was Jay-Jay trying to tell me he had been sexually abused? Should I ask him? What was this threat of death about? We had both fallen silent again, looking at each other. He was still fidgeting. In my head I was trying to order the words to ask him. How the hell do you ask a kid something like that?

'Jay-Jay, are you telling me you were . . . sexually abused?'

'Yes. That is the thing,' he said with relief. 'I don't like to say. It makes me feel bad.'

He waited for me to ask another question. I didn't have one. Jesus. I was just a sports writer. I was ready to talk about childhood dreams of football stardom, to offer sympathy about being scammed by an agent, wondering what it was like to miss family members. Jay-Jay filled the silence, emboldened. A weight had been lifted. He began to tell his story again. We pieced it together. We both stumbled over the right words, stuttered and shared silences. There was no chronological coherence to our conver-sation. We flitted back and forth in time. And it was about to get a whole lot worse.

'They want to hurt me, to kill me. Because I do these things. I don't do things like that. Nobody want to touch me or play with me. I was not allowed to play football. My sister told me that I should go to the police. The police do not investigate. They don't want to help me. My family slap me and punch me. My father was there. My father has a big family. They were beating me because they believe these rumours. I didn't go to school, I didn't play football. I stayed at home crying, crying, crying.'

'What do you mean they wanted to kill you? Who?'

'My father's family. They said things I did were bad. I am Muslim. I had done bad things for the village. They made the threats to kill me for what I did.'

'So because of these rumours they threatened to kill you?'

'Yes. I don't want any problem for me in the village. The guy took me away from the village and to the city. I told him about them killing me. He said, "Come with me." He said we would go and I would play football. He said he could take me to Europe to play for a big club, he said I was very good player. And I didn't know we were going to come here [London]. We went to capital city of Guinea [Conakry]. For me I was very scared about people from the village coming to find me, so I went. I thought it was best for me.'

'So the man said that he would take you to Europe to find a football club?'

'Yes. I thought I was going to play football in Europe. And if they saw me with him they would kill me. I was frightened of the man. He took me to a big house in the city and we stayed for a month. Then he took me to another place. He took my picture and my name and my family name for a passport, and after that he said we will travel somewhere and I said, "Where?" and he said, "Somewhere." Then he took me to the airport and we got on an airplane.'

'Was it a Guinea passport?'

'I don't know which passport it was. He spoke French. It may have been a French passport.'

'What was the house like?'

'The house was very big, he was very rich. I just stayed there crying, crying. He gave me food. I was not the only person there. There was a driver for him. Driver of the car. That was it. After that we went to the airplane. I asked him, "Where do we go?" He said, "Come on, we have to leave because you have a problem with your family and they say things about you and me. Cannot leave you here." But he never said where we go. We took the airplane.'

'Where did you go?'

'When we got there it was dark. I didn't know which country. He didn't tell me but it was very cold.'

'So you got on a plane in Guinea and you didn't know where you were going?'

'Yes.'

'It was a long flight?'

'Yes, it was a long flight. The flight stopped somewhere. And we took many hours there. And I was staying there sleeping, sleeping, on a b . . . bench? A bench, yes. I spent many hours. I think it was maybe a ten-hour wait. And then we got on another plane. And we came here. It was very, very cold. Oh, so cold. I was very, very cold and, er . . .'

'Was it winter?'

'I don't know but it was very, very cold. It was time for cold. After that he took me to some place, it was a big, nice house. Big, nice. But after like a couple, a few days, he start to say something to me, you know, he have er . . . he say . . . this is a rich house and there is some guys coming here and they are my friends, they want to do, I don't like to say . . . I think he say three guys or four guys, they want to do the thing that people in my village say, the sexual with me.'

I asked whether the Frenchman had taken him to a house in London so men could have sex with him.

'Yes. And for me, I don't know if it was London. After the plane we travel a long way again. I don't know if it was Gatwick or Heathrow. That day we travel by train and then by car.'

Jay-Jay reverted to a whisper. He looked at the floor and nervously pulled at his hands. Was he scared?

'I was very scared. I spent two weeks there. I never left the house. After he said to me his friends were coming I was very scared. I said, "No. The village tried to kill me, to do these things . . . I don't know how to do any of these things." I was just crying . . . after that the guys were coming. It was a big room, a living room like that, sofa and chairs like that. He take me into the room. The guys were there. I was very quiet. They didn't touch me. The guy was very nervous, was very nervous because he say something to me, he was pushing me and, er, shouting at me. He was speaking, you know, the language like that.'

'Shouting?'

'Yes! Shouting. Very quickly. It was English. He do something like that. Before that, he was giving me the good food but after that he stopped. He didn't give me nice food. I had chicken and rice but after that not good food for me. I stayed there a week, I didn't eat properly. He said I have to go because this house is for the people who can do the sexual with the guy. That is what the house is for. He said he would take me to another place.'

'Were there other boys in this house?'

'Just me. And him and his friends who come with him.'

'How many friends?'

'Four.'

'And they wanted to have sex with you?'

'Yes.'

'But they didn't touch you?'

'But when they show me that I'm crying the guy says, "No."'

'Did he stop feeding you completely? Just bread and water?'

'Yeah. The food when it come wasn't good food.'

'What happened next?'

'He took me again, long travel. Got on a train. He called someone and in a few minutes I saw a car come, I saw him write something to give to the driver, and the driver took me to go to the other house where I can go and explain my situation. I don't know where I go, I didn't speak English. I only study English when I am here. I am tired and hungry. I need to eat and it was very cold! The driver left me somewhere with the paper. And I saw the house where I should go. And I went there. They saw me and they asked me what my name was. Where I was from. I told them in French. They took me somewhere to sit. They asked me questions in French.

'I stayed there one day and after that I went to another house and they ask me how did I get there? What happened to me? And I explain to them. They give me someone who can help me. I said, "OK." They give me the food. Good people. They look after me.

'I tell them I want to play football. They say they can help me play football. They give me training boots. They were nice people. They will look after me. They ask me how I get there. And they interview me about that house. They understand my situation. They give me a key worker and a social worker . . .'

Jay-Jay stopped. Then he said, 'I didn't give the man any money. His name was Marcel.'

'Did Marcel work for a company in your village?'

'I don't know, but he was something to do with them. Where he was living there in the village it was a very big and expensive house. I didn't give any money to Marcel.'

'Did he do it to other boys?'

'He told me he didn't do other boys, but he told me he liked boys like me, for him. If he go for other boys he likes young people, similar, yeah. He said he liked the boy like me.'

'Did he take other boys from Guinea?'

'Just me I think.'

'What did he look like?'

'He was tall, big, strong. For me I can't describe hair colour . . . like brown, darker than your hair. Long hair. He wore big sunglasses.'

'He never abused you in England?'

'But when I was back home he tried to make me touch him. But he tried this before when the rumour come in the village. Yeah, I was very scared. He said, "No, don't be scared. I'll give you some kind of thing . . . liq, liquid?"'

'Alcohol?'

I had been willing Jay-Jay to say yes. Alcohol would have been a blessing. But of course it wasn't alcohol. And I knew it wasn't going to be. Jay-Jay's story was sickening and graphic.

'No. Like some sort of thing I can put for my hand, to touch him. Lotion. "Don't be scared," he said. But do you know the first time he taught me that I didn't tell anybody. Just my friend who I knew in the village. I told him I was very scared, and this guy taught me to touch him. I was very scared. I told my friend. For me the goss . . . goss . . . gossip? How you say? I think it came from him. I didn't tell anyone, not my family. I told my family the guy gave me football kit and they were happy. But when they asked about the rumour coming they said that he had given me these things for the sexual. When he took me away he said he would help me get away from my family because they wanted to kill me, and he said I was a good player and he would help me to play.'

So now you've met Jay-Jay. How do you feel? Sick to the stomach and shaken to the core? That's how I felt. His story was not straightforward at all. If only it had been. He had been sexually abused and suffered death threats from his own family. Then he had been sex-trafficked to London by his abuser who, having promised him a football career, offered him to homosexual men. He was let go when he refused and offered asylum in the UK on the grounds that if he returned home he would be murdered.

Jay-Jay had not seen or heard from his family since arriving in England. He received £45 a week in benefits. He studied information technology at a local college and worked part-time in a charity shop. He shared a two-bedroom, ground-floor flat in east London. 'I have my own bedroom.' He wanted to stress that. He shopped at the 24-hour supermarket around the corner. He ate pasta every day. He had saved his money to pay for football trials and had been tested at Cambridge United and Brentford.

'Will you help me get a trial with a club?' he asked.

'Absolutely,' I said.

I wanted to help Jay-Jay. Who wouldn't? So this will not be the last time you hear from him. It was through the prism of his story that I would view the world of football at its exploitative worst.

2

Foot Solidaire

The wind had been surprisingly chilly for a spring night in Geneva. I hunched my shoulders, looked at my watch and cursed Jean-Claude Mbvoumin. There had been no sound or sight of him for hours. 'He should have been here by now,' I grumbled, eliciting an odd look from an elderly couple on a stroll. Surely he would show up this time?

I had been in the same situation the previous winter. Hunched, clock-watching, cursing. The venue was the Gare du Nord in Paris. Jean-Claude had invited me so he could explain more about the growing problem of football trafficking and what his organisation, Foot Solidaire, was doing to combat it. Since early 2000 Foot Solidaire had supposedly been at the fore-front of the fight against football trafficking. They knew everything. They had made contact with thousands of boys who had been victims. Jean-Claude had appeared in numerous articles in magazines and newspapers across Europe. He had spoken about the problem for a BBC documentary. He had engaged with politicians and football administrators. He had travelled the world. A meeting with Jean-Claude was the obvious starting point for me.

When in Paris I had sent copious text messages asking where he was. I called and called. No answer. Eventually a woman answered. She said she thought he might be in Paris but couldn't be sure. 'He is supposed to be meeting me!' I said. 'I discussed this with him yesterday.' There was no sympathy. 'Well, obviously he has left his phone here so I don't know how you're going to contact him.'

I was not entirely surprised. A contact who had met him suggested he was unreliable and disorganised. Jean-Claude and I had tried to meet in London previously but he had failed to respond to messages.

I roamed Paris for a few hours, had a steak dinner and called my contact. 'Who is this guy? What's his problem?'

'You know something?' he said. 'That's really weird. When I tried to meet him the first time I had the exact same thing happen. No show at the Gare du Nord, unanswered calls and then a woman picking up and saying he'd left his phone behind.'

If Jean-Claude's inability to keep an appointment had any bearing on the success of Foot Solidaire, it was not difficult to understand why it had drifted in and out of existence since its inception. There had been a Paris office at the beginning but that had been shut down. Jean-Claude worked from home. Foot Solidaire then moved to Lausanne, Switzerland. Roger Milla, the former Cameroon striker and star of the 1990 World Cup, had been a 'roving ambassador'. He hadn't roved for some time. Foot Solidaire had survived on handouts and partnerships. When it had money it was active. When that ran out, it wasn't. The African Union and France's national Olympic committee had supported the charity in the past. So too had Fifa. In 2008 the two combined to contribute to the International Conference on Young African Footballers, which focused on the protection of underage footballers. Sepp Blatter, president of Fifa, proudly announced that Foot Solidaire would receive 'full support' from football's governing body. The Fifa website still claims that Foot Solidaire is 'backed' by the world governing body.

But on the eve of the World Cup in South Africa, Foot Solidaire said Fifa broke its promise. In a letter to Blatter, Jean-Claude wrote: 'Since August 2009 Fifa has not followed this up, arguing budgetary constraints and delaying its response until December when it finally abandoned the project. If this campaign is not instituted we fear that after the 2010 World Cup the trafficking of young minors will not only be a long-term feature of the African sporting landscape but indeed it will become worse: it will be institutionalised.'

Foot Solidaire, however, did not have an unblemished record in maintaining agreements either. In 2013 it signed a deal with the International Centre for Sport and Security (ICSS). The ICSS was a sort of self-proclaimed police force for world sport, funded by the Qatari royal family. Its aim was to be a one-stop shop for all manner of sporting security and corruption, from stadium safety to match-fixing and, of course, trafficking of minors. Foot Solidaire was to provide vital information to ICSS investigators to enable them to go out in the field and track down the traffickers. Foot Solidaire was able to provide, in some cases, the names, telephone numbers and email addresses of rogue agents and scouts because they had hundreds and hundreds of testimonies from trafficked boys. The ICSS received little.

The partnership had started well. Jean-Claude had written to the ICSS in one of his first communications suggesting they conduct 'sting' investigations to root out offenders. He also provided a neat summary of the problems which needed to be solved to rid football of the scourge: 'Rogue agents produce false clubs' invitations and request the payment of fees for visas,' he wrote.

The most affected countries we know are Cameroon, Senegal, Nigeria, Ivory Coast and Ghana. It is organised into networks.

What's needed is to trap these people, asking, for example, to meet them or pretending to be a young player's parent.

We may not entirely trust [African] FA officials. Many of them are involved in most of the drifts (issuing false international transfer letters and sometimes false player passports, confiscation of Fifa training compensation due to small academies, falsification of ages and identities of young players). Several officials . . . are owners or shareholders of academies, [a] conflict of interest causing widespread abuses. In addition, FA officials, pretending they are independent from public authorities – which themselves do tend to take control of the football business – are rarely concerned with issues related to the recruitment of young players.

It's a taboo subject, and anyone who mentions the trafficking of young players is seen as an enemy. That is the reality. In African FAs, corruption is still present at all levels, particularly in countries whose teams regularly participate in the World Cup. Serious levels of mismanagement, conflict of interest, abuse of power, negligence, financial irregularities and possible criminal activity are daily recorded. But always impunity under the umbrella of Fifa, in the name of Fifa. These people [are] never worried, they also have political support at the highest level.

Only an independent entity could alert all stakeholders via information and awareness directly towards young players, academies and families, but also police forces when necessary.

Combating rogue agents and trafficking in Africa means clearly going against some FA's officials. This is how they'll see it. But it must be done.

It was good stuff. It was odd, though, given his knowledgeable and impassioned summary that nothing came of the agreement with ICSS. Jake Marsh, their head of youth protection, had been tasked with liaising with Jean-Claude, but rarely did he reply to emails or phone calls. 'I never heard back from him,' said Marsh.

Perhaps Jean-Claude wanted to concentrate on bigger suitors. The United Nations had thrown its might behind Foot Solidaire in 2014 and the organisation had been rejuvenated. It was 'back from the brink' again. Jean-Claude had organised 'The Right Paths to Integration and Success for Young African Athletes', a conference to be held on Young African Footballer Day at the UN. It was backed by names and organisations which were meant to impress: Wilfried Lemke, special adviser to the UN secretary-general on sport; Thorbjørn Jagland, general secretary of the Council of Europe; the Permanent Mission of Italy to the UN; the African Union Permanent Delegation; and the International Organisation for Migration.

There had also been plans to stage a charity match. Jean-Claude had hoped that Samuel Eto'o, George Weah, Yaya Touré and even Roger Milla, reprising that 'roving' role, would lace up. But that idea was shelved. Jean-Claude had asked the ICSS for $25,000 to sponsor the game. They said no. Still, Eto'o, Weah, Yaya and Milla were 'expected to participate' according to the invitation. I was in Geneva, not hopeful of a glimpse of those footballing stars but of the elusive Jean-Claude Mbvoumin.

At least on this occasion I had managed to speak to him. 'I will call you back in five minutes,' he said. He did not. 'I will be there in two hours.' He wasn't. Then he ignored my calls. I called on the hotel phone so he wouldn't notice the number. He picked up straight away. 'Yes, yes I am coming. Sorry, sorry.'

Jean-Claude arrived by car, early evening. There was a young African boy with him and a man in his fifties who introduced himself as Mathieu. Jean-Claude shook my hand, and apologised profusely. His eyes darted left and right. He had a lean face and a distinct, chiselled jaw-line, which made his mouth and nose protrude as if he was always craning forward. He had a keen look about him. 'This is Amane,' he said, pointing to the African boy as we walked back into the lobby, 'we must do our interview now, yes? I am sorry. I am very busy but we will sit down and talk, I promise, I promise. But first . . .'

He turned on his heels and beckoned me, Amane and Mathieu back outside. He wanted help carrying boxes of leaflets and books for the conference. As we were unloading the car, a Japanese boy got out of a taxi. 'Jean-Claude?' he said. He looked about 18 or 19, greener than the hillsides of Lake Geneva, and pissed off. Jean-Claude was supposed to have collected him from the airport. Jean-Claude and the Japanese boy spoke in French. Amane appeared to know him and gave him a welcoming pat on the shoulder, which seemed to appease the new arrival. Jean-Claude, Amane and the Japanese boy went to check in at the hotel. It was called the Hotel Century, part of the Best Western chain. It was not the Hotel President Wilson. Remember that. It is important. The Japanese boy was called Shinji. That's important, too. He and Amane went up to their room on the other side of the hotel.

I sat down with Jean-Claude in the lobby to begin the interview. He then said he had to go back to the airport because he had forgotten someone. 'Was it Shinji?' A snide dig. He didn't understand what I said. He said he would be back in half an hour and I should wait.

Mathieu, who was originally from Cape Verde but lived in Paris, sat with me. He told me about Amane. He had come from Ivory Coast when he was 16. He made the trip by road to Morocco and then took a perilous passage on a migrant boat to Spain. 'These kids, they risk their lives and for what? Why don't they stay where they are and make the best of it? They work so hard in Europe. I have seen kids work so hard. But they are not prepared to do that in their own country.'

'So Foot Solidaire is helping Amane?' I asked.

'The French,' he said, waving his hand dismissively, 'they are taking care of him now. Place to live, you know. I'm just a volunteer . . . we're all just volunteers.'

An hour later than he said, Jean-Claude returned. He booked more people into the hotel. One was from a film crew. He took them up to their room, telling me he would be back in five minutes. Mathieu went with him. I didn't see Jean-Claude again until 1 a.m. 'It is getting late now . . . we can do it at seven tomorrow,' he said. We did. But we spoke for only eight minutes before he had to go, telling me to travel to the conference with Mathieu, Amane and Shinji.

Amane was a scamp. He had a constant smile on his face and was beside himself at the prospect of visiting the UN. He found it hilarious that I could not speak French. Shinji, whose English was average, tried to act as interpreter and each still-born conversation was greeted with a snigger and wide grin from Amane. When we arrived at the UN, Amane managed to speak the few English words he knew. 'You get me club? In England?' He raised his eyebrows as if to suggest that it should be a formality. Shinji gave him a jokey rebuke. 'He is writer. For magazine. Not football,' he laughed, revealing a crooked, gummy smile. Amane sniggered again and thrust his hands into his pockets. Amane was to be the star of the show that day. He courted media attention and conducted scores of interviews for press and television. They loved the cheeky chap from Mali. He was wearing a brand new Atlético Madrid shirt. It still had that 'fresh out the packet' sheen. His hair had been neatly sculpted into a mohawk. He was bright eyed and bushy-topped. Amane was Foot Solidaire's poster boy.

Shinji, who was 20, was a mystery. He wasn't a footballer. At least he said he wasn't, if he understood my question correctly. Communication was difficult but he seemed to say that he was a football student. I took this to mean he was studying sports science, or somesuch, at a French university. He was a Japanese cliché: meek and mild and unnecessarily polite. He was always bowing and scraping. He never spoke unless someone spoke to him. And that wasn't very often as everyone else, apart from Amane, in the Foot Solidaire entourage seemed to ignore him.

There were passes for Yaya Touré and Samuel Eto'o at 'Pregny Gate, Access Door 17' but not for me, Amane or Shinji. Touré and Eto'o would not be attending after all. We had to go through security, fill out forms and then have each of them stamped by an official who looked like he could make life uncomfortable if he didn't like what he saw. This was the UN, after all.

Amane needed help filling in his form. He strained his neck to look at mine, as if he were trying to cheat at an exam. Shinji became increasingly anxious. He had left his passport in the car and his bottom lip looked as though it was about to wobble. But he didn't speak up. I had to ask what was wrong and then take him to Mathieu and explain for him.

I sat between Amane and Shinji in the conference hall. It was a grand affair. The orators were raised on a stage, they puffed out their chests and lifted their noses in importance as the throng below waited for their wisdom. They were flanked by the ubiquitous blue flags of the UN. Amane was like a schoolboy in assembly, unable to sit still or listen. His English was almost non-existent but he was able to lampoon William Swing, the director general of the International Organisation for Migration. 'Willy swing!' he laughed, poking me in the ribs. Swing, in the gravelly American tone you might hear in a movie trailer, had been reminding everyone how a migrant boat had recently sunk off the coast of Italy leading to a great loss of life. The timing of Amane's joke was off. It would prove to be a rather crass afternoon. My investigation would begin with confusion and contradiction after contradiction. Little did I know at that point that it would set the tone for the whole story.

Jean-Claude had invited the chief executive officer of ICSS Europe, Emanuel Macedo de Medeiros, to speak. Given that Foot Solidare had failed to provide the information the ICSS required, and they in turn had refused to sponsor Jean-Claude's match, there appeared to be little credibility to Medeiros's appearance.

Jérôme Champagne, at one point a candidate for the Fifa presidency race in 2015, corrected Jean-Claude, who had spoken about corruption within African football associations. 'I rebel against this caricature that the African federations are very badly organised,' Champagne said, ever the politician. It would not have been a vote winner to have agreed with Jean-Claude but it was surprising to hear him disagree with a man whose specialist subject was football trafficking. Such hubris was a caricature, surely, of the man he once hoped to displace, Sepp Blatter.

Most crashing of all was the presence of officials from Benfica FC and the Aspire Academy in Qatar. Gonzalo Gomes boasted how the Portuguese club had 1,600 participants in four grass-roots programmes in Angola, three in Cape Verde, and 11 in Mozambique. There was also an academy in Guinea-Bissau. 'Eusébio came to us from Mozambique,' he triumphed, before reeling off a long list of names they had also 'inherited' from Africa. Perhaps I had missed the point of the conference but it seemed to be sending a mixed message. 'We want to reduce the amount of boys leaving Africa to go to Europe, but if they're good enough, hey, let the big clubs trade them.'

In Benfica's case, just like every other club on the planet, their aim was the pursuit of talent for financial gain. They wanted to find stars and then sell them or improve their team's chances of winning trophies. And therefore make money. Money was the root of the problem in all of this, surely? So they should not have been there.

It may have been only the start of my journey but at least I knew that European clubs coveted the African footballer: he was faster and stronger and cheaper. Everyone knew that. The Bosman ruling in 1995, which had allowed out of contract players to move clubs for no fee, had given clubs free rein to target players from the continent. This was the source of the problem. In 1997, for example, there were only five players in England's Premier League qualified to play for African countries. By the 2014–15 season there were 39. Since 1997, 177 had appeared. There had been a sharp rise across Europe of the import of Africans after Bosman. There were fewer than 200 playing on the continent before 2011 but in the next two years 625 more were signed on professional contracts.

And what of the Aspire Academy? In 2008 Jean-Claude had compared their operation to 'modern-day slavery'. Aspire had targeted 13-year-olds in Africa from as early as 2007, hoping to turn them into professionals. It was part of their mission statement on their website. Bora Milutinović, who worked as an ambassador for Aspire, had subscribed wholeheartedly to the confusion that afternoon. Milutinović said Aspire's objective was to 'give opportunities to young players from developing countries to reach the heights of international football'. It was something of a fall from grace for Milutinović who, with Carlos Alberto Parreira, was one of only two men to have coached five different teams at the World Cup. He spoke with the bluntness one would expect from such an experienced manager. 'From 2007 to 2013 3.7 million children have been screened!' Screened was the term Aspire liked to use to describe the process of talent scouting in Africa, Asia and South America before selecting the best and taking them to Doha or Senegal to groom them for careers in the game.

Then there was Shinji, who sat dutifully, quietly through the whole charade, listening intently to the translations through his headphones. At the end of the conference, when Jean-Claude was having his picture taken by the UN flag and the rest of speakers were congratulating one another, Shinji stood alone. He was anxious again, waiting for something to happen. 'The game?' he said to me. At first I was unsure what he meant, then he showed me his boots. He thought he would be playing in the charity match that Jean-Claude had abandoned. With Eto'o and Touré.

'There's no game,' I told him, almost incredulously. 'No. No. No. Finished. All talk. No football.' He sighed and sank his chin into his chest.

Jean-Claude, Shinji, Amane, Mathieu and other Foot Solidaire volunteers headed off into the Geneva night to celebrate their success at a restaurant. Jean-Claude had escaped again. I should have been perplexed. But there was clarity. A bunch of suits in a conference room were rarely capable of revealing what lurked under the fingernails of grubby hands. You had to examine them yourself. Jean-Claude wouldn't talk to me, but he had given me an idea. All I needed to put it into practice was a little knowledge on how and why footballers were being duped by the traffickers.

3

Anatomy of a Con

Jake Marsh had a dream once. Then he woke up. At the age of 14 he was on the books of Southend United. In the club canteen he ate lunch alongside Stan Collymore. For his school, Brentwood, he played in midfield with Frank Lampard. Up front was Neil Harris, who would score 156 career goals, the majority for Millwall. 'When I played with those guys,' he said, 'I knew I wasn't going to be good enough.'

Instead Marsh became an investigator, specialising in fraud and sport. He worked for Quest, a private investigations company owned by Lord Stevens, and was part of the team that conducted the inquiry into the Premier League transfer bung scandal – 'you can call it bungs, I can't' – the Formula One race-fixing case in Singapore and an investigation into doping by the German showjumping team at the Beijing Olympics. Now he is the head of youth protection for the International Centre for Sport and Security (ICSS). His job is to help safeguard vulnerable young footballers. 'I was one once,' he said. 'When I wanted to be a foot-baller, at age 13 or 14, had I got an email from an agent saying, "I can get you a trial at Arsenal or wherever," I'm not sure how I would've reacted. Would I have fallen for it?'

He was talking about a scam which, to most people, would have so obviously appeared to be fraud that they would not have given it a second thought. It was not one of the two types of football trafficking, although it was inspired by it. Just like a young player might give money to an agent, who would then take them to a trial abroad only to abandon them when they failed, or pay an agent for a trial abroad, travel and then never hear from them again, the hoax relied on broken or false promises. It was important to understand its anatomy because it gave clues to how footballers could be exposed to genuine football trafficking and end up abandoned in a foreign city. It was crude but it showed succinctly how desperate young boys were to become stars in Europe.

'It all starts with an email to a player,' Marsh said. 'That player, typically, is in Africa but it could be Spain, Portugal or South America. It says, "You're a great player, we've got these four big clubs in Europe and they want to sign you, but first you need to fill in these forms and send some money so we can get your application up and running."

'You and me, we're thinking about those emails that go round about winning the Nigerian lottery. But kids don't think about that. They want it so badly that they fall for it. I've known kids hand over up to €3,000. To get to that point is quite detailed. There are email exchanges between agents and players of up to 50 or 60 threads. The scammers are probably talking to another 20 at the same time. They keep going and going, they hammer away. It's not just one email. Think about it. It's a 14-year-old on the other end, probably quite intimidated, naïve and unfortunately it appeals to their wishes and dreams in the sense they've finally got the break they're looking for.'

In three years, Marsh had learnt the tricks of an unscrupulous trade. The lengths that the scammers, and those who had been scammed, would go to was extraordinary. There was the bank account set up in Stratford, east London, using the name

Liverpool Football Club, which enticed thousands of pounds out of kids. 'I heard about how, in one village in Africa, a family sold one of the younger kids to raise the money so the eldest could go on one of these trials. They would buy him back later when he [the elder brother] became a big star.' Then there was the youngster who travelled to Manchester City's training ground from Australia, wrongly believing an agent had used his money to get him a trial. 'He turned up and said, "I'm here for my trial." "Sorry, we've never heard of you." He'd handed over a few grand. He was distraught. But he was lucky. City took pity on him, looked after him and put him on a flight home. Others aren't so lucky.'

The scam was simple. The email addresses of the hopefuls were found using Facebook or YouTube, where kids, according to Marsh, 'upload videos of themselves training every day'. There had also been a surge in attempts to defraud footballers on a website called Fieldoo, a football social media site. It offered the chance for footballers, agents and scouts to connect. Players could message agents asking for a trial, send videos and their CVs. It was a sort of football 'dating' site. Almost 150,000 registered users paid for membership costing as little as €9.99 a month.

It was while investigating how Fieldoo had been corrupted that Marsh discovered that the real names of agents were being used to trick players. It was identity theft. The scammers had simply used Fifa's website to find licensed agents, where hundreds were listed per country, some with addresses, telephone numbers and email addresses. One of the names used was Cyrille Regis, the former England striker.

Money was requested, ranging from €300–€1,000, for medical insurance, registration fees, passports and visas. 'Impossible for someone else to get a visa,' Marsh said. 'You have to apply in person or through a company which will need you to sign forms in person and provide a passport.'

The fraudsters were able to collect the money because of a flaw in the UK banking system. The payee name and account name on money transfers did not have to match, which enabled 'agents' to use names such as Liverpool FC and convince their targets everything was legitimate.

'You or I could do it in half an hour, here and now,' Marsh said. 'It's so simple. These people might have 30 or 40 kids on the go. They would only need four or five, paying €300 each, to come off to make big money.'

The email addresses had been traced to Lagos, Nigeria and the Ukraine. Fieldoo, which had passed information on to Fifa, claimed to have developed an algorithm to block suspected fraudsters. They also said that their website offered advice to players and agents in an effort to prevent the scam. However, articles in their 'magazine' section made no mention that users should not hand over money, and if they wanted to check whether an agent was legitimate, then they should simply look on Fifa's website.

'Unfortunately there's no one who can do anything about it,' Marsh said. 'A Premier League club came to us and said, "Can you do something with this?" They had a whole file of cases. They were getting almost one a week telephoning or emailing them. We've spoken to clubs and federations, the Spanish, the English, the Dutch, among others to say, "Look this scam could happen to your players, please let them know."' At the time of writing the English FA had failed to pass on an official warning to clubs.

Disturbingly, Marsh believed that some of the scams originated from within football. 'Compared to other online scams where you used to get someone saying "you've won ten million dollars" these are sophisticated. The English is very good, there are fake contracts which are 15 pages long, medical forms, visa registration forms, which I know aren't real, but not everyone is going to know that. So the level of detail suggests they've either got contacts in the football industry or they've been operating frauds in the football industry at the same time. It's just too much of coincidence.'

Joseph Kaltim wrote:

My very pleasure to write to this management, am a player from Nigeria. Please sir, I want to achieve my dreams, I want you to help me with my career by being my manager, I promise to give you my best. I look forward to hear from you sir.

Daniel Klog: hello, player . . .

Joseph Kaltim: Please sir be my agent

Daniel Klog: Thanks for your message i want you to know that i have read your CV and i like it and i want you to know that i will Forward your CV to the List of the Club Below:

1. Arsenal Fc (England)
2. Liverpool Fc Club (England)
3. Chelsea Fc (England)
4. Barnsley Fc (England)
5. South end Fc (England)
6. Manchester City Fc (England)
7. Reading Fc (England)
8. Queen park rangers Fc (England)

Joseph Kaltim: So what will I do sir?

Daniel Klog: SEND YOUR CV AND PASSPORT

Joseph Kaltim: Hello sir, hope you received it

Daniel Klog: I got your message. I am sorry for my late response. I just got back from the meeting with the listed club sponsors and after reviewing your CV, only QPR Football Club will like to have you for some 3 weeks trial. i never get any reply back from Other Club . . . I will be having some meeting with my sponsors tomorrow about you and some other boys that we are recruiting for these clubs and we want you to get prepared for the training and we want to see you put on your best performance at any of the club you choose to play with.

YOU HAVE TO MAKE YOUR REGISTRATION FEE THROUGH VIA MONEY GRAM OR WESTERN UNION MONEY TRANSFER

'Klog' had attached two forms, purporting to be official documents from Queens Park Rangers. They were slick. There was the club crest, address and telephone number. A watermark of the club badge had been added, running beneath professional-looking data and tick boxes for Joseph to fill in his name, address, date of birth, next of kin, next of kin telephone number, career details (including favourite position), former clubs and academy manager contact. A barcode had been added to the bottom of each page and on the first page there was a section to 'affix passport photo here'.

Joseph did not fall for the scam. Eby Emenike, a London-based agent from Nigeria, told him not to pay any money. She forwarded me the above email exchange and had used it to warn players of the dangers of scams. In 2014 she had set up a charity called STAR (Stop Think Ask React), to educate young footballers in Ghana and Nigeria. Joseph was 16. 'He's desperate to come,' Emenike said. 'He calls me, he emails me, he's sent thousands of messages. A lot of these boys think I can help them get a club. I can't. They think I can be their mother.

So he said to me, "I'm coming for a trial at QPR." Initially I thought, "OK, let me know when it is and I'll come to watch you." Then I thought, "That doesn't sound right." I started asking questions about whether he had a visa, whether there was any money involved. Joseph doesn't have any money, that's for sure.

'I don't know about that QPR letter. I never got a response when I emailed the guy [Daniel Klog]. If I'd have wanted to take it further then I'd have gone to the FA. I don't think it was fake, I called QPR and they said they were running trials.'

I called QPR, too. I thought they would be interested to receive information about their club being used for a possible fraud. They were not. When I spoke to their public relations department they told me not to bother sending through the forms which Joseph had received.

It was, undoubtedly, a fake. There were two mistakes. First there was the header 'personal informations'. Then the question 'wing of play?'. Both were examples, surely, that the author's first language was not English. Then, of course, there was the biggest clue of all. Daniel Klog was listed on the Fifa website. His address was there – Cricklewood Lane, London – but there was no email address or telephone number. It was a case of stolen identity. The real Daniel Klog had been a victim.

It was something of a surprise that Joseph had not fallen for it. He was, as Emenike said, persistent. Several weeks before Joseph received the QPR 'application', Emenike had put me in touch with him. I had wanted to understand why he was so desperate to leave Nigeria and why he thought he was good enough to play professionally. It proved to be a mistake. He bombarded me with call after call, early morning and late at night. He sent countless emails. 'Please dear, be my agent.' 'Just give me a chance.' 'I won't let you down dearest, tell Eby to be my agent.'

'I can't be his agent!' Eby laughed. 'The first thing I said to him was, "Joseph, how are you going to get a work permit? You don't play for the national team." This is the big thing I publicise. If you don't play for your national team you are not going to get a club in the UK, so if anyone promises you a club and you have no national caps you're not going anywhere. You have to play 75 per cent of your national side's matches over two years. There are some cases where if you've played 50 or 60 games then the club can fight for you. But you have to be a big star, a big prospect.

'Most of the kids I speak to have no idea about that. It is worse when one actually falls for it and you tell them about work permits, or the underage thing, Article 19 – they can't go if under 18. They cry. They're embarrassed. They feel foolish. Some say they knew something was not right but they were too ashamed to say, or that they were worried that, if it was genuine, they would pass up the opportunity and one of their friends would get picked instead. That's the other thing, they don't talk to anyone outside the family about it until it's too late.'

And yet the scam kept working. It was getting smarter. Eby showed me a contract offer from Emirates Club, the Arabian Gulf League team in the UAE. The basic salary was $1,500 a week for two years. Bonuses were to be negotiated. There were two lump sums of $1,200 and $1,350 payable to the player for medical cover and transportation.

'The agent found the club and sent the salary package,' Emenike said. 'And he even said, "I don't want to take any money but you'll have to buy your own flight. You do it all. I'll sort the accommodation for you. Just book your flight and when you've done that I can get your visa." So the player thought, "This sounds good. They don't want any money from me." But the agent told him he had to book it with Emirates, that was one of the conditions. So he did it. But he said he tried to contact the agent and he wasn't responding. There was something wrong. It didn't feel right. So he went online to check his flight status and it said it had been refunded. So he contacted Emirates and they said, "Yeah, it's been refunded into your bank account." "But I paid cash. It hasn't been refunded to me." That's a clever one. Not seen that before.'

There was no doubting the gravity of the 'online scam'. Families had been bankrupted. In some parts of Africa, as Marsh said, kids had been charged up to €3,000, which was almost three times the annual salary. But when a child actually gets on a plane, flies to Europe, arrives at an airport and the 'agent' is nowhere to be seen, it is clear there are more serious frauds in operation. Families had been bankrupted by that, too.

'Yeah, that's the big problem. The actual trafficking,' Marsh said. 'It's basically illegal movement of players, completely fraudulent. With the "online scam", no one goes anywhere. It's a simple con. It's important to make clear the difference. But with trafficking, an "agent" will go to a club in, let's say Africa, and approach a player or manager – he might already be working with a manager, having moved players before – and say to the player, "I've got an offer for you, a potential trial in Europe." He talks to the parents, talks to the manager and he'll try to get money out of the club or parents to pay for flights and accommodation in return for promising, "If I get him a club you'll never have to worry about money again." And then obviously he moves them to Europe where they can end up being dumped because they either don't go to a club or they were never going to a club in the first place. The "agent" is using the person as a commodity to get the money out, get the kid over and then just leave them.'

According to Foot Solidaire and Jean-Claude Mbvoumin, that has happened to 7,000 African children since 2005. And all of them to France. 'That's the number I've heard him say,' Marsh said. 'I've met some of those kids, too, in Paris. They were all from Mali. They all had the same date of birth in their passports. That's the other thing, you see, the visas and passports are illegally obtained. These people get visas from Ghana, Gambia, Zambia, these sorts of places, and people think they're getting fake documents but they're real documents illegally obtained. I heard of a story of a relative of an agent working in the embassy. The agent gets them to sort out the documents. It's a real visa, they just don't know the derivation of it and that's the illegal part.'

It was clear that it was important to know how to get these 'illegal' passports and visas. They were essential tools for the trafficker because, without them, no player could go anywhere. Without them, football trafficking would be severely reduced.

'A lot of people, when they hear about this problem, they say, "Oh, it's not that bad,"' Marsh said. 'Well, in the last 18 months the more you look into it it's a serious problem. I wouldn't be surprised if it's at least maybe 2–3,000 youngsters a year who attempt to move or are targeted to move outside of Africa. They won't just be going to Europe, they could be going to Asia as well. It could be upwards of that, I'm being quite conservative.

'These are youngsters who are told they'll have a future, and they've got no chance whatsoever but don't know it. I would say that it's at least 50–100 a year that are ending up in France under the guise of football when, in fact, the chances of them setting foot on a pitch are incredibly slim.'

It begged the question, if they weren't travelling for football purposes, then what? 'We think we've got criminals doing it and moving them into drugs, prostitution,' Marsh said. 'Do we have football people doing it? Wouldn't surprise me. The governance in African football is almost non-existent. Anything goes. But of all the work I've done in sport, this is the hardest. It's impossible.

I can trace computer IP addresses, money flow from bank accounts, but people? These kids are getting picked up and moved from remote parts of Africa. How do you track that? Then they end up in Europe and they just disappear. They vanish. Absolutely impossible.'

The only man who could find them, seemingly, was Jean-Claude Mbvoumin. 'If I was being honest,' Marsh said, 'Foot Solidaire do need to be seen to be transparent, and it needs to be clear what they're doing. When I speak to people about them they will often say they don't understand exactly what they're doing.'

Emenike said that Jean-Claude was 'looking at the cure'. She didn't know why children were being moved out of Africa once agents had the money in their pocket and were fully aware that they couldn't get them a club. 'I have no idea what's going on there,' she said. 'It's always puzzled me. Some of them are not dumped instantly. They trial them in clubs and then realise they can't do anything with them. The guys that take them are unscrupulous. It's a business and they just don't care about the family or the boy. That's difficult to get to the bottom of.'

'Impossible'. 'Difficult'. Maybe. But it was vital to track down the people who were moving kids from one continent to the other. Now I understood more about the methods, I could put a plan into action.

4

Ben's Story

'We got off the airplane and we went to a hotel, in Roissy, Paris. It was near the airport. I think in the north of the city. The agent had booked me a room. It was an OK hotel, not very expensive but nice. He said, "I am just going somewhere, I will be back very soon." I thought everything was good. I was in Europe, I had my place to stay and the agent was taking care of me. But he never came back. I called and called. He didn't answer his phone. I didn't know what to do.'

It was an expensive plane journey and first night in a European hotel for Ben, who was just 16. It had cost his family €3,000. It had been paid to an agent who had promised that their boy had something special, that he could earn big money playing as an attacking midfielder in Europe. Racing Club de Lens, the top-flight French side, was one club that the agent claimed he had special connections with. Ben could get a trial there. It would not be a problem. Other clubs were mentioned. Maybe Paris Saint-Germain, Lyon. It was four years ago.

Ben was from Yaoundé, the capital city of Cameroon. He had grown up watching the Indomitable Lions, the nickname of the national team, and had wanted to emulate players like Samuel Eto'o, Benoît Assou-Ekotto and Alex Song who had left to play for big European clubs. They were just like him, he thought, so why couldn't it happen to him?

Whenever Ben had a spare moment he would play football. He played after school on the street – 'Monday to Friday, from four until six' – and on the weekends and holidays in organised matches. 'Sometimes,' he said, 'some professionals would join in and they would say I was a very good player.' He joined Dragon Club de Yaoundé, a second division club, and played for the youth team.

'Football is a way out,' Ben said. He spoke softly, almost in a whisper, in good English. 'Everyone wants to play. We don't have a very good football structure in Cameroon, so even if you play at a high level you want to leave. You want to leave and live your life in Europe. That is very important.'

Ben was not born into poverty. He was from a middle-class family. His father ran his own business. 'We lived well, yes,' Ben said. 'We had a good life, we were at home with everybody – my sisters, my brother, my parents – we were happy. We had a good life, yes. Poor? No. It was sufficient.' Sufficient enough to afford €3,000 to pay an agent. It was equivalent of half the annual salary in Cameroon.

'One day I played a good match and afterwards a man came to me and said that I should not be in Cameroon. My place is not here and that I should go to Europe. He said he wanted to be my agent and that I should call my dad and tell him.

'But I was still at school. I didn't like school. Sometimes it was fun but it wasn't very exciting. I wanted to play football. I said to my dad it was football or nothing. The agent said he needed the money to make my visa, make my passport and the plane ticket.

'My father paid. I was training very hard then because I knew that when I come here, to France, I will be playing football at this high level. The man was calling me all the time: "Train hard, you know I'm counting on you." And I said, "It's OK, it's no problem."'

The agent flew with Ben to Paris. On the flight, an excited Ben asked the agent about the clubs he would be having trials with and what he could expect. But the enthusiasm was one way. 'He said I had been playing well but he said, "Let's wait and see what happens." We arrived and we went to a bar. We were talking and talking and it was about eight o'clock and then we went and took a room in the hotel. He told me that, "I am coming back soon." From now I don't know where he is.'

Ben was left alone in a strange city with no money. In an unconvincing rasp, a note up from his whisper, he attempted to take offence at my suggestion that at such a young age he might have been scared. 'I was not afraid,' he said. 'How did I feel? Like a boy. That is all. I knew I was alone. I went down [to the hotel reception] and asked to use the phone. I called my parents back in Cameroon. I tell them where I am, the man left me in the hotel, I don't know what to do, I don't know what to do. My mother said, "OK, calm down, I will call one of my friends that is there. She will see if she can come to the hotel." She took me to stay with them and then after I will see if I can manage. That's how it happened.'

And how had Ben managed? He had no football club, no job and no money. He lived with his mother's friend. He got up at ten in the morning and spent the day training in a local park. 'I have nothing,' he said. 'I do not even have my independence.'

5

Scout Network

Scout Network was an English operation on the hunt for players. African players. They weren't interested in those older than 18. If they had been any good, they would have been signed up by that age. They wanted the raw, unearthed talent. The black diamonds who could be polished. And they wanted them for clubs in England. They didn't care about Fifa's transfer rules, that a player under the age of 18 could not be moved internationally without the parents of the kid first migrating for non-football reasons. They didn't care about visa or passport issues. There were ways round those problems, right?

The 'vision' of Scout Network was to exploit an opportunity in the international transfer market for lower league English clubs who were desperate for a new talent source. It was no secret that in England the bigger clubs, particularly the Premier League academies, would hoover up the exciting players as young as nine, under the controversial Elite Player Performance Plan (EPPP). Those with a spare £2.3 million qualified and were allowed to cherry pick the best, freed from a rule which said they could only sign youngsters within a 90-minute travel radius. They could pick a starlet from a lesser club at will, potentially starving the small fry of their lifeblood.

So the clubs outside of the EPPP needed to find a new tactic. Scout Network provided it. They told the agents and the scouts who worked in, or out of, Africa that they represented ambitious clubs who recognised the need to find new talent in new territories. Most of the agents they contacted were Fifa-licensed.

John, the founder of Scout Network, emailed scores of potential partners: 'We plan to travel to Africa to check out the talents.' He claimed to have 'good contacts' with league clubs in England. Indeed, Oxford United, the League Two outfit, had already signed up. 'We're tasked with finding them players,' he wrote. The response was strong. Of the twenty who replied, only one bluntly refused. 'They won't get work permits.' None mentioned Article 19, Fifa's rule which did not permit the transfer of under-18s. Agents sent videos of players, profiles, CVs. There were defenders with 'international experience', national B-team players, 'players of the season' in Ghana. Some were as young as 15. Almost to a man, the agents had offered to organise friendly matches or trial games so John could have his pick.

Scout Network did not exist. John did. Sort of. He was me. Inspiration had come from Jean-Claude Mbvoumin, who had suggested that the only way to truly understand the nature of the problem and expose individuals was to set up a sting. 'What's needed is to trap these people,' he said.

From the conversations with Jake Marsh and Eby Emenike, the methods and tactics used by the fake agents and conmen had been made clear. There was a blueprint. They could be beaten at their own game. Scout Network was to attempt exactly that, relying on the belief that the hopeful young footballer and the agent were bedfellows. The player wanted a deal with a football club. The agent wanted the cash that the deal would bring.

The tactics taught by Marsh and Emenike could be used to expose those who sought to exploit players. The targets were those who worked inside football, who Marsh had tantalisingly alluded to. The men who did tempt players with offers of trials abroad, who did deals to move players under the age of 18 in clear breach of Fifa regulations. They were football's traffickers.

The fake letters from the clubs, like the one purporting to be from Queens Park Rangers, could convince naïve, young men. Would the agents be as susceptible? They too wanted their shot at glory, and there in black and white was an offer. An agency working for a League Two club had been in contact. They wanted his players. They wanted a partnership. They saw dollar signs.

Attached to emails sent from Scout Network's account was a letter from Oxford United. It had the club crest, address, telephone numbers, website, email, and company registration number. It was signed by the youth and community director. It looked genuine. It was far more convincing than the bogus QPR letter. Even a seasoned agent might have believed it was real. That's because it was.

Simon Lenagan was the youth and community director at Oxford. I had enlisted his help, tugging at his heart strings by telling him the fates that could befall the boys after the conmen had deployed their tricks. 'Of course, I'll help,' he said. 'Anything you need.'

The letter read: 'This is an official document to confirm that John Hawkins is acting on behalf of Oxford United Football Club. He is a bona fide representative of Oxford United tasked with scouting new player talent in all territories, whether that be individuals, academies or other sources. If further information is required do not hesitate to contact me from the details below.'

It had to appear to be as professional as possible. Lenagan's willingness to vouch for Scout Network was crucial. When working undercover and meeting agents face to face there had to be back-up. If targets doubted 'John', they might do background research. This way, if they contacted Lenagan on the 'details below', he could confirm John was working for Oxford.

How did Scout Network get the addresses of the agents? In exactly the same way the perpetrators of the 'online scam' had trawled the internet for targets to exploit. Most were taken from the list of licensed agents published on Fifa's website. This was something that Marsh and Emenike had said the conmen had done. Scout Network reversed the process. The football 'social network' site Fieldoo was also used. The hub where players, agents and scouts could meet online was open to abuse. John had joined as an agent and began posting messages to others who could partner him in transferring players to Oxford United. All that was required to convince Fieldoo that he was genuine was the letter from Oxford. In truth, I could have spent half an hour making a 'genuine' fake letter, if you will. Mine had the blessing of an Oxford official but it would have been child's play to copy a crest from the internet and cut and paste the club's address.

An email address was set up. I did not need to worry about having a licence or being recognised by a football association because I was a scout. There was no licence required to be a scout. I was faceless, part of an unregulated army who chugged up and down motorways or hopped on and off budget flights looking for the next big thing. Anyone could say they were a scout.

I sent email after email. Jake Marsh said the agents 'hammered' the players. I turned the tables, indulging in exchanges up to 30 or 40 threads long. The difference was that they needed little convincing. I hadn't asked them to part with any money. I wanted their help to find players. I wanted their help to solve the difficulties surrounding moving an underage player from one continent to another. 'We need your expertise with visas and passports,' I said.

It was hoped that this homemade sting would enable me to 'learn more', as the Archbishop of Westminster had ventured at the anti-trafficking conference in London. But I also wanted the agents and scouts to come to me. So I set up a false Fieldoo profile of a 17-year-old Nigerian footballer called Som Kalou. The idea for 'Som' had come from the desperate pleas of Joseph Kaltim, the footballer Eby Emenike had introduced me to. Som contacted agents and scouts in an effort to root out those who were trying to charge young players sums for documents and offer trials at clubs at which they had little chance of success.

I was ready to meet the people responsible for trafficking in person. Those who bent the rules and those who had no idea what the rules were in the first place. They would help me to gain a fuller picture of an unsavoury business.

Charlie Baffour was a London-based, Fifa-licensed agent. He had come to the attention of Scout Network because in 2012 a Ghanaian player had fled from Istanbul, claiming that he had suffered death threats after reneging on signing a contract with the club Adana Demirspor. Richard Mpong, a winger who was 21 at the time, had said the contract was a 'slave contract' and had been written in Turkish to deliberately confuse him. Baffour was his agent.

A slave contract is one that is heavily in favour of the club and the agent. It might include a meagre salary, or in some cases no wage at all. Often expenses or the rent for an apartment are all that is offered. There might also be clauses which allow a large percentage of the player's salary to go to the agent who set up the deal, or others involved in the transfer. It is not unusual for an agent to take a percentage of a player's salary but slave contracts would take more than the standard ten per cent. Writing such a contract in a language which a player could not understand, claiming the version in their own tongue would be produced once it was signed, was a common trick.

Mpong said he was threatened when he wouldn't sign, and his club in Ghana, Medeama, paid for a one-way flight to Accra, the Ghanaian capital, after he escaped the 'clutches' of the agents in Istanbul. Medeama threatened Baffour with a lawsuit. Baffour denied any wrongdoing. He told a Ghanaian media organisation, 'This is a totally unfounded and untrue story. Yes, I brought the player to Turkey to further his playing career. His attitude here in Turkey is beyond comprehension. When all parties involved agreed on the contract, including Medeama's fee, which I negotiated on behalf of Medeama, I told Mpong [and] Moses Parker [the owner of Medeama] . . . that we will wait for the English version which Richard agreed. All I will say is if Parker and Mpong told lies I will leave them to God to judge them.'

Baffour's career as an agent seemed to have concentrated on setting up friendly matches. In 2013 his company, Divine Sports Management, was in discussions with Sunderland and Asante Kotoko, one of Ghana's most successful teams, to organise a youth game between the sides. Baffour claimed he had a meeting with Gordon Chisholm, Sunderland's director of youth. There were also plans for Asante to play Motherwell. Baffour referred to his company as 'my outfit'. According to Companies House, Divine Sports Management (DSM) was struck off the register in 2007 and dissolved. Its registered address was the same as Baffour's, the only director, and it had never filed accounts.

It was through a DSM email address that I had been able to make contact with Baffour. Whoever replied to the mails never gave their name, although it could have been Baffour, referring to himself in the third person. 'Our associate Charlie is in

England right now, perhaps you can meet up with him and discuss more about your project.' When I asked DSM for his personal email (it was strange that I would have to go through a middle man to arrange a phone call with him) they replied, 'No! We do not have an email for Charlie. As we said he is in England and we can pass on your phone details to him should you wish.' Baffour did call but withheld his number. He did that every time we spoke.

I met Baffour in a Fulham wine bar. We were going to attend the Nigeria versus Scotland friendly at Craven Cottage together. It was a game which made headlines before a ball had been kicked. The National Crime Agency had announced there had been an attempt to fix the result by a betting syndicate.

Baffour was no more than 5 feet 10 inches and had a slight frame. He was wearing a light green jumper, the colours of Nigeria. 'People will think I'm Nigerian. I'm not.' He was cagey from the beginning and eyed me with mistrust. 'You have a very famous name,' he said. I took this to mean that he had googled 'John Hawkins' and, unsurprisingly, had found no evidence of Scout Network. 'I think you mean it's a common name,' I said. I made up a back story. I told him I had no background in football and that my business partner was the expert, having been on the books of Arsenal and Southend. We had met at school. His job was to identify the players, mine was to do the logistics; I had the contact at Oxford United, for example.

'Your sort of email we get every day,' Baffour said. 'Every day. All day long. And the only reason I took the time to see you is 'cos, one, you're here in England and, two, when you said you know the director of the club I thought, "OK, let's go see him and at the end of the day whatever he tells me, you know, I'll listen and see what can be done." The players aren't a problem. For me that's not a problem, I mean I've had a lot of people over the years who will call you up. They want to meet, say they can do this and do that, and at the end of the day you find out that they're not genuine. You get people trying to pretend to be agents.'

Baffour was heavy on promises but light on detail. Each time he was pressed for more information about the players he had access to, he changed the subject, preferring to ask the same question – 'When can I meet the director at Oxford?' – but in different ways. In between this broken record Baffour boasted that he had 'the top, top players'. He was talking about players aged '16, 17, 18' and wouldn't move a player to England more than 21 years old. 'The younger ones,' he said. 'I'll go along with getting them into England.'

'How many have you got?' I asked.

'A lot of players.'

'Who's on your books at the moment?'

'Currently I've got . . . I've got three youngsters that are very, very good and I'm looking to ship them out ASAP. OK? So—'

'Tell me about them.'

'They're in an academy in Ghana.'

'Do you think they'd work for our project? So you'd want to pitch those players?'

'That's what I'm saying. We need to meet your guys at Oxford.'

And round and round we went. It was a relief to end 'negotiations' and go to the match. On the way to the ground Baffour said he knew 'the manager and management at Fulham' and talked about how he did most of his business in Holland because he had partnerships with agents there. He would not give the names of players he represented. If agents had a reputation for the hard sell, Baffour was soft. It matched the fare on the pitch. Nigeria had the cut and thrust of a rusting lawn mower. Scotland matched the passion and effervescence of the inebriated Tartan army, but also their touch.

Baffour didn't seem to know who he was watching. I was surprised he didn't know who every player was, particularly the Nigerians. He had to check on a team sheet and was asking those around him. When he did spot a player he knew, he was impressed with himself. 'I know that guy,' he said with delight. 'The left-back. Yeah. He plays for, um . . .wait . . . Monaco! . . . What's his name?' He asked a guy in front with the team sheet, who pointed out the name. Elderson Echiéjilé. 'Yeah, I said I knew him.'

A few weeks later I organised for Baffour to meet Simon Lenagan, 'your director friend'. Lenagan was on the board at Oxford United and his father, Ian, who owned Wigan Warriors rugby league club, was the chairman. Lenagan was also an actor. He had been in *Outnumbered*, *Coronation Street* and *The Bill* among others and was 'Big Man in Bar' in *Basic Instinct 2*. In real life he wasn't that big. He wasn't even stocky. He came with a sizeable reputation in football, however. He had rebuilt Oxford's youth structure after years of neglect. For ten years the club did not produce a first-team graduate. Within five he transformed their fortunes. By the end of the 2014–15 season, five of his graduates were playing first-team football.

We met at a London hotel. Baffour spent the hour contradicting himself. All that was required for Oxford to sign a player under 18 was a letter of invitation from the club to the British embassy, which would help the player get a visa. 'You send that to me,' Baffour said, 'then I go to the British embassy.' He never mentioned Article 19 or, just as important, work-permit regulations. Later, Baffour said that it was 'nothing to do with him' and that Oxford would have to go to the embassy. Either way, it was inaccurate. But basic details were not Baffour's forte. When pressed, he said, 'No, you can't play him but you can just have him in your youth squads.'

Baffour also claimed he had players that he 'owned', which would have been illegal under the Football Association's third-party ownership rules.

'That's that whole joint ownership thing. How does that work?' asked Lenagan.

'It's a straightforward thing, you know, we own the player fifty-fifty per cent. If I put him in a club for you it's fifty-fifty.'

'So you have other associates who own players?'

'Yeah, we work together.'

But when asked for details of how a joint ownership worked, Baffour refused to say. Later he claimed he didn't have ownership of any players. 'I don't own him, I don't own anyone.' He would never give any examples or information about deals he had done. He also said there were occasions when, as an agent, he would want a fee from a club for bringing a player to a club. When Lenagan pointed out this was against Football League rules, Baffour said he would never ask for money.

It became comical when Baffour turned his frustration on Lenagan, saying that it was 'completely new to him' that Oxford would not take a player on trial without having first scouted him. Even I knew that was irregular.

'Which British clubs have you placed players with?' Lenagan asked.

'Um . . .'

'Which British clubs have you placed players with?'

'I haven't . . . I don't work with British clubs.'

'You've never placed one of your players with British clubs.'

'No.'

I thought of Baffour's lecture about time-wasters when we first met. It turned out he was one of them. 'He's no agent,'

Lenagan said to me when Baffour had left. Maybe. But he was licensed with Fifa through the Ghana FA. What was interesting about Baffour, who was clearly a peripheral figure, was the total lack of knowledge and understanding of how a player could be transferred from a country into the EU. The invitation letter from Oxford to Baffour would not be enough to obtain a visa for a club to sign a player. He would have to be over 18 for a start. If he wasn't, he would need to meet Fifa's transfer criteria. Remember's Fifa's Article 19? He would also need to satisfy work permit regulations. Clubs cold only sign non-EU passport holders if the player was an international from a country ranked within Fifa's top 70 and had played 75 per cent of their country's international matches in the last two years.

If Baffour had genuinely suggested bringing a player from Africa with just an invitation letter from a club, then he had unknowingly given an insight into why there could be so many kids lost in Europe's cities. A club cannot play, or sign, a kid on a tourist or student visa. They can give him a trial, he can train with them – but he cannot play. So the agent is peddling a myth to either the player or club or both.

Previously Baffour had told me of a Ghanaian player in Cyprus whom he represented. It sounded as though he was in the limbo created by players travelling on short-term visas which did not allow them to work or, in other words, play football. Baffour claimed to have had nothing to do with moving him to Cyprus. Gabriel was his name. The club he had 'signed' for couldn't actually play him, so he trained alone.

Baffour might not have been the shady character that the story about the slave contract in Turkey had suggested. He said he was not involved in moving players under the age of 18. He said he only wanted to do 'legitimate, above board' work. So all Baffour had shown he was guilty of was not knowing the rules and regulations, but it was still a jigsaw piece.

So what if an agent *did* know what he was doing? What if he was able to exploit players willing to travel for a wholly unrealistic shot with a professional club? I thought I'd found one. By coincidence he happened to reside in Cyprus.

His name was Hamid. I had found him on the website, Fieldoo. Or rather Som Kalou, my fake footballer, had. Hamid had offered Som the chance to go to Cyprus, so long as he sent him €1,000 for a visa. 'You must deposit for me €1,000 so I issue for you visa for a trial,' Hamid told Som. Given what Jake Marsh had told me about how visas could only be obtained by the individual who needed them, Hamid seemed like a man who might know something about the trade in players. 'John' made contact. Hamid said he could stage a trial match in Larnaca with only African players. He would need only a few weeks to arrange it. 'You can come when you like, select the players,' he told me on the telephone. I told him I thought that was very quick. How would he be able to get all the players over from Africa in time? 'Don't worry,' he said. 'They're already here.'

6

Drawing the Sting

Hamid's penchant for rolled cigarettes and black coffee made his breath smell of the streets. It wafted across the table as he talked. 'Tomorrow, maybe day after, we can stage trial for you. You can see the talents. I just have to fix the referee, the pitch. It's not that organised, John, this is Cyprus.'

We had been waiting for Imari to arrive. 'I do the managing of the players,' said Hamid, the agent. 'He [Imari] finds the players.' Imari was the talent spotter. 'I look after them. I trust him.' Hamid, whose knee-length khaki shorts did little to detract from his short stature, had been eager to impress. He had taken me to a beach-side bar, paid for all the drinks and food. We watched the passenger jets fly low over the strip. 'It's beautiful, no?' laughed Hamid. This was Larnaca on the south coast, Cyprus's third-largest city. Next to him was a fresh-faced young goalkeeper, Dimitri, who towered over us both. He didn't get the joke. He was from Greece. 'This is very good player,' he said, tapping me on the knee. 'You watch him and if you like you can take to Oxford and we can do a very good deal.'

It was time to impose John's scouting credentials. 'We've got lots of good keepers in Oxford,' I lied. 'But if he is good . . .'

'Ah, he is very good. Great shot stopper, passing—'

'But can he command his six-yard box . . . ?' I broke off and directed my query at the young man. 'Hey, can you? You know in

England we want our goalkeepers to be strong and vocal. I want you in this match to clear everything in the six-yard box. You kill everything to get the ball. Do you understand?'

Dimitri nodded. He didn't look as though he could punch his way out of sodden cardboard box, let alone a mêlée in front of him.

'You listen to John,' Hamid said, wagging his cigarette at him. 'Do as he says. He knows what he's talking about.'

Hamid took a call on his mobile phone. It was Imari. 'He is driving here now,' Hamid said. I asked how he and Imari had started in partnership.

'He's a famous African player,' said Hamid. 'You heard of him? Mohamed Imari? He's here soon. We can talk about players, scouting them and bringing them.'

I had heard of a Mohamed Imari. If it was the Imari I had been told about by a contact then he would know intimately about the illegal movement of players. I would recognise the face, too, from newspaper cuttings.

'For Imari it's easy access in Africa,' Hamid said. 'So this boy he can go scout in Africa and he can go to four or five countries 'cos he's African. I know he has good eyes and he makes good deals. The good thing in this kind of co-operation is that we have the same target. You want young players to invest, we want to give the chance to young players, and there is a club who is going to be patient with them, not rush them like Cyprus, who in six months . . .' Hamid rubbed his hands together dismissively.

'At Oxford they can be patient. That is what they're all about. They have a very good academy,' I said.

Hamid ushered away the young Dimitri to sit at the bar and began to tell the story of his 'big misses', the deals that almost changed his life. No doubt every agent has the same sort of stories. There was the transfer of a Brazilian to West Ham United whom he was due a share in. 'All was agreed,' he said. 'The player just had to sign. Big money for me. But it went bad. Ah, some complication at the very, very last second on contracts. There was another one of my guys, went to play in the Middle East for . . . one. Point. Six. Million. Euros.'

Imari arrived, bringing an end to Hamid's monologue. I recognised him.

Mohamed Imari was a former footballer from Ivory Coast. In 2002 he was detained in Cyprus with two teammates following their arrest by immigration officials. Imari was apprehended when he flew to Cyprus from Russia to find a club. He had been having trials with a Russian team in July that year, an arrangement organised by Thomas N'Kono, the former African footballer of the year and Cameroon goalkeeper. N'Kono was also once a teammate of Jean-Claude Mbvoumin, the founder of Foot Solidaire.

In what would appear to be a classic football trafficking tale, Imari had left Ivory Coast without the permission of his club. He failed to win a contract in Russia but 'received a call from a Cypriot who claimed he could find them a club'. Naturally, upon their arrival in Cyprus, the agent did not show up. Imari's club asked the Ivory Coast foreign affairs ministry to help bring him home.

Imari did not go back. There he was, sipping a drink in a Larnaca bar, ready to talk about bringing more players from Africa to Europe for my fake project. He was aloof at first. He shook my hand limply, didn't look me in the eye or smile. It was not until I explained the idea behind Scout Network that he began to engage. We wanted young players under the age of 18 because the best clubs in England were 'hoovering up' all the talent. So clubs lower down the leagues needed to find new territories to identify talent.

'I [can] go to three to four countries to bring three to four young talents,' boasted Imari. 'And I mean young talent. I played for my national team, I'm an ex-footballer, played with the biggest stars in the world. I know football. I know what kind of players they want here. If you want players for England you have to know what type of players they want. If you don't know this then you lose your contact.' Imari had made his pitch. The words 'lose your contact' were said with a narrow-eyed stare. He was saying, 'Don't waste my time.'

'That's fortunate because we've been commissioned to look for new players because these clubs need to find new territories,' I said, off-hand, with an aim of reassuring him I meant business.

Imari leaned forward in his chair and steadied himself as if he had something important to say. 'I spoke with Craig Bellamy. I was in Sierra Leone when he went to fix an academy there. He said Africa is the best place for you to find somebody. Use your eyes. See the talent. You have to have somebody behind you, a good African who knows Africans and how to see young players. Craig Bellamy is clever. You know what he did? He didn't only look in Sierra Leone. He had an academy base there but he had eyes in Ivory Coast, Nigeria, Ghana, all these places. And they see one good player and they send him to this academy. And from there you take this young player. Bellamy is interested in the Scandinavian side, to Norway, Sweden. If you are willing to do something like that then we will offer our support.'

Bellamy, the Wales international who played for Liverpool and Celtic, among others, stated he funded a foundation in Freetown with £1.4 million of his own money. It was a not-for-profit organisation, focused on educating young boys, rather than just developing footballers. Bellamy had said that it would be a 'bonus' if it found a future star. There is no evidence of self-interest or profit as motives for Bellamy's academy or intention to move players to Scandinavia as alleged by Imari.

'We want to have our own academy,' Imari said. 'I've brought more than 50 players to this island. I have no fear that I go for the best. I know what type of player is good. Quick feet, technique and stability. Bam! If you want the best midfield they come from Ghana, if you want the good strikers you have to go to Mali, Senegal; the best wingers you go to Ivory Coast. Ivory Coast, they like running . . .'

'"They like running,"' Hamid laughed.

'In Sierra Leone they have technique . . .'

'And defenders you can find,' added Hamid. 'So the teams tell us what we want and then we go to that country. It's not like we bring the first player we find. For us it's time and money.'

Ah. Money. It hadn't taken long to get to the nub of the issue. How much did they want to find Scout Network players?

'If you make the expenses, I go with you,' Imari said. 'We go to Ghana, we go to Ivory Coast. We have tournaments. You tick the players you like. We play another tournament, you tick, we go to Sierra Leone, you tick.'

'He needs €5,000 in expenses for one, two, three countries,' Hamid said.

'The money to bring them here is not huge,' Imari said. 'But how you look after them? These are the expenses. You have to put them in a house. African players can be four or five in one house. Even if they are from different countries. They are like brothers. We understand each other. By bringing them to Cyprus you have to put a guarantee in the bank, pay the ticket, send them to Nigeria or Egypt to get a visa. One player can cost €2,500–€3,000. If you want to bring four players it can be €10,000 to bring all of them.'

'Feeding them, their house, everything,' Hamid added. 'For me and for him to scout we spend €50,000 every year. He needs at least €5,000 for one trip [to Africa] for ten days. He scouts, he finds. He goes after two months again to see the progress. The scout says the player must come. It's €15,000 for one player in one year. I want to make this easy for you but I need my expenses.'

Hamid and Imari had painted themselves as the good guys. Altruists who paid money out of their own pocket to give the young African a shot at glory. I didn't believe it. The numbers did not stack up. If it was costing €15,000 per year for one player, then Imari's claim that he had brought more than 50 seemed improbable. That equated to €750,000. Neither man appeared wealthy enough for that sort of spend. Hamid drove a battered three-door Honda. Imari, wearing board shorts, flip flops and a vest, had moaned that the lights on his ancient car were broken. Surely it was more likely they were being paid by the footballers to come? Hence why Hamid asked for €1,000 from the 17-year-old Som Kalou.

'Do players pay their own way?' I asked.

'Sometimes,' Hamid said.

'Yeah,' Imari said. 'Please take my son, the parents say . . .'

I asked how young the players could be for Imari and Hamid to bring them from Africa.

'The younger players get picked up earlier,' Imari said. 'At 17 years, I can bring him to Cyprus. Two or three months before 17 he can travel. Someone has to be his guardian, someone has to adopt him.'

'Are you able to be the guardian?' I asked Hamid.

'Yes, but not for too many players. Maybe maximum two.'

This was important. Fifa's Article 19, which prohibited the movement of under-18s, could potentially be sidestepped if a player's parents agreed that a resident of the country he was going to play in could adopt him. Without the parents agreeing, a transfer would be halted because they would have to be living in the country for reasons other than football. And what of their real age? The African footballer is constantly questioned about his date of birth. The players are always said to be older than they claim to be, which put an interesting perspective on the trafficked teen. Can we trust their passport? I asked.

'All the players from Africa are between six months and one year older than their passports,' Hamid said. 'They are born in a city like Accra in Ghana, for example, and it is very tough for families to get a passport.'

Imari launched into an impassioned eulogy about the commitment of the African footballer: 'From the age of 15, you become strong for your age. A player wants to do 1,000 sit ups, he wants to look fit and strong, he wants to take off his shirt. That's why you see a 16- or 17-year-old African and he looks 21, 'cos he works too hard. We play on the bare ground, with rocks, we have perfect ball control, we slide on the bare ground and tackle and burn our legs. You wash it with salt and hot water and you have a scar. You come the next day and you drop again with the same tackle. When the African comes here he is killing himself to make it: "I will kill myself to play here because I don't want to go back." If we had all these facilities in Africa then it would not be easy to take these players. Ghana is in the World Cup, Nigeria is in the World Cup. All their players play out of Africa. For any player it is their dream to come out and make his life.'

Imari explained the best way forward for our 'project' was to create an academy and bring the players to Cyprus on six-month student visas. It was his 'dream' to have an academy, like Craig Bellamy's foundation, which would be full of young Africans: 'Train boys, have contact with team in England and get them to take players. You sell this player, for the future this is my cut, my profit.'

Hamid was not so sure. He was shaking his head, muttering about visas. 'Problem in Cyprus is they are very, very tough about the African. I don't know why. They can give [visas] to Russia, USA, Scandinavian, Australian, to anyone, but when an African come to this island they scan it from up to down. Imari knows the procedure, he can explain it to you.'

Imari said he would have to pay €650 'to the town munici-pality' and give details of a player's address, salary and expenses. 'Everything must be covered before he can come.' Imari would then be given papers to take to the immigration department which would be stamped. They would then forward these to the Egyptian embassy.

'Why Egypt?' I asked.

'We only use Egypt to come straight to Cyprus because they don't care whether they give the visa or not.'

'Egypt is loose?'

'Egypt only takes profit. A plane every day. Any African players want to come, they come.'

'Egypt is the hub,' I nodded.

'Of course,' Hamid said.

'The first player I will give you,' Imari said, taking charge again. 'If he is no good then you don't have to work with me again. Football is business and we have to bring good products.'

Products. Commodities to be bought and sold. It was easy to forget that we were discussing human beings. Hamid and Imari were trading in people. They were not the sort of traffickers who abandoned boat-loads of immigrants in the Mediterranean, having charged princely sums. But they were moving footballers, responsible for the continental drifters who, one day, could find themselves without a friend, without a club, without somewhere to stay. What happened to those boys who were not good enough to earn the interest of one of Cyprus's professional clubs? What did Hamid and Imari do with them then? Presumably their scheme, if their story about paying the extortionate expenses were true, was to claim money back through a percentage take of a player's salary or from a transfer fee. As Imari said, 'This is my cut, this is my profit.' Perhaps they were taking their cut of the visa fees. Hamid told Som it would cost €1,000, but Imari said the fee was €650.

It was getting late. 'I have to go,' Imari said. 'I've no lights on my car and don't want to be stopped by police.' Hamid walked with him and started discussing arrangements for the trial match. When he came back, he told me of another meeting he had arranged. 'John, my friend, listen,' he said. 'There is an academy director here from Ghana. She can meet with you, we can discuss the partnership. We can meet tomorrow morning? She has good young players. Some are here.'

'This is the most amateur president of an academy in the world,' laughed Hamid, pushing Lois on the shoulder. She took the joke in good spirits. We had been talking barely half an hour and Lois had, tantalisingly, revealed she had players under the age of 18 in Spain and Italy. 'I know,' Lois said. 'I'm still learning.' She giggled at this and her shoulders shook, followed by the rest of her. She was a big woman. The bracelets and bangles on her wrists jangled.

'When she starts to learn she's gonna be 100 per cent more careful than now,' Hamid said. And we all laughed again. I did so through gritted teeth. I was anxious to get back to how Lois had managed to get African boys to Europe. She was difficult to question as she took umbrage at repeated enquiries, seeming irritated. She was being careful with the information she gave.

Lois ran an academy in Accra, Ghana. She had been doing so for four years. She had two scouts who found the players, sometimes she bought players from other clubs. 'We train four times a week, aged 15–20, about 55 boys altogether. They play together. I have about eight boys at aged 15. A lot at 18 and 19, and just a few at 20.'

Her aim was to provide talent to the professional leagues in Europe. 'Those who are 21 we want to play in Ghana in the league,' she said. 'Younger than that we want them to go to Europe. The funding comes from my pocket, my savings. I have four players in Cyprus, one in Spain and one in Italy.'

'Oh yes,' I had said. 'What are their names?' But she was coy. She played with her jewellery and gave a sort of 'hmmmm' sound.

Hamid and Lois spoke about two boys she had brought that week from Ghana. Frank and George. Strikers both. Hamid excitedly told me they would be playing in the trial match. More feigned interest on my part. Lois made that sound again. Instead of talking business she claimed to have been the former girlfriend of Stephen Appiah, once the Ghana captain, when she had lived in Cyprus. She called him 'her guy': 'When I was in school I was dating [him]. I would travel around to watch him play. That's how come I had an interest in football.'

Hamid, perhaps also sensing that Lois's mouth would take us in a direction which would not be beneficial for 'our partnership', tried to get us back on track: 'John, one question: Are you prepared to come to Africa and look for players?'

'Yes,' I replied.

'This is good for us,' he said.

'That is our expertise,' I said. 'We can spot players and we are doing that all the time. We need to do that in Africa. But where we struggle is getting them out of Africa.'

The bait was taken. Lois was not the wallflower she pretended to be. She wanted to brag. But on her terms. She gave the name of one of the players. As she said it, another passenger jet screamed just above our heads. Same beach, same bar as the night before. The player, she said, had been signed at the age of 16 by a club in the Spanish second division. He had also played for a B side of a famous La Liga outfit.

Lois had, finally, warmed to the task: the conundrum of helping Scout Network move players from Africa. She continued. 'Maybe Italy or maybe Spain. Everybody is taking players to Spain. It would be easier in Spain if a player had an invitation from a club.'

'Is that how you got your player to Spain?'

'Yes,' said Lois. She was more relaxed now than she had been earlier, despite the one-word answer.

'How did you get them to take a 16-year-old to Spain? Much harder?' I ventured, nervously, as this could have sent her scurrying back into her large shell.

'Not hard if you have an invitation from a club,' she said. 'Not hard. But then I have a reputation with people in Ghana, the embassy.'

'Reputation'. That was an interesting word to use. Was Lois teasing again? It was, of course, vital to know what she meant. A cynical mind would reckon she was hinting at something underhand. That was exactly what I thought, anyway. After a short pause she felt compelled to fill the silence: 'My sister works with the Ghanaian embassy, in Egypt, she works for the foreign office. So I always take letters from the Ghanaian embassy and I present that and in the next one hour they call us.'

'So you've got an inside person,' I said.

'Yeah. The same thing if I have to take a visa from the Greece embassy in Abuja [Nigeria]. I have to contact the Ghanaian embassy in Greece, take a letter from there and attach it—'

'Surely with your sister in the Ghanaian embassy we can get them to England quite easily?'

'Yeah. Any time. You need to [let] me know . . . so I know what the scheme [is].'

'She can ask her for the procedure,' Hamid said. 'She knows the procedure better than us. I will send through all the details of what an African needs.'

Clarification was needed, however, and I noticed that Lois was getting weary again by the questions. A harder tone was needed. These were, after all, the fine details required for the foundation stones of any partnership.

'It doesn't matter about age?' I asked.

'No.'

'You can get anyone out?'

'Yeah . . . I prefer young boys which they [clubs] can then pick up.'

'What age? Up to 16?'

'Sixteen. Sometimes with a 16 there is a problem . . . or 18, I prefer. Seventeen to 18.'

Despite Lois's confidence, Hamid mused on the problem of getting a player to England from Africa. He said it was 'very hard', although countered that 'the sister of Lois can help'. Lois said she got three-month visas when she was bringing players to Europe. If they stayed beyond that they would be illegal. They could stay, Lois said, if they found a club.

'But the maximum they can stay legally is three months,' argued Hamid. 'After that and you are still searching for a team and they can register you. But if not and police catch you, you are illegal.'

Unexpectedly Lois offered an idea. She appeared to be suggesting a 'ghost' club, to arrange with a team in Europe to take the player for a certain amount of time with Scout Network, or a club associated with Scout Network, paying the expenses.

'Then it would be easier to get them to England,' she said. 'The best thing is to find a headquarters in one country, like a club.'

'That's Oxford?' Hamid said.

'No,' Lois said. 'Not in England. England is impossible to go straight. You need a headquarters in Cyprus, Greece, anywhere that can give invitations to your players to get into that country and be a regular in the club in that country.'

Hamid was excited. He rubbed his hands together and smiled. 'We can do in Greece only and I explain the reasons,' he said. 'First of all foreign players in Cyprus can only register with teams in first division. So the premier teams, they are not giving the invitations as easy as Greece, as they can only use 20 for each team. Out of the 20 invitations to Africans they can register five, or they must go back or to another team.

'In Greece we have first, second, third division [teams] that can register foreign players, so they are able to issue invitations. Also in Greece I have much, much better contacts with clubs, because in Cyprus they don't pay. I don't bring players from other countries to Cyprus unless it's a big transfer.'

'So your club in England,' said Lois, waving her hand at me, 'should have an operation with the one in Greece.'

'What you are talking about is having a holding club?' I said. 'They are registered to that club but they are not actually going to play for them. And they do that for six months?'

'Yes,' said Lois.

'I tell you the most simple thing is that Oxford scout the player from Africa, you choose which players to move to England,' Hamid said. 'Out of this we have an agreement with a third division team in Greece. They play six months in Greece and Oxford can continue to scout them.'

'So it'll be like they are on loan,' said Lois. She then named European clubs she believed used the method to take players to Scandinavia.

Hamid slapped his hands on his knees. 'John!' he cried. 'We have a good understanding.' Lois chuckled away and began to scrutinise the lunch menu. She had a final thought, though. 'Don't take African boys to England in winter, they will suck . . . the weather.' She laughed.

'You are OK?' Hamid asked me.

I was delighted. After two days in Larnaca I had, somewhat unwittingly thanks to Lois's arrival, found a 'cell' which was working to move under-18s to Europe from Africa. Hamid and Imari, as agent and scout respectively, had no qualms about bringing players to Cyprus despite being fully aware of the difficulties in obtaining visas, the associated costs and the odds being stacked against players of finding a club. It was important to remember what Hamid had said. Only 20 invitations could be sent by clubs in Cyprus and only five players could be signed. Hamid and Imari were playing the numbers game. Players had been brought over, failed to find a club and had nowhere else to go. Unlike Charlie Baffour, who didn't appear to be aware of the rules, Hamid and Imari just seemed to ignore them. It was evidence as to why there were so many young, disenfranchised African footballers without clubs in Europe. It did not take much thought to extrapolate the Larnaca example to other countries, like France, Spain and Portugal. If there were people like Hamid and Imari willing to take a punt in Cyprus (which seemed to be a favourite destination because EU residency could be granted after five years as opposed to ten in Greece) there were surely similar gamblers elsewhere. Admittedly, it was not the minutiae of detail that one would have hoped for. The anatomy of the problem had not been dissected. But then why would it by two chancers in a beachside bar. This was more of a mantra than a *modus operandi*.

Surprisingly, it was Lois who provided more of the latter. She had the most insight of all. Lois had boys in Spain and Italy and more than hinted at embassy corruption with regard to getting visas for players. It was just as Jake Marsh had said when he explained how players were brought from one country to another. Visas and passports were legitimate but they were illegally obtained because of agents having embassy staff working for them. Most intriguingly, Lois had raised the possibility of one club using another in a different country as a base to then bring them to England. This was known as a 'bridge transfer'. Only a few weeks before the meeting with Lois, Fifa had for the first time issued sanctions against clubs, in Uruguay and Argentina, for the scheme. Fifa described a bridge transfer as 'clubs collaborating to transfer players through a bridge club to a destination club where the player was never fielded by the bridge club for other objectives'. 'Other objectives' might include tax scams or a club avoiding paying transfer fees due, such as sell-on clauses. In Lois's probably flawed example, the objective was seemingly for the player to bide his time at the bridge club to satisfy work permit regulations or to gain EU residency. It was possible that a 'bridge club' had been used for the transfers of the players Lois said she had in Europe. It could have been bluster, of course. After all, what Lois hadn't explained was exactly how a club was able to bypass Article 19 to sign a player. Perhaps her sister at the embassy was able to make her players older than they were. Perhaps the clubs didn't officially sign them until they were old enough.

'Before I go,' Hamid said. 'You should know, for the trial match, any player you see is not registered. They've been here longer than their visas. There are many players who come and they didn't find a club.' In other words, they were all illegal immigrants.

7

The Illegal Match

Frank and George, the two boys Lois had brought to Cyprus to find their footballing fame and fortune, had been sharing a one-bedroom apartment. It overlooked a car park. It was owned by Marc, a local player who Hamid and Imari said was an 'explosive midfielder'. There was a Playstation in the kitchen-cum-living room, which was just big enough for a two-seater table and sofa. There was a sofa bed on the balcony.

Frank was quiet and unassuming. He was about 5 feet 9 inches and lithe. He looked the 19 years he said he was. He was wearing a Borussia Dortmund shirt. 'Where is George?' asked Hamid. 'He needs to meet John.' Lois and Dimitri, the goalkeeper, were sitting outside. Lois was engrossed with Candy Crush Saga on her mobile phone

Although polite, Frank was not a talker. He could manage only one-word answers. What's your dream? 'Footballer.' What is life in Accra like? 'Hard.' Who are your heroes? 'Messi.' He told me he was fast, could play up front or on either wing, and had good movement.

Did he pay for himself to go to Cyprus? 'No, my mother did.' He pointed to Lois, absorbed in her phone. Lois had told me she often adopted boys who wanted to join her academy. It was a standard practice in African football. Poor families were happy to let their children leave because it was one less mouth to feed and they were being given the chance to make it as a star. And if they did, they would never have to worry about feeding all those mouths again.

'You have to give something to the family,' Lois said. 'Or I pay their school fees. You feed the players. Once in a while I give the parents something.'

'When did Lois spot you?' I asked Frank.

'At 17 when my mother died. I have been in her academy for two years. I would like to play professionally in Cyprus.' He said he would be here for two weeks. (Seven months later, during a conversation on WhatsApp, Lois told me he was still there, looking for a club, hoping for his big break.)

George emerged. He looked old enough to be Frank's dad. He was lined and his hair appeared to be thinning. He had the build of a 30-year-old. He told me he was 21. I was almost embarrassed by the lie and looked away. I remembered what Hamid told me about the age of African players. They are always older than their passports stated.

We got ready to go. Lois fussed, looking for her boys' shin pads. 'Have you the right socks?' she asked. Lois stayed behind. Frank, George, Dimitri and I squeezed into Hamid's Honda. The three boys in the back. We hit the dual carriageway. A sign for Ayia Napa, the nightclubbing capital of Cyprus, said '38 kilometres'. 'Anyone who wants to play football should not go there,' Hamid shouted. 'That is where bad things happen. Down there. If you are a footballer you don't come back.'

Hamid's driving left a lot to be desired. He barely looked at the road, preferring to 'text and drive' with apparent impunity from hazards and other road users. He rested the wheel between his knees. Each time I looked over, his eyes were on his phone.

The town of Oroklini, Hamid said, was home to 2,000 British ex-pats. It was difficult to spot the attraction as it was neither close to the sea nor nestled in the hills. Sandwiched between ugly apartment blocks was the football stadium, shared by a third and a fourth division team. There was razor wire around the perimeter. We had to wait for 'the man with the key'. The first player to arrive was Adam, who looked like a surfer bum with his pony-tailed brown hair and whispy beard. He was heavily tattooed; on his right arm Jesus Christ, on the left the Virgin Mary. Hamid said he used to play for the Cyprus national team. A car full of African boys was next. They swaggered over from the dusty car park, shorts halfway down their backsides, baseball-capped, shirts off. Apart from one, who was smartly dressed. This was the giant Ugandan who Hamid said had the fiercest shot known to man. Surprisingly, his accent was cut-glass English. He had obviously been expensively educated. He was studying sports management. He had been in Cyprus for two years and played for a lower league team. He had also played in South Africa. He said he wanted to become a football agent. 'This guy is 1.97 metres tall,' Hamid said, expecting me to be impressed.

A steady stream of African boys followed, car by car. By the time 'the man with the key' arrived and we entered the stadium there were 21 of them, four Cypriots and one Lithuanian. One of the Africans was Marc, the owner of the apartment. He was known as 'the black star' because of his association with the Ghana national team. He seemed to know everyone and was laughing and joking. Hamid said he was 20. He was another who looked as old as me. His face was weathered and his demeanour was certainly that of someone wiser than his supposed years. He was the alpha footballer at this gathering.

The stadium was dilapidated. There was concrete terracing behind one goal and the changing rooms at the other. Bleachers ran down one side with a 'punch and judy' stand perched above. The pitch was artificial. The sun was blazing and it heated the surface like a hot pan.

Hamid asked me to say a few words to the players beforehand. A team-talk? 'Yes,' Hamid said. 'They need to hear from the scout, what he expects of them.' That was out of my comfort zone. As a football supporter I had often wondered what a manager might say to players before a match. Did he try to rouse them with Churchillian prose? Should I rant and rave, demanding blood, sweat and tears? Football is a closed, secretive world and never has that been more true than when it comes to the dressing room. What went on in there, stayed in there. So I was nervous. I could be exposed if I appeared weak or naïve. I settled on swearing a lot. If there was one thing I thought I knew about dressing-room team talks, it was that there was surely profanity. And shouting. Plenty of shouting to try to disguise any wobble in my voice: 'Play for the fucking team, not as individuals trying to impress. Pass for the team and dribble for the team, not yourselves. And demand the fucking ball so you can give yourselves every opportunity. I'm watching you off the ball as much as on it, so don't be fucking lazy.'

Fearing that was somewhat short, I remembered what I said to Dimitri, the young goalkeeper. 'Where's the goalkeeper? Fucking kill everything in the six-yard box.' This little speech was repeated in the other dressing room. When I said the last line, Dimitri nodded. Otherwise the players were largely unmoved by my rhetoric. In fact, I was not sure most of them had listened.

Before kick-off, there was a further test of my scouting credentials. One of Hamid's coaches asked me what formation I wanted the two teams to play. I stumbled. I should have just said 4–4–2 like any good Englishman: '4–3–2, er . . . 4–3– . . . er . . .'

'4–3–3?' he asked.

I nodded nonchalantly.

'Do you want that as a diamond or—'

I cut him off. 'Fucking diamond, innit.'

Imari told me the four players he wanted me to keep an eye on: Appiah, a right-back, 20, from Ghana; Taylor, centre-half, 22, from Sierra Leone; Abdul, 20, also from Sierra Leone; and Iche, 21, wearing number 11, from Nigeria. 'You use your own eyes for these players,' he said. 'But I think they are the best.'

Abdul got off to a poor start. His touch was heavy. One pass from his centre-half, although fizzing, ran over his foot and out of play. As the half wore on he was increasingly cumbersome. The first goal arrived in a few minutes. Imari's right-back was out of position, playing an attacker on side. Imari screamed at him as the inquest began. 'It's you! It's you!'

There were four more goals in the first half. Adam, the Cypriot national, curled in a free-kick with his left foot. John, a Nigerian, roamed round the park chopping and hacking. 'Why he have to play nasty?' said a guy on the sidelines who, Imari advised, also used to play professionally. 'If he is going to make it a bad trial, we take him off,' Hamid said. Dimitri dived bravely at the feet of the Ugandan striker. He was then beaten at his near post. But the star was Frank. His first touch was superior, as was his movement, pace and turn. He didn't give the ball away once. He allowed the ball to run over the outside of his boot beautifully to free George, his roommate, who was all hustle and bustle, no class.

At the break, the coach agreed that Frank was the best player. He asked me if I wanted to give any instructions to the teams at half-time. I said I wanted to see if Frank had the ability to beat a man. 'He needs to play wide left,' I said.

Oddly, I was taking it seriously, chewing gum in the dugout, writing notes and exhorting and directing Frank. I was shouting at him to hug the touchline and telling him to time his runs to be played in on goal. I don't know why I cared. You are not a scout, I told myself. You are not a real scout. Hamid and Imari, having sensed the scout's interest in Frank, started to demand more passes

72

for Frank and encouraged him to make more runs. When a Cypriot player failed to play him in they cursed him. It turned out, eventually, Frank could beat his man. A jinking dribble resulted in a goal.

Towards the end of the match, however, I had become distracted. Imari was in a close, hushed conversation with a friend by one of the dugouts. He mentioned the police and an arrest warrant. He also talked about 'bringing players from Paris'. There was a nagging feeling in my mind. There was something not quite right about this trial, aside from the fact that it was for the benefit of a fake scout. The desire to impress was wholly lacking from all but three players – Frank, Adam and the Lithuanian – and there seemed an ulterior motive for the rest being there.

Marc, with whom everyone seemed to want to speak, dashed back and forth to different groups of players. I saw him take money from a friend of Hamid by the corner flag, carefully counting it. Before leaving he handed Frank a wad of notes, trying to disguise the exchange with a handshake. Hamid had said all the players, bar Frank, George, the four Cypriots and one Lithuanian, were illegal immigrants. They had overstayed their visas. So what were they still doing there? No longer did it seem they were desperate for a football career. Could it be that they were also working illegally as well?

There was some sort of an answer in the form of Gabriel, the player who Charlie Baffour claimed he represented. He was in Paphos, a two-hour drive away from Larnaca. He was 22 and had been in Cyprus for two years. He had been scouted in Ghana and brought over to play for a first division team. Soon after his arrival, the club suffered financial difficulties. They would be unable to pay him.

Gabriel had left Ghana expecting a footballer's life but he was, it seemed to me, a slave. He did 'some work' in a hotel as a caretaker but he wasn't paid. Instead he was given free food and lodging. The man who scouted him, Gabriel claimed, was a director of the club. But after the club had run out of money, he took pity on him and gave him a room at his hotel. 'He said I'm good so he likes to help me. To take care for me. If I need money I ask him and he gives me. When there is something in the hotel I can help. Sometimes I go there and help with something. Play volleyball in the pool with the guests. He has been so good to me. It is closed end of November and opens in April. So I am there on my own. I am a kind of caretaker for him, he's a good person. Because I've been there and not done anything bad, sometimes he feels bad that I'm going through this. He doesn't want me to go back, he wants me to stay and find something. I don't want to bother him too much. I don't want to ask him for money.'

Gabriel was not allowed to train with the club, who resided in the third division, so he trained alone, running on the beach at half-five in the morning before returning to the hotel gym to do more work. 'Sometimes I feel bad that I am not doing what I want to do,' he said. 'I will be there [the hotel] alone, no one to talk to, I sit on the internet and then put on my running shoes. It's very difficult for me to go back [home] because I don't have the money for my flights. I am here for good now, I guess so.'

Baffour had been trying to find him a club. 'He says, "Keep on training, keep on training." He says, "You never know." He is checking on me.'

I doubted that Baffour would be able to do much for Gabriel, so did he know of a scout in Larnaca called Imari?

Of course he did. 'Imari from Ivory Coast? He is a very good person,' Gabriel said. 'He tried. He took me to a team and played a friendly but it was no good. He took me from Paphos to Larnaca. He feed me, take me training and I was very happy.'

Just like the African players who turned up for the trial match, Gabriel's prospects did not look bright. They were the forgotten footballers, discarded by the scouts and agents who had brought them to Cyprus because, quite clearly, they were not good enough to play football. All they were good enough for, in Gabriel's case, was to work for nothing as a caretaker in a hotel. And they had all overstayed their visas. They were illegal. Some of the players who played in the trial had been in Cyprus for two or three years after their six-month papers had expired. 'If the police catch you, you are illegal,' Hamid said.

My time in Larnaca had come to an end. I had learnt about some of the tricks and cheats scouts and agents would attempt to circumnavigate Article 19. I had listened to Imari and Hamid talk about the '50' players they had brought from Africa in the hope of finding one or two gems. Interestingly, they were not too concerned about the ages of the players. They didn't have to be kids, yet there was only one African player at the trial over 21. A commodity was a commodity at 17 (Imari's preferred age), 19 (Frank's age) or older, like Gabriel. The point was that you didn't have to be under 18 to end up lost in Europe. Young men were being targeted, too. It was, obviously, more disturbing for children to be moved from country to country and, although noting that any footballer could be a victim of trafficking, I was keener to focus on the former. I had, however, seen what happened to those who had hopes of playing in a European league, only for them to be dashed. And what they had been reduced to. It was the player trade in inglorious technicolour. It was surely why so many had ended up wandering the streets of foreign cities. It was time to try again to speak with the man who was supposed to help them.

8

'I Have Integrity'

This time I knew Jean-Claude would turn up. There would be no excuses or distractions. I had offered to help him find a way to fund Foot Solidaire's new website. So he was punctual, welcoming me from across the lobby of the Paris hotel like his new best friend.

Despite being the head of a charity, the 42-year-old had not been charitable with his time for someone he didn't believe was worth it. For those who were, he was quite the raconteur, a story-teller whose face beamed as he spoke. The nervous persona of Geneva had disappeared. He was not the man who was looking over your shoulder for someone more important to talk to. But then this was not the United Nations. It was a three-star hotel not far from the hulking structure of the Stade de France, in Saint-Denis, the place where Foot Solidaire's story began.

It was there, 14 years previously, that Jean-Claude would meet African footballers who had been duped. They would train together and swap survival tips. At the time, Jean-Claude was something of a celebrity in the African diaspora of Paris, a former Cameroon international plying his trade for nondescript lower league clubs.

'One day my friend at the Cameroon embassy called me and he said, "Jean-Claude, can you come? I have a problem and only you can help." So I went and I saw a lot of young players with their football strips. My friend said, "I have this team of 14-year-olds, they are abandoned on the streets, they come to ask for help." I say, "Why?" And I speak to one of the boys, and they'd been recruited for a tournament in Paris. An agent had promised the family he would take them to trials after the tournament. But after the tournament he never returned, his phone was off, they had no money, no flights home. So they walked 15 kilometres to the embassy because they had no money for the metro. All the families in Africa were panicked. I thought, "This is incredible." I was given the name of the agent and had never heard of him. I called my friends in France and they had not heard of him.

'So we begin to investigate and then somebody said, "Oh, Jean-Claude, you know there are a lot of young players like them at Saint-Denis?" So I went. I got the surprise of my life to see a lot of young Cameroonians, young Africans training. And the same story. "The agent promised me trials, took my money and abandoned me." Because I was a former Cameroon player everyone wanted my help – "I don't eat anything for two days"; "I have nowhere to sleep" – I take my credit card . . . *boff-boff-boff*. That was catastrophic. I give, I give, I give. I buy the hotel for one night. I try to help. That was the beginning of the problem. I was playing at the time. It was 1999. One year later, in December 2000, I decided to create Foot Solidaire because there were a lot of these young kids. Sometimes they come to my home. They stay and they eat, my woman make the food. It was very strange. Sometimes the people disappear with my shoes, my clothes, my computer. So we said, "It's not good to continue." Sometimes they call on the phone – "Yes, Mama, a guy called Jean-Claude help me . . . it's not too bad" – and the phone bill at the end of the month! Ah! They cut me off.

'So one of my friends was a journalist and I was telling him my problems. He said, "No, Jean-Claude, it is not possible, you will be destroyed if you continue. You must create an organisation. Ask for help for the authorities. You cannot solve it on your own."'

The emergence of Foot Solidaire had coincided with the demise of Jean-Claude's career, which had promised much but delivered little. There was a hint of bitterness that he'd made his name off the field rather than on it. 'I was one of the best players in Africa in my position,' he said. 'If I had gone to the World Cup in '98 I would have gone to a big, big club.'

That had only been a latent ambition. At the beginning, there was no dream. Jean-Claude's aspiration was only to play for the love of the game and his hometown. 'I never thought about playing for my country or for money. I wanted to represent my city.' That city was Yaoundé, the capital of Cameroon, where Jean-Claude grew up. Just like the boys he helped, Jean-Claude, aged 'six or seven' played barefoot football in the street with an orange wrapped in newspaper. They played until sundown. His friends called him 'Maradona': 'You know, the first time I heard him talk I couldn't understand why he wasn't speaking my language.'

Jean-Claude was not alone in playing football for fun only. In Cameroon at the time few held the ambition of being a professional footballer: 'I remember at church the preacher said, "We have four problems in our community: you have the prostitution, you have the alcoholics, you have the gangster and you have the football. It's not good for our children." Football was seen as something for thieves and gangsters. It was a joke and our families would remind us of a former player who finished his life in the poverty, no money. So it wasn't the future. It was not aspiration. The family said you have to go to school to study and go to university.'

Jean-Claude's first club was a church team: The Small Pilgrims of Zachary. 'I played everywhere, but mostly in defence.' He progressed to the regional under-17 team, where a coach advised him to change his age to make him younger. 'It was the first time I met corruption,' he said. 'I found out why later when I went to the under-17 World Cup with Cameroon. We played Ghana. They were not under-17. On the pitch it looked like you were playing with your big brother.'

Upon his return he signed for Canon Yaoundé, his home club. It was 1989. The club paid his school fees, a salary of £150 a month and gave him an apartment. 'I could play football for my city and I could learn and get a job in a bank like my father wanted. It was good.'

One year later Cameroon put African football on the map. In one of the biggest upsets in World Cup history, they beat Diego Maradona's world champions 1–0 at the San Siro in Milan. Overnight African football was legitimised. Spontaneous street parties were held across the continent. Roger Milla, Jean-Claude's 'roving ambassador', and 38 years old at that tournament, went on to score four goals at Italia '90. 'I'll tell you something,' he said, after Cameroon were finally knocked out, 'if we had beaten England, Africa would have exploded. Ex-plo-ded. There would have been deaths. The Good Lord knows what he does. Me, I thank him for stopping us in the quarter-finals.'

Suddenly credible, football in Cameroon changed immediately. The world had seen what their players could do and they wanted them. The players themselves saw what they could do and they wanted to see the world. 'I played with four or five of that Cameroon team at Canon Yaoundé,' Jean-Claude said. 'They were all heroes, gods, and everyone wanted to be like them. People wanted to be footballers. Football was not for thieves and gangsters any more.'

The significance of that 1990 World Cup in terms of fuelling trafficking was not lost on Jean-Claude. From Cameroon at least, he believed it provided the impetus to begin the trade in players. 'Everyone thought about going to Europe,' he said. 'That was the start. And players thought about other countries.' He experienced it first-hand. An agent approached him to go to Gabon, where 'the money would be better'. Even his father, who had previously preached the importance of getting a good job, had been tempted by the possibilities. 'He said, "Jean-Claude, you can do better."'

It was a prophetic moment. Jean-Claude would be one of the first young footballing hopefuls to be encouraged by a family swayed by the possibilities of a professional career abroad; to earn more money, to send it back. Thousands would follow him. And just like them he would fall prey to a scam. Jean-Claude was trafficked in his teens. He seemed surprised when I pointed this out, as if he hadn't thought of it in those terms. 'Yes,' he exclaimed, 'like I was trafficked!' He told the story as if he had done so a thousand times, laughing, slapping his knee or tutting at the stupidity of his younger self at the end of every sentence. It was quite a tale.

'So I travelled to Libreville in Gabon, with no visa,' he said. 'We paid money to the guards at the border. It was the first time I had lived the life of an illegal migrant. All I had was some money and my football shoes. It was mad. But then the car we were in was, *pfft*, broken. The agent said, "I will give you the address and you can find the guy in Libreville." I said, "I cannot go alone." A guy overhead this conversation and said, "You can come with us. Give us 10,000 francs." I give him the money and off we go. He was a very strange guy, he was driving very fast. He was talking with two other guys in the car and they were saying, "We have to kill them, we have to kill them."

'We were stopped by the police. They took my identity card. They asked, "Why do you have no visa?" I said, "No, they let me enter, I paid the police at the border." They say, "That is not a good thing to admit to." We were all put in jail. But the three guys, I think they were gangsters, paid off the policeman. So we go in the car again. Driving in the night, driving in the day. We arrive in another city, somewhere, we stay in a hotel and there were rats everywhere. "When will we get to Libreville?" I thought.

'When we leave the hotel the next morning we were stopped by another gang. The three guys had stolen 50 million francs from this gang. They wanted their money back and the three said, "We have to go to Libreville because we don't have it here. So we will have to go and get it." Bizarre. The gang said, "If you don't give us the money we will kill you, we will kill you ALL." I said, "I don't know this guy, they just took me on the road." So they say, "Here, take this person, you keep him and if we don't come with the money you can do what you want with him." So they go. And I was left in this small village in the jungle. I had no money left. I wanted to find work to pay and they said, "No, don't move. You are a hostage. If they don't come back we will kill you." My God. I was sitting awake throughout the night hoping they would come back. My captor asked me what I did. "Ah, you are playing for Canon Yaoundé? What are you doing with these men? They are thieves, gangsters, they have stolen lots of money. That's why we are chasing them and you are a hostage." I said, "I'm not a hostage because they won't come back. They don't know me. If I die they don't care."

'So he let me go. I took a bus to Libreville. I was very tired. I couldn't sleep. When I arrived I was red with the dust from the road. I went to the address I had been given and there was no one there. I found another Cameroon player who was in the city and he took me to some trials. But I was tired and had not eaten so I didn't play well.

'I had nowhere to go. My family were asking for me. The fans at Canon Yaoundé were saying, "Where's Jean-Claude?" because I was the best player the previous season. I wanted to work but I had no visa or work permit, so I paid someone to get me the documents. He disappeared. Never came back. The Cameroon player said if you want to stay you'll have to find a wife, there are prostitutes who will do this. I didn't want this so I went home.'

Jean-Claude moved to France – 'in an illegal way' – in 1995. The exodus had begun. The groundbreaking Bosman law, which allowed players out of contract to move for free when their registration had been previously held by a club, had oiled the hinges on the immigration gates. And with Cameroon's credibility as a football nation confirmed, Jean-Claude was suddenly able to dream. After all, an African footballer could not leave for Europe without one. He wanted to play in the 1998 World Cup. He was 'one of the best defenders of my generation', making his name as a left-back for the Cameroon under-20s at the World Cup and Africa Cup of Nations.

He began playing for Beauvais, a second division club. He stayed for one year, and then started to become one of those footballers hampered by the derogatory label 'well travelled'. He went to Dunkirk and broke into the national team a year before the World Cup. The coach of Cameroon, Henri Depireux, a Belgian, wanted him to play at a higher standard, so he moved to Brussels to first division club RWD Molenbeek (now called FC Brussels). That was where Jean-Claude's career stalled. He broke his foot, missed out on selection for the World Cup as a result, and was never the same player again. He ended up at L'Entente Sannois Saint-Gratien, a third division amateur club in the north-west suburb of Paris which trained for three days a week and played on Sundays.

'At that time I discovered the real world,' Jean-Claude said. 'When I was injured I needed to feed my family. I worked at the supermarket for nine months but I thought, "This is not my life."

You wake up at 5 a.m.! Is that possible to wake up at 5 a.m. and go to work? Then I worked for a person selling cars. And I thought, "I used to be a star!" We were earning €1,200 a month. How do people live on that amount? I discovered real life. In football you don't see it. Football maintains you in a situation to make you believe you are a big man.' The call from the Cameroon embassy came soon after.

'I begin to go around Paris, to meet the boys and to talk about their situations. How they get there, who did they pay, where is your visa, and passport. I interviewed them all. My first conclusion was that the agent promised things to the family, they pay the money and then . . . nothing. These children were in very bad situations. Some were working in the black market.'

In the years that followed, Jean-Claude saw it all: the late-night phone calls from a Cameroonian to meet him near the Gare du Nord to try to sell him a stolen car; the Ivorian who brandished a new phone and then came knocking on Jean-Claude's door when his 'good Samaritan' tried to sell him into prostitution; the Senegalese who contracted TB working in just a T-shirt in a freezing abattoir. Jean-Claude could spin a good yarn. He was less garrulous when it came to explaining exactly what Foot Solidaire did, preferring instead to talk about the problems the organisation faced.

'But it is like a bush fire,' he said. 'You put it out here. Here. Here. You cannot think. The funding was very sporadic. We had small donations. Since the creation we had some projects. We do a project when we get funds. At the beginning we were not well organised. When you start you need good communication, a fundraising policy.'

I suggested to Jean-Claude that communication was still poor and there was no fundraising policy. 'I speak to people in football and they are unclear what Foot Solidare does?' I said.

Jean-Claude dodged the question. 'At the beginning I thought everyone would help Foot Solidaire because it's essential, it's useful, it's about the children and because it's sports and education and solidarity. Because it's the community. But at a certain level [there is] a political problem. In the football world not everyone agrees. People who are interested in the recruitment [of players], they don't see things like you. That was our first big stop.

'Other parties were saying that I was trying to harm their business. It was maybe clubs, maybe agents mostly. The people involved in recruitment. This was the general attitude: "You're harming our business." Some agents called me: "We'll kill you." I get a guy who called me and he said, "If you go to Saint-Denis, we'll kill you." So I couldn't go alone. I needed to be with other people. Dangerous for me.'

I asked Jean-Claude whether he thought Fifa had bowed to pressure from clubs to cut their funding of his organisation. For the first time, he shifted uncomfortably in his seat. The Jean-Claude of Geneva had returned: 'With the Fifa it is very difficult. Foot Solidaire is nothing to Fifa, they have all the power, all the money, all the politics.'

'You are nothing, they are everything, so why can't they fund you?' I asked.

'It would be easy, yes, for them to fund us. I'm not angry Fifa let us down. You can be angry when you don't have the experience of this world. But with my experience, you have to know how the world is going. Maybe because of some mistakes, maybe because of the number of contacts inside Fifa, you need the lobbying to help. We don't have any contacts at Fifa. We have good relations. Sometimes I send an email to the secretary general and he replies. I'm not angry because maybe it's our mistake. We have to improve our management.'

'Why your mistake? [Sepp] Blatter said he'd give you the money.' I remarked, reminding Jean-Claude of the agreement between Fifa and Foot Solidaire in 2008.

'Maybe we didn't know how to ask for the money.'

'But he said he'd give it to you.'

'Maybe we don't have the strategy. I cannot say they don't want to help. Maybe if I ask they will. With the conference [the International Conference on Young African Footballers in 2008] Fifa helped us. After that they didn't help us. Maybe because some people in football said, "Don't help Foot Solidaire."'

Possibly. Or it could have been that no one was sure what Foot Solidare stood for. Did the mistakes that Jean-Claude referred to include a failure to pass on the names of 'agents' to the police or Fifa? Jean-Claude was suddenly very interested in an invoice from the company building his website. Or was it an ill-advised 'partnership' with Top Spot Ltd, a company which organised football tournaments in West Africa to identify young players? Top Spot had done nothing untoward but Foot Solidaire's involvement was wholly contradictory. Legal or not, an anti-trafficking charity should not have been linked to such a scheme.

'Their guy said, "Supported by Foot Solidaire." It is not true, it is not true,' Jean-Claude said. 'I know this guy. We meet in a conference and we talk a little and he sent me a project, but we were not with them.'

I was beginning to get frustrated. So I tried again, asking what Foot Solidaire did. It elicited a surprising response.

'Foot Solidaire, you know, we cannot do anything. There are organisations for education and for helping migrants. Foot Solidaire is for information advice to the young player. That is our main task. Then we can help children. We can talk with them and sell him another service. We are an information advice service, we can say that.'

'Foot Solidaire cannot do anything . . . sell the player a service.' Two interesting statements, which led neatly to Foot Solidaire's new project. It was called the 'Foot Solidaire Player Passport', a booklet which would advise the abandoned boy how to survive. It would have to be purchased. If Jean-Claude was to believed and there were 'five to six boys a week' in Paris alone contacting him, then it would be in demand. The plan was to distribute the 'passports' in major European cities. 'Are there any boys in London?' I asked. 'One.' This 'one' turned out to be Jay-Jay. Jean-Claude had never met him and had only briefly talked with him on the phone. Jay-Jay had been told about Foot Solidaire by someone he worked with in the charity shop in east London. Jean-Claude bemoaned not being able to visit him. 'Perhaps you could go to see him?' Jean-Claude was not aware of Jay-Jay's harrowing story.

'If we don't have the good result with the passport I will have to begin work part-time,' Jean-Claude said. 'I don't get holidays, all the time I work on this. I was working for a guy who sold Indian food.'

Jean-Claude hoped Foot Solidaire would grow. He reckoned it would need €200,000 a year to be run properly, enabling him to take a salary. 'Maybe two or three salaries,' he said. 'We tried it before but it was not a good experience because you need to pay the tax. But if you have funds then you can make more funds.

'I want to be useful and be useful to the community. You know in Africa today you can buy everything with money. You can buy humans. Sometimes some clubs try to give me some big funding, some agents try to give me money. I'm not rich, I don't want to be rich, rich, rich. That is why I remain with my integrity.'

9

Jay-Jay's Chance

I had texted Jay-Jay the night before. 'Be ready to go at 7 a.m. tomorrow. It's a long drive.' A reminder was needed as he had told me previously he had missed trials at clubs because he had got the wrong day or left too little time to travel. He replied immediately. 'That is good opportunity, friend. I am excited for that.' I was excited, too. It was a chance to see the talent that he had hoped would change his life but had so far blighted it.

There was a trial day at Cheltenham Town, a club in the bottom division of English football and one which had only joined the elite of the Football League in 1999. It was the size of club where players like Jay-Jay would have the best chance of being spotted. At that level clubs like Cheltenham, who averaged little more than a meagre 2,500 attendance, had to unearth their own talent to survive. They could not splurge six-figure fees on transfer deals. Instead they scouted players, coached them, improved them and then attempted to sell them on or receive compensation from a bigger club.

Two forms had been sent by Cheltenham to Jay-Jay to fill in. He had to sign a declaration that he was fit, had no allergies nor was taking any medication. The second was a 'player profile'. He called himself a 'striker/winger' and listed his former clubs in Guinea, adding details of the two trials at Cambridge United and Brentford, plus one at AFC Wimbledon, another League Two outfit. He had not mentioned that trial before. He signed his name and indicated he required one night's accommodation at a hotel which Cheltenham would organise. The cost was £35. The trial cost was £60. I paid these by cheque.

Jay-Jay claimed he had been to a similar trial before. He paid £65 for a trial at Cambridge, a club which was non-league at the time. He also said he paid £60 for a two-day trial at Brentford, who had been higher up the pyramid in League One. When I first met him, he rather proudly produced paperwork from those two trials. He kept them in a plastic wallet. 'Look here,' he said. 'I played for Cambridge and Brentford.'

The document for his trial at Brentford was headed 'Brentford Academy – individual player notational sheet'. It was divided into four sub-headings (technical, tactical, psychological and physical) and gave an insight of what Cheltenham could expect. Jay-Jay 'consistently performed the required technique from a static or moving position during opposed practice'. Tactically, he made 'inconsistent' decisions but he did display the ability to 'concentrate for the majority of the session'. The physical category recorded his speed over 20 metres, 'arrowhead' agility left and right and a vertical jump.

Cambridge and Brentford did not 'pursue their interest', to use the football parlance, in Jay-Jay, although he was still hopeful that both clubs would get in touch. 'I've asked my social worker to call them,' he said. 'The trial for Cambridge . . . definitely I was thinking good things for Cambridge. I thought they wanted me. Their manager was there for the first day. We do warm-up exercise and then we play match. We won the match. But I was thinking, "Are they going to say something to me?" After the match the coach came and he said, "Well done, Jay-Jay, you played very well." I thought they would say something to me. All the other players said so because I am very fast. I had two opportunities to score but I gave the pass and they scored. "After we finished we will let all players know." They said this. After two weeks no player was told. All the time I said to my social worker, "Any chance with them?" But they didn't give anything. Then it was the Brentford trial two weeks after that. It was the same. I cannot understand that trial. We didn't warm up properly.'

After he was granted asylum in the UK, Jay-Jay was a football nomad, playing for several amateur south London teams in the Saturday and Sunday leagues. He would train on his own. 'All I do is train, train, train. To be ready.' Either he was deluded about his ability or he was supremely confident. He never stayed at a team for long enough to make an impact. 'Why don't you stay at one club, score lots of goals and then you might be scouted?' I asked.

'The coach of one team asked if I wanted to play Sunday league. My dream is to play football. I played every Sunday and on Saturday. Both together 'cos he really liked me to play. This team was in south London. He always want me to play but I say, "I can't play here, it is not my level." The players were too poor. I was very tired. I don't wanna play for that team. I told my social worker. I didn't feel very good there.'

So Jay-Jay had all the talk. But could he walk the walk? He at least looked the part when he walked towards my car that morning. He was tracksuited, wearing sunglasses and oversize headphones. He looked the archetypal footballer making his way to the team bus for the big game. Behind the glasses could have been the cold stare of a finely honed athlete, totally focused on the job. When he saw me, however, he offered a wide smile, took off his glasses and gave me two thumbs-up. He dropped his bag, couldn't work out how to open the boot and when he took his seat beside me he beamed. 'Thank you, thank you, friend. This is kind of you to take me to trial.' And off we went.

I discovered I was anxious. I fired questions at Jay-Jay, hoping that he had prepared properly. Had he slept well? Had he eaten a healthy breakfast? Had he been eating more than pasta, like I'd said? 'Here, eat these bananas they are good for energy.' 'Yes, friend. Thank you, friend,' Jay-Jay replied. He asked me how my family was and how long the journey would take. We spoke about his 'dream' again and how his favourite player was Lionel Messi. Did he play like Messi? Jay-Jay laughed. 'No, no, no. He is trickery. I fast, *faaaast*. And powerful and a big shot. That is my game. Not like Messi.' Like Didier Drogba? Jay-Jay squealed with joy. 'Yeah, yeah, just like Drogba. He is *gooood* player. I am like him. He is from Africa, like me.'

There was, however, that sadness to Jay-Jay. It was always there. He could laugh and smile but it was not permanent. His face would break and his eyes tighten. Not for long. The slightly downturned mouth would return. His doleful eyes would settle again and he would stare ahead, a slight crease to his frown. I wondered in those moments what he was thinking. Did the abuse he suffered torture him? Was that a stupid question? Was he thinking of home? Of his mother who sold fruit and vegetables in the village market? Of his father, a taxi driver? And of his brother and sister? After a particularly long silence, I asked if he was OK. 'You seem sad today, Jay-Jay? Are you OK?' I was right, he was mulling over things back home.

'Have you spoken to them?'

'No. Last spoke to them when I was back home. When I was 17. I am 20 now. Haven't spoken to them in three years. This is very hard for me. They don't know where I am. I don't know if they want to find me. I will tell them where I am. They won't attack me! It was the other family – my father's family – that wanted to kill me. If I tell my mother and father I am here now they will be pleased I am safe. I don't know if they are safe.'

Ebola had been beginning to wreak havoc in West Africa and Jay-Jay was aware that his family could be in danger. Guinea had suffered almost 1,000 deaths from the disease and the small villages, like the one he came from, were particularly badly affected.

'Our village is very small. It is not like London. We don't have many things. I have not heard from my family. I worry about the Ebola because they could be ill or dead. I don't like to think about it. It is hard for me, you know? This not knowing what is happening. I can't telephone them. No email. No writing letters. Did you know Ebola is very dangerous? If you get it you can die very, very badly.'

Football would provide a welcome distraction for us both. 'Let's not talk about all that,' I suggested. 'You should focus on the trial.' I tried to give him a pep talk. Enjoy it. That was the thrust of my advice. It was important to be relaxed and loose limbed, not tense. 'Don't be tense!' I shouted, because Jay-Jay didn't appear to have been listening. He stared blankly ahead again. 'That would be bad for you.' Then I worried that by demanding he not be tense that might have the opposite effect. 'Jay-Jay! Are you list— Listen, do you want some food? We can stop? You need fuel for the trial? Some more bananas for energy.'

'I am fine, thank you, friend.'

Any parent, or anyone who, as a child, trialled for a school sports team or can recall being asked to turn out for practice at a prospective new club would have recognised the atmosphere at Cheltenham's training ground that day. The air was thick with apprehension. Including friends and family, there must have been 60 people there, all congregated outside the small clubhouse, huddled around picnic tables or leaning against the wall.

Very few were talking. Those who were did so in whispers. The young hopefuls looked serious, terrified, sad. They were trying to act cool. Some chewed gum. Other jaw muscles pulsed purely from anxiety. Jay-Jay sipped from a bottle of Lucozade. Two boys wearing fading Crystal Palace tracksuits sat on the steps, scowling. Three French kids, one with the diminutive stature of Lionel Messi, and tousled hairstyle to match, grunted and shrugged to each other in the corner, away from everyone else.

The hush was occasionally interrupted by a clearing of the throat or sniff of the nose. The sort of noise people feel they have to force out in tense situations. There was the odd snort of attempted laughter as a mum or dad tried to pretend that they were all relaxed. Their boy should be relaxed. Don't be tense.

The tension did not befit the tranquil setting. The training ground was off a well-to-do residential street and was overlooked by the rolling hills of the Cotswolds. Prestbury Park, the home of the Cheltenham National Hunt Festival, was just around the corner. It was a beautiful day. Boys from Cheltenham's youth teams swaggered around with angry brows, hunched shoulders and hands thrust in their club tracksuits. They eyed the interlopers with suspicion. Rightly so, they were potential rivals. Only one per cent of them would make a living from the game, and two-thirds of those fortunate enough to be given a pro contract would be jettisoned by the time they were 18.

One of the Cheltenham's academy staff emerged. It was James Murphy. I had spoken to him previously on the phone. He unfolded a table and produced a piece of paper with the names and addresses of all the triallists for the day. In an unmistakable West Country burr he asked them to stand in a queue. Slowly, silently and sullenly the boys formed a line. I counted 30, each paying a minimum of £60 each. One by one their name was checked off by Murphy, who was struggling to contain the piece of paper blowing in the wind, and they filed into the changing rooms. One boy, who could not have been more than 18, paid cash.

With the players out of sight, the stress level dropped. Parents began to congregate and gossip, discussing trials at other clubs. 'You can tell this is going to be good,' said the father of a scamp-like boy who was barely above five feet. 'Oxford asked him to go for a trial but it was poorly organised, not like this at all.' A South African ex-pat told me she had allowed her son to attend on condition he enrolled on a college course. Another mother was bemoaning her son's stubbornness about turning down the chance to play for a small non-league club who wanted to sign him.

'That's only four leagues below Cheltenham,' said her friend.

'We've told him . . . Stratford, Evesham and Pershore are all after him,' she replied. 'He's turned them all down.'

'That's a good level is that.'

'We've told him but they don't listen, do they?'

Jay-Jay was last out of the changing room. He wore black shorts, black socks and a bright yellow training T-shirt. He will be easy to spot, I thought. France's miniature Messi had shorts down to his calves. The two boys who wore Crystal Palace tracksuits had changed into Crystal Palace training gear imprinted with their initials.

One of the coaches told the boys: 'We're gonna split you into two groups. Do some passing and dribbling skills and then some running drills. We'll take about two-and-a-quarter hours today. Give your best but be careful in tackles. We don't want someone with half a leg missing, we've had some tasty games in the past.'

The boys drifted on to the training pitch, a waft of heat rub following them. Jay-Jay was, again, last out to warm up. I took his Lucozade bottle from him. I noticed, for the first time, how tall he was. More than six foot. And he had broad shoulders. Physically, he had all the attributes to be a footballer.

'Are you OK?' I asked. 'Nervous?'

'No, friend. Excited. You will watch and see. I hope I do well.'

After warming up with all the relish and discipline one would expect from a group of dispirited young men, they were taken over to a pitch for six-a-side matches. It looked as though it was two touches only – control and pass it on – but it was difficult to make out. Parents and supporters were not allowed to stand on the touchline of the pitch and had to remain by the clubhouse, presumably because Cheltenham's coaches didn't want the kids to be screamed and shouted at by a desperate mum or dad. 'If he does that again I'll cut his fuckin' 'ands off,' shouted one as his son misplaced a pass. Jay-Jay, now something of a dot, seemed to be doing OK. He was able to neatly control the ball and he did not give it away.

The group was then split into three to be tested on three different 'circuits'. The first was a shooting test, the second a dribbling drill and the third examined close control. There was no hiding place. A coach stood with a clipboard over each test and made notes on the player. A powderpuff shot, a dawdle of a dribble or wayward ball control could see a player written off.

Jay-Jay began on the dribbling test. He moved with no little purpose and negotiated the challenge of controlling the ball around several cones without disaster. He was fast. He dropped his shoulder deftly and had a surprisingly low, hunched running style for such a big frame. With pace and no little power in those shoulders, I began to see why Jay-Jay reckoned he had something special.

It would be a lie to say that I took Jay-Jay to the trial for purely altruistic reasons. To give the poor African boy a day out. No. I reasoned (hoped) that it would be a great story if Jay-Jay was the pro-in-waiting that he thought he was. Perhaps he would so impress Cheltenham that they would offer him an extended trial. Perhaps there would be a happy ending to this grim tale. The chances, of course, were skeletal. I knew that. Brentford, Cambridge and Wimbledon had not wanted to see more of him, let alone sign him. But just maybe . . .

I began to feel like one of the parents as he approached the second test: close control. I was willing him on. I wanted him to look over so I could give him a thumbs-up. I stood there biting the knuckle of my thumb as he took his turn. He was standing in the middle of four advertising hoardings, which had been arranged to form a square. He was to pass the ball against a hoarding and when it returned to him, control it, turn and pass it against the next hoarding, moving round and round. The quicker the better. The boys who excelled would spin quickly. With the hoardings shielding their feet and the ball to spectators, they looked like they were dancing, and the pounding of the boards was their drum and bass beat.

Jay-Jay started off slowly. He'll get quicker, I thought, he's just finding his feet. But the tempo remained the same. His beat was more New Romantics. Jay-Jay's was a slow dance, one which turned back on itself every now and then, to retrace its steps, as he miscontrolled the ball or stumbled. I didn't know whether the coaches were marking each boy on a 'pass' or 'fail' basis but Jay-Jay had not done well.

Still, he never said he had good ball control, did he? He was a Drogba-style player. He had pace, he said. And that had been proved correct so far. He had a powerful shot, he said. The standard of the shooting test had been woeful. There had been more shots off target than on as the boys had frequently sent efforts hopelessly wide. They had about six or seven strikes each. The balls were lined up just inside the area and either side was a pole which they had to run round alternately before approaching the ball to shoot. Left and right foot were tested. Jay-Jay devoured the ground towards the pole. It was coming back which was the problem. He slowed right down. Surely the point was to attack the ball at pace and fire it home? Should I have told him that? Should I have said, 'They are trying to replicate a match situation'? Surely the coach with the clipboard told him that? His feet stuttered, unsure, as they approached the ball, exactly like an amateur hurdler does the obstacle. Jay-Jay was not a natural. His first three shots went over the bar. One went wide of the post. His final shot was pouched comfortingly by the goalkeeper. With each shot, my wince grew wider. I read Jay-Jay's lips to the coach. 'Did I do OK?'

Jay-Jay was no pro-footballer. He was a victim. That was all. He had been sold a hopeless dream for someone else's sordid fantasy. With each sorry stumble on the ball and sad shot sailing through the blue sky past the goal, his story became more tragic. His staccato, naïve approach to kick the ball reminded me of when we first met and he couldn't bring himself to utter the words about his abuse. All he had in his footballing favour was an athletic physique, his height and broad shoulders no doubt attractive. And yet it was this frame which would have first caught the eye of the man who defiled him.

Above all, he was just a boy. A boy who had no one to advise him about the best path to take in life. I thought of those two young Chelsea wannabees outside his kitchen window. Jay-Jay was just like them, with their boundless, chaotic enthusiasm, trying to kick the leather off the ball. The difference was those boys would go home and they would, probably, have a mother or father, aunt or uncle, to guide them. Jay-Jay did not.

Should I tell him? That was what I was thinking when I drove him back to his accommodation. Was it my place to say, 'Look, I think you're wasting your time'? I didn't. I reasoned that there was still the full match the next day. Perhaps Jay-Jay had had a bad day, and in the cut and thrust of a match situation he would be a better player, more physical, more instinctive. After all, I was no scout. This time I wasn't even posing as one. It was the job of Cheltenham's coaches to tell Jay-Jay whether he was good enough. In the information letter about the trial, the club had promised to give feedback.

Looking back I realise I was being a coward. I didn't have the guts to tell Jay-Jay what I thought. I thought it might break him. His football dream sustained him and, no doubt, at times it kept his mind from wandering down the dark path which had led him to England. In that regard it was a healthy fantasy. Over a Big Mac and fries at McDonald's that night, I was praying he wouldn't ask me whether I thought he was a good player. I needn't have worried. He didn't. I did ask how he thought it went.

'Disappointed with myself. It was not good for me. You see . . . I have not been training, training, training. I need to do better in the match tomorrow. Show more of my skills. Show them my very *faaaast* running and powerful shot.'

Jay-Jay did not do much better in the match. The hope that he would prove that day one was an aberration disappeared quickly. With his first touch of the ball, he gave it away. His second saw him chest the ball down, move off from the wing and take a wild swing. He missed it completely. His third touch he retained possession, holding off a tackle before passing it wide right, his fourth he fell over, his fifth ran over his foot for a throw-in, his sixth he fell over. As the game progressed I made a note 'falls over a lot'.

There was a time, midway through the second half, when if this was a movie we would switch to slow motion. The music would be cut. There might only be the sound of a beating heart. The viewer would know that it was the defining, pivotal, glorious moment of the story. When our hero becomes exactly that. Jay-Jay was clean through on goal. There was hope. Despite his technical failings, if Jay-Jay was a finisher, a goalscorer – that precious commodity in football which insiders will tell you cannot be taught – then he had a chance. 'His overall game needs work,' the coach would say. 'But, boy, can he finish.'

The ball skipped off the turf away from Jay-Jay. It was his lack of control again. He collided with the goalkeeper and the ball spun away harmlessly. He picked himself up, dusted down his shirt and gave a thumbs-up to the boy who had provided the pass. It was the little French kid. He was one of the best players, although he was guilty of hogging the ball, trying to beat everyone with dazzling tricks and turns. We all played with one of those in the school playground. What that kid needed was a pep talk before the game, someone to tell him to play for the team, not himself. 'He thinks he's fackin' Messi that one,' said a dad. 'Pass the ball, son!' The two Crystal Palace boys were also good. They seemed to have that little bit more time on the ball than everyone else. With the ball approaching they weren't thinking about controlling it, that was a given. They were thinking about where to pass it.

When waiting for Jay-Jay to emerge from the dressing room, showered and changed for the drive home, the Palace boys were sitting, still scowling, outside. I wanted to ask them a question.

'Was it normal to have to pay for a trial?' I wondered.

'Nope, never done it before,' one said.

'Nah,' replied the other. 'And we won't be doing it again, neither.'

10

England Exploits

The sight of the boys standing solemnly, dutifully in line at Cheltenham Town had pricked the conscience. They had a replica shirt on their back, boots in a bag and hope in their heart. But most importantly, money in their pocket. Just like the victims of football trafficking they were proof that all dreams have a price. There was a difference, though, between them – the clique of French kids, the surly boys from Crystal Palace – and those who had been unceremoniously dumped in foreign cities. Their dream was cheap. At just £60 it was paltry compared to the thousands that some had been persuaded to part with.

Cheltenham had been happy to take it. It was a transaction between two consenting parties. Both wanted the same outcome. Cheltenham hoped to find a potential professional, each of the boys wished, desperately, they were it. But that didn't make it edifying. Quite the opposite. From a boy stuffing notes of cash into the hands of the kingmakers to the palpable sense of trepidation in the air, it looked like exploitation, it felt like exploitation.

The will to exploit young people's aspirations is at the core of this story. It is the motivation for agents to ship kids from one continent to another so they can take a slice of their contract if they impress on trial. Likewise those who extort money on the false promise of a trial. One would expect to find it in South

America or West Africa, where stories abound that 'anything goes', but the sleepy Costwolds at one of English football's bottom feeders?

Disturbed by Cheltenham's scheme, I spoke with managers, directors, scouts and youth coaches in the lower leagues to check whether it was commonplace for clubs to charge for trials. Thanks to Jay-Jay I knew he had paid to try out at Cambridge, Wimbledon and Brentford, so there was a possibility that it was normal practice for the football industry. To a man they said it was not. Chris Wilder, the manager of Northampton Town, who were in the same league as Cheltenham, said he had 'never heard of that before'. Simon Lenagan, the director at Oxford, said it was 'wrong, totally wrong'. The look of disgust and disbelief on the face of the scout and coach, who wanted to remain anonymous, when asked for their opinion was memorable.

Although Cheltenham had done nothing illegal, there was a moral and ethical debate to be had over a club taking money from players. As stated, both club and player willingly entered into the deal, but there was an imbalance. The club had all the power and none of the risk in the same way that agents held sway over youngsters they would be prepared to traffic. The rationale in staging trials for money and moving players was exactly the same.

A club giving a chance to a young player exposed itself to no liabilities whatsoever. In fact, with the nominal fee they had the opportunity to make a profit. There was also the chance, no matter how slight, that they could discover a talent. Young footballers represented cheap labour but the potential upside could be huge. Cheltenham could find they had a player who could blossom into one good enough to play two or three leagues higher, thus earning themselves a chunk of money from a transfer fee. It was a numbers game, the same one Hamid and Imari played.

For the player the risk was not on the same spectrum. They could suffer an injury or loss of confidence. Do not forget the £60 gamble, either. That might not be much to an adult but to an under-18, who would also need to find travel expenses, it was a significant amount of money.

What suggested a lack of principle was that the club must have been acutely aware of the desire of players without a professional club to succeed. That they would do almost anything to have a career in football. So why not give them a chance and charge them for it? Was that their thinking?

Firstly, there were the huge odds of any of those boys getting a contract. Cheltenham knew exactly how to push the buttons of the young players, offering what they craved. The price included, they boasted, 'the opportunity to win a professional contract'. Secondly, what other industry charged for what was, essentially, a job interview? Think of your dream job. Would you pay £60, with 30 other applicants, to be assessed on your suitability? Maybe you would, but it is unlikely you would think it fair or decent. Cheltenham also promised 'written individual feedback for each player after the game'. Jay-Jay did not receive that feedback. Nor did a Swiss player, Rejuan, who told me so by email. 'No, they didn't send me anything. I think this trial was just about making money.'

With each of the 30 boys paying a minimum of £60, Cheltenham would have received £1,800 that day. In the upper echelons of English football, that wouldn't buy you a player for even half a day. But for a club on the bottom rung of the professional game, one that attracts about a couple of thousand supporters every other week, it was a big deal. It was not a one-off either. Cheltenham had held up to three trials a year previously for 16- to 23-year-olds, and the uptake had been greater. James Murphy, who ran the trial when Jay-Jay attended, had told me that they had hosted 60 earlier in the year. 'It's quite low,' he said. 'Normally it's 80–120.' If Cheltenham were staging three trials a year and they had an average attendance of 80, it meant they were making almost £15,000 a year from aspiring young footballers.

There was a more disturbing aspect to Cheltenham's policy, however. Murphy had told me on the phone, rather proudly, that some boys 'come from Africa. We've had some from Australia, New Zealand and Canada.' If that was true then not only had Cheltenham engaged in something ethically dubious, they had offered paid trials under false pretences because they would not have been able to sign anybody from outside the European Union, even if they did impress enough having handed over their money.

The players from Africa, Australia, New Zealand and Canada that Murphy spoke about could not have signed a professional contract. If they were under the age of 18, Fifa's Article 19 prevented clubs signing players of that age from another continent. If they were over 18, they would have had to have played 75 per cent of their country's international fixtures over the last two years to qualify for a work permit. And how likely was it that a player who met that criterion would have been reduced to paying for a trial at a nondescript club?

To confirm that Cheltenham would take money from a non-EU foreign underage player they could not employ, I sent an email from a fictitious player called Penfold Black. He was 17. 'I am a great striker. I am coming from Nigeria for the trial to achieve my dream.' Cheltenham were happy to have him. They invited him to their next trial, attaching the fitness declaration form and player profile. Would the club help him pay the accommodation fee as he was coming from another continent? No. Would they accept cash? Yes. 'Our bank account details are as follows if you want to make a bank transfer. You can bring cash on the day, but no cash, no play!!'

Was it harsh to pick on little old Cheltenham, whose supporters might argue that in their own small-minded, provincial way, they were just trying to make ends meet? After all they were one of the poorest clubs in the country, something which their chairman, Paul Baker, also a Liberal Democrat borough concillor by the way, reminded supporters about.

So what about Brentford? In the 2014–15 season they were a club on the brink of promotion to the Premier League, the land of milk and honey. In 2013 they had a turnover of nearly £4 million. Comparatively they were a giant to Cheltenham Town in terms of finances, resources and support. What was their excuse for charging kids £40 for a trial in May 2015? Why did they feel they had to lure kids on their website with the promise that: 'a professional contract at Brentford FC will be up for grabs'? Their last trial, in November 2014, had 200 attendees. The next one, the following year in May, had space for 400. If all of those were filled, that was £24,000.

Brentford were also guilty of being prepared to take money from an under-18 they had no possible hope of giving that 'professional contract' to. Our fictitious friend, Som Kalou, who had introduced us to Hamid, emailed the club at the start of 2015. He said he was 17, was from Nigeria and wanted to attend the paid trial. A club aware of Fifa's Article 19 and work-permit rules should not have countenanced taking money from someone like Som, let alone encouraged him to travel to a different continent.

Their initial reply stated: 'All information regarding the trials can be found on our application form on our website. Please follow the instructions carefully on how to apply.' Som emailed again, reiterating that he was coming from Nigeria and it would be 'hard' for him to post the application form that needed to be downloaded. He was told: 'We must receive the £40 payment along with the application form.' Som replied, asking: 'So if I send the money I can come for trial?' 'Correct,' was the response.

When I asked Brentford for an explanation, they wrote back: 'We get applications from all over the world to attend our trials and do not bar anyone who wants to attend. There has been a rise in dual-passport holders in recent years and the club would not be in a position to know whether an individual would qualify to work or play football in the UK until an application was made to do so. We also have education provision available for those of the right age.' They also included a blurb for a two-day trial in May 2015 for 16- to 21-year-olds. It boasted how they gave players 'from all over the world an opportunity'. The fee was £40. Cheltenham were also contacted but they failed to answer my questions.

So Cheltenham and Brentford were both culpable of attempting to charge players for the chance to earn a professional contract when the reality of the sport's rules and regulations meant they could offer no such thing. It begged the question, how many more clubs were doing the same? How many more between Brentford at the top of the Football League and Cheltenham at the foot would encourage a 17-year-old from Nigeria? I conducted a survey of every Football league club. Som Kalou emailed each of them (70 out of the 72 in total as Cheltenham and Brentford had already been asked), asking for an opportunity to trial.

Dear sir

Please can I come for trials? I am 17 and a very good striker from Nigeria.

I have my CV below.

I am fit and hungry to score goals.

Please tell me trial details and how much I have to pay for the trial. I can send cheque or cash.

Thank you

Som

Fourteen clubs responded and only one offer of a trial was forthcoming. That was from Watford, another Championship club. They wrote: 'The trials are free, just make sure you attend for the best chance of securing a place.' None of the clubs told Som that he was wasting his time, failing to quote the rules about transfers of minors or work-permit regulations. Stevenage, in League Two, were closest to imparting the correct advice. Som was not suitable because he 'lived too far away'. There was encouragement from some clubs. Oldham Athletic told him 'not to give up' and suggested two non-league clubs to contact. Plymouth Argyle were similarly positive and told him to register with a website for young players searching for clubs. Derby County, MK Dons and Blackburn were hardly discouraging in their replies. The response of each of the 14 clubs is recorded here:

Birmingham City: unfortunately we do not have any place for a boy of your age.

Blackburn Rovers: all I can do is forward your email on to somebody who works with that age group. It is down to them if they contact you.

Bury: if you were based in England you could have trials but we don't have the funds to get you over for trial.

Charlton Athletic: in an effort to avoid your disappointment, Charlton Athletic Football Club will not invite a player in for a trial unless one of our scouts has seen him play and thinks he is of the required standard.

Derby County: we will keep your details on file and contact you should there be any interest.

MK Dons: please follow the trial procedure on our website.

Oldham Athletic: sorry, you are too old for this club. Do not give up though. [Try] a semi pro club like Curzon Ashton or Droylsden.

Port Vale: thank you for the request – we are not looking to add to the youth squad as we have a full team.

Plymouth Argyle: we are not holding any trials at this moment in time. Unfortunately, we are unable to offer you a suitable position within our set-up. In the meantime we do hope that you have success in finding yourself a club. To assist your search for a club, may we suggest that you visit 'All About Ballerz' at www.allaboutballerz.com. This is a platform for footballers at all levels to showcase their talents – a place where you can upload video clips of yourself and be seen by a wider audience. A number of clubs, managers and scouts discover fresh new talent and experienced players by using this growing popular platform.

Rotherham United: many thanks for the email, I cannot offer you a trial.

Stevenage: we can't accommodate you as you live too far away from our club.

Swindon Town: unfortunately we are not running any trials, as we have offered a scholarship to a number of players that have come through our academy, which will take us up to our full quota for the 2014–2015 season.

Watford: the trials are free, just make sure you attend for the best chance of securing a place.

Outside of the professional game, charging kids for trials has become an industry. Thanks to the glamour, glitz and gold of the

Premier League footballer's lifestyle, often the ambition of a young boy to make it as a star is today matched by his parents. To cater for this hankering, soccer courses and academies have sprung up all over the country, offering trials with the promise that scouts from professional clubs will attend.

One company heavily involved is FootballCV. As their website states: 'There are hundreds of thousands of youngsters who have the same dream but only a few will be able to boast in years to come, "I played the game for a living." And what a living that can be for the top professionals.'

FootballCV were of interest because they ran trials in association with the Football League and the Professional Footballers' Association. The founder and director is David Mallinger; its managing director, Graham Starmer. Mallinger was a director at Corby Town FC of the Southern League Premier Division and Starmer was the vice-chairman of the club. Mallinger was also listed as a director at Kettering Town FC.

FootballCV organise trials for children as young as six, charging £15. The top price for a trial listed on their website was, at this point, £85. There was also the option of attending camps – for players aged 12 to 25 – which ran over four days, at a cost of £430, and a residential academy course from £609 per week. Included in the cost was the chance to impress scouts from professional clubs. There was even a two-year course at just under £25,000 per year at a dedicated academy at Steel Park, Corby. Students would receive training from professional coaches, play in competitive matches against Premier League and Football league clubs and be watched by up to 50 scouts. Education formed a large part of the programme, with A levels and B-Tech courses available. Alongside each of these details were reminders of the 'lucrative living to be made'. 'Beckham . . . Rooney . . . Gareth Bale . . . so who will be next? FootballCV may have the answer and give you the opportunity to be the next star of the future.'

Would that opportunity be available to international players like Som? Yes. In a reply to his email asking to attend a trial it was recommended he 'play football in the UK for as long as your budget will allow to give yourself the best chance of being discovered'.

Attached was a 'how to' guide for players without a European passport to attend a FootballCV trial. It said that FootballCV would provide an invitation letter 'which can be used to apply for temporary visas once a trial has been booked and successfully paid for'. There was a £20 administration fee for an invitation letter and, if the player wanted an original copy, there was a £70 charge for a courier. There was no mention of Fifa's Article 19 rule or work-permit stipulations in the document. There was no mention that even if one of the scouts that Som had paid to impress wanted to sign him, they could not.

Graham Starmer was asked why Som was encouraged. 'We are very stringent with how we operate re. visas and comply with all Home Office rules.' He also said that players from outside the EU can sign and play for clubs 'below Step 5' in England. He is correct. That is six levels below the bottom division of the Football League, hardly the stomping grounds of Messrs Beckham or Bale. Som was not told this. The 'how to' guide that FootballCV sent to him also failed to mention that he would have to make do with a club no higher than a division like the Spartan South Midlands League.

So it was apparent that, at best, there was little regard in the English game for the rules when signing minors and work-permit regulations. At worst it was evidence that football was an industry obsessed with money and how clubs would do anything to gain an edge over rivals, find the next star or, more prosaically, win three points on Saturday. But there was nothing revelatory about the latter. It was another important piece of the jigsaw, however, as it provided a reason as to how and why it was possible for players to be moved from one country to the other without a realistic chance of playing. Already I had learnt that there were agents who had displayed an alarming disregard for football's laws which had been drawn up to prevent mass migration for nothing. Charlie Baffour, the London-based agent, thought that a club could sign an under-18 from Africa and stick him in their academy. 'No problem,' he said. Hamid had actively scouted players from Africa and encouraged them to go to Larnaca, Cyprus. It resulted in scores of them kicking their heels, without a club and with little chance of finding one precisely because they did not meet the criteria. It was why so many turned up that day for a 'trial' match under the shrewd eyes of John in that sleepy ex-pat town.

When agents don't know the rules or wilfully disregard them and the professional clubs do the same, then you have the recipe for football trafficking and exploitation. Although only three clubs – Cheltenham, Brentford and Watford – had offered a trial to Som, the consequences of such erroneous decisions could be far reaching. If Som had been real and he wanted to come to England from Nigeria he would need an invitation from a club, or a company like FootballCV, so he could get a visa. Check. Entry into a country is one of the biggest barriers to football migration and here it was being leapt with ease.

Let's extrapolate Som's 'story'. He is desperate for a chance to prove himself in Europe. He has an agent who says he can get him a trial. Som is delighted. The agent spends a couple of hours online searching for clubs in England who offer open trials. He emails them. They say 'yes, he can come', ignoring his age and where he resides. He also approaches FootballCV. Crucially, he has invitations from three sources. A visa should not be a problem. The agent goes back to Som with the good news. 'I have three trials for you, one at Brentford, one at Cheltenham and another at a place called FootballCV in front of many, many scouts.' Som cannot believe it. Finally, he will get his chance. The agent names his price for his work. It would probably be in the thousands. Som travels to the UK, attends the trials. No club signs him. The agent abandons him.

11

Sulley's Story

The hunger in Sulley's eyes had nothing to do with football. He said he not eaten that day. His was a frame which would have needed plenty of fuel. He was tall, at least 6 foot 2 inches, and he had the sort of rangy legs and arms which made it easy to imagine him striding around the midfield, bossing and barging. He looked a bit like Yaya Touré, the captain of Manchester City and Ivory Coast. Apt. 'Yaya is my favourite player,' he said. 'He plays so easily, like me.'

Sulley was 21 and hailed from Bobo-Dioulasso, the second-largest city in Burkina Faso. He had ended up in Paris by way of Portugal and Belgium. It was a journey which began when he was scouted at 17 by an agent who had claimed he could be a big star. He had just the right club – in the Portuguese second division – where Sulley could begin his ascent. It ended predictably. There was no offer of a professional contract. The agent took his passport, not that Sulley had money to return home. He slept on friends' floors and had to borrow money.

Sulley's ambition had not been superstardom. He didn't speak of being the next Yaya. He just wanted to earn 'a good salary playing ball' in order to send money back home to his uncle, who had raised him after his father died when he was six. He had a brother and sister. 'Both are older than me but I want to earn for them. My uncle was not rich at all. He didn't have money for a lot of things. It wasn't easy. In the school holidays I would work in a clothes shop with my brother for money. I wanted to help them, too.'

He had started playing football at the age of nine, in the street with the other kids. He pretended he was Ronaldinho, the Brazil star. 'Playing football was great for me. It relaxed me. I could have many, many worries but when I played I forgot them all. It is still like that now, even if I have worries about food and money and a place to stay.'

In Bobo-Dioulasso, Sulley had stood out. He had joined an academy after leaving junior school and his strength, close control and assured passing had brought him to the attention of scouts and agents. It was no mean feat to shine in a city renowned for producing football talent, such as Charles Kaboré, the powerful midfielder who played more than 120 times for Marseille and in 2013 transferred to Kuban Krasnodar of the Russian league. He also played almost 50 times for the Burkina Faso national team. Then there was Bertrand Traoré, who Chelsea signed from Auxerre, the French club, and then loaned to Vitesse Arnhem in Holland. Sulley had gone to school with Traoré. 'We played together from the age of ten, at school and in the street,' he said. 'We were in the same class at school. He went to the UK after he left high school, I think. I saw him in June. His brother lives in Paris.'

'Could he help you get a club?' I asked.

'I've not spoken to him about getting a club. But he is my friend. He plays in Holland now. He was a different player to me, so I cannot say whether he was better. He was an attacker.'

Traoré was luckier. He was spotted by a reputable agent, Sulley was not; he went to the Portuguese second division team and started off playing in the under-19s. 'I was doing well and I soon moved up to play with the seniors,' he said. 'I felt so motivated. It was my dream and I think I should have been able to play in the first division.'

The club provided an apartment and all of his meals. He was even able to send home some money – 'three times' – from the little he did earn. 'It was rare we got paid,' he said. 'I spoke to some of the senior players and they had not been paid for three months.'

It was the beginning of the end. Before Sulley could make an impression, the club suffered financial problems and withdrew funding for the youth teams. It left Sulley without a club. According to Sulley, the agent, aware that it would have been too much work to find him a new club, showed his true character. He told him to sign on for benefits and pocketed the money himself. When it ran out, Sulley never saw him again. He told me his name but had no telephone number or email address. He was not listed as a Fifa licensed agent.

A friend from Senegal, who had been on trial at the Portuguese club but was not taken on, suggested he try his luck with a club in Belgium he was playing for. But they would not even offer him a trial so he went to Paris to join the thousands of other young foot-ballers wandering the streets. 'I heard about Foot Solidaire. I was told they could help,' Sulley said.

He spent his days searching for a club. 'It's my job,' he laughed. 'It's what I do. I get up, I look on the internet and if the team is close by I go there. That was what I was doing before I came here to see you. I have been out all day, looking and searching.'

Paris's roads lead nowhere. Sulley, one day, will run out of clubs. 'I have no real job,' he said. 'I have no money.' He told me he lived in Paris's northern suburbs, sleeping on the sofa at a friend's apartment. The friend had a wife and five children. He could not stay there for ever. 'But sometimes I can eat with him,' he said. 'Maybe I will eat tonight.'

12

Slave Trade

The man lay prostrate on the road. His body was twisted. Arms and legs pointed and jutted awkwardly as if directing the cars, one of which had just mowed him down. Then sped off. He was dead or dying. No one came to his aid. A group of people stood shouting and gesticulating at the injustice. I was stunned, rooted to the spot. Other cars manoeuvred around him carefully before the rasp of the accelerator drowned out protestations. The police turned up. Bovver-boy-booted and clad in camouflage they got out of their car with all the urgency of an early morning constitution. Life was cheap in the slums of Accra.

It was my first day in Old Fadama, the largest slum in the city, and you could buy anything there. Anything. More than 80,000 people jostled to exist in the space of 40-odd football pitches. 'This is where it goes dead,' said Samuel, my guide, as we had passed over the Odaw River, choked with the rubbish and detritus from a community which had bigger concerns than being neat and tidy. Samuel was studying to be a lawyer but he had been previously been a scout, still worked as an agent and had a small stake in lower division clubs in Ghana. He knew football in the country inside out. I was undercover again, posing as John from Scout Network in a bid to understand the footballing culture in West Africa. To understand why so many boys dreamt of playing in Europe.

'You couldn't come to this place alone,' he said. 'Probably be robbed. I've been here at night. Happened to me. They don't rob their own, though, you know that? That's because in there,' he pointed to the slum, 'they have ways of dealing with you.'

It was the sort of place that a tremulous white man, or 'blond' as they sometimes say in West Africa, would reckon he would not make it out of. Was there menace in the air? Something had throbbed and seethed in that intense heat, shimmering off the roofs of the corrugated iron shacks. People there didn't have homes. After a hard day's work, they put their head down, sometimes with up to 20 others, in one room. It might be, if they were fortunate, a wooden kiosk. Others had tarpaulin for a roof. The huts and hovels were tightly packed and tessellated into an unfathomable jigsaw. The alleyways and paths were labyrinthine. Sanitation and running water was hard to come by. The gulleys and streams which ran behind the homes, or sometimes through the middle of its 'streets', doubled as a rubbish dump and toilet.

The locals called Old Fadama 'Sodom and Gomorrah'. The prevalence of religious hoardings everywhere suggested it was trying to fight its reputation: 'The divine finger of God is pointing at you'; 'Jesus Saves!' There was another billboard. It was of Asamoah Gyan, the Ghana striker, cajoling the people to support the 'Black Stars' in the African Cup of Nations. 'Jesus saves . . . but Gyan always scores the rebound,' Samuel laughed.

It would be a cliché to call football a religion in Old Fadama. They love it, of course, crowding round any television set showing a game or packing out the small bars which do the same. But they don't live for it. It's an escape from the drudgery or a potential route out.

'It didn't used to be that way,' Samuel said. 'When Michael Essien – he was from Accra – signed for Chelsea and everyone here read in the paper that he was earning £70,000 a week, everything changed. Everyone wanted to be a footballer. Even the middle-class parents send their kids to a football academy now.' Samuel was right. The Ghana FA said that in Accra alone there were 240 clubs (holding the registration of 20,000 players), an increase of nearly 20 per cent from the previous decade.

'That is why we have this trafficking problem. Opportunists. People are very clever. They spot a social or cultural change and they exploit it. People here are desperate. Some are desperate to be footballers.' That's what was in the air. Desperation. It was a dumb 'blond' moment to immediately think of oneself and feel threatened. People wanted to improve their lives. 'Football trafficking is bad,' Samuel said. 'But is it so bad? Getting out of this place?'

Indeed. The life expectancy for a child born into a place like Old Fadama is 60 and, along with a third of the country's population, they get by on less than £1.50 a day. The crooks and charlatans, therefore, have rich pickings in Accra's city of sin.

Before travelling to Accra, I (not John) had spoken to Erin Bowser, who worked for the Ghana office of the International Organisation for Migration, the anti-trafficking charity headed by William Swing, or Willy Swing as our friend Amane called him at the UN conference in Geneva. Having listened to her experiences of the subject, it was clear that football agents were not the biggest problem. There were worse individuals at play. 'We know about the football side of things,' she said. 'But the situations people are trafficked into vary greatly. Often it is sex exploitation and forced labour. Domestic servitude is most difficult to prove. The harvesting of organs is probably one of the worst.

'What happens is that the parents sell their children to these people because they are desperate for them to have a better life.' The fee for a child – a life – was nominal according to Bowser. It might be as small as $55 a year, with 'some cattle, sheep, fish or foodstuffs' thrown in. 'It's also one less mouth to feed,' added Bowser. 'There's a sense they want their children to have more. They are in poverty, they can't feed their child enough so maybe they can eat regularly if they give them up, they can go to school. It's not seen as strange to send a child away. It's the culture here. The traffickers come and they have these great offers – "They'll go to school, they'll be looked after, maybe a bit of work."'

The offer of an education is one that is not often turned down. In Old Fadama around 65 per cent of under-18s do not go to school, and almost 50 per cent will never go. Just like the tantalising dream of football, the prospect of education is dangled like a cynical carrot. The stick is brutal. In Ghana, Bowser said, there have been 1.2 million kids trafficked internally to forced labour. Some of them have ended up at Lake Volta having been promised football trials – a fate worse than an empty hotel room in Paris or Madrid.

Lake Volta is the largest reservoir in the world. It was man-made, after 3,000 miles of forest were flooded in 1965. Children as young as four have been sold to the fishermen who've used them to untangle their nets from trees below the water line. 'They have to dive down to free the nets,' Bowser said. Some of them get caught themselves and never resurface. Their bodies are buried in the sand by the lake. The daily hardship of Old Fadama is almost a luxury by comparison.

Farook, aged 11, did not go to school. He wears, day in and day out, a fake Barcelona shirt. He works at one of the largest digital waste dumpsites in the world. There's a fair chance that if you've ever discarded a laptop or mobile phone it has ended up here, waiting to be discovered by Farook's small and scarred hands. The kids of Old Fadama take apart the old electronic devices to sell as bits of scrap metal at the market. They might use a rock to smash and strip out the copper wires or burn away the plastic, exposing them to harmful toxic fumes.

When work allows, Farook plays football with his friends with a ball made from rags and string. For Farook to realise his dream of being a professional footballer, he would need to be spotted by one of the small academies that operate by the roadside, on the beach or any piece of scrubland going. When driving by one of the slums (or more likely stuck in traffic) one can spot them. They are known as 'neighbourhood teams' and operate on an informal basis.

On our way to Old Fadama, Samuel had taken me through Jamestown, a slum more famous for producing boxers: seven world champions and counting, including Ben 'the Wonder' Tackie. 'This is where all the next huge football stars will come from,' Samuel said. 'Places like this. They have the fight and desire to get out. To improve their lives. They'll do anything. In Jamestown they are particularly angry. This is the people who used to have all the money in Accra but they wanted the easy life and retreated out to the beach, giving up all their lands. Now look.' He pointed to a group of 15 or so boys on a training run, dodging the rubbish on the sands, all wearing yellow bibs. 'Another academy.'

There have been estimates that there were up to 500 academies in Accra alone, but those who've worked in the bona fide football industry in the city said the number was exaggerated. They are called 'illegal' but only because they are not recognised by any football association. They are not registered with the Ghana FA, so there's no way of checking what happens to their players or where they might be transferred to. An industry has been created outside of an industry. For example, Lois, who I met in Larnaca, Cyprus, ran an 'illegal' academy in Accra.

They are mostly run by chancers with little or no pedigree. The proprietors might claim to have played professional football in

Ghana – difficult because 90 per cent of players are amateur – but can rarely produce any proof. The 'roadside academy' managers scout players like Farook, hoping their ball skills match the dexterity of their finger-bleeding work. If they do, they might buy the child from the parents for a small fee, offering the exact incentives that Bowser told me about. Many, Samuel said, saw it as a free bet: 'They want to find the next Essien. The next Gyan. A lot of money can be made, you know? These academies, if they are smart and do things the right way, can receive a big payment from a club or a scout.'

It was, according to Samuel, a misconception that these managers had extorted money from families. Stories that they have conned people out of life savings or houses were wide of the mark. 'No African would sell their house or give monies to a local person,' Samuel said. 'That is done by the criminals, the trafficking scams you read about in the papers. Those people would disappear. You think you could get away with that in Accra if you were from Accra? No. The academy scouts and managers? Everyone knows their business.'

Even Samuel 'has boys', the colloquialism for training footballers. 'You must come and see them,' he said. 'Tell me what you think.' He noticed my look of surprise. 'There is nothing bad,' he said. 'They go to school and eat because of me. I can afford it. They might be the next big African star. Play in the Champions League. The money that can be made is huge. Don't judge us. It's the way of life here.'

The turf at the Carl Reindorf Park Stadium, home to Liberty Professionals, was hallowed. It didn't look it. It was patchy, uneven. There were tufts of grass in the penalty area big enough to cause embarrassing 'bobbles' for a striker. But it was where Michael Essien, Asamoah Gyan and Sulley Muntari, who plays for AC

Milan, learnt their trade. 'They are like gods those players,' Samuel said. 'So here is very special to the people of Accra.' Essien trained there every day when he was in Ghana.

Liberty are a Premier League club but they have never won the title. They don't care. They are not even that bothered about winning games. In 2014 they just about staved off relegation. All they want to do is produce young players to sell to Europe. 'That is what football in Ghana is all about,' Samuel said.

It is a simple concept to grasp, albeit an anathema to a supporter of a Premier League club in England where a top-four finish is utopia, mid-table mediocrity is considered success and relegation a fate worse than spending August to May in purgatory. The Premier League in Ghana is the top echelon but it is not the promised land.

'If a player plays in the Premier League in Ghana for too long it is bad,' Samuel said. 'Some of the big players barely played. I think Sulley Muntari might have played less than five games. If they play in the Premier League they have not been scouted, no one wants them. The best players we never see in Ghana.'

There is little incentive to play in the Premier League. A professional contract, which is rare indeed, is worth no more than $200 a month. Instead, the rewards go to young players. In Ghana's under-17 and under-20 World Cup campaigns, Samuel said players had been paid $1,000 and $2,000 respectively if they won a match. The message is clear. It is aspirational in Ghana not to play for the Premier League but to be the next young emerging talent, one who could move abroad and inspire a new generation. These players dance in the dreams of the youngsters resting their weary heads on the bare ground in Old Fadama. The coaches at Liberty share the reverie. If they find the next Essien or Gyan it means, at a base level, they are paid. Their families eat. The bills are taken care of and they are not sucked into the slums. Liberty

Professionals survive to unearth more talent next year. That is the circle of footballing life in Ghana.

George Lamptey had been round and round. He is the grizzled old coach of Liberty. As Samuel and I sat on a bleacher watching the morning training session, he barked and growled at players taking part in a one-touch exercise. He had to stop it on two or three occasions to deliver an Alex Ferguson-style 'hairdryer' rebuke. 'Simple! Simple,' he shouted. 'Bang! Bang! Bang!' He pumped his fist to denote how he wanted the ball to be passed quickly.

'They are showing off,' Samuel said. 'Because they see a white man and they know you are a scout. George is furious with them. He knows that.'

Most of the players had come from the 'roadside academies' or teams in the north of the country. Liberty call them their feeder clubs, paying up to $500 a season and sending kit and balls to have first refusal on the talent.

Samuel pointed out some of the players. By the corner flag, diligently going through his exercise routine was Daniel Adjei. He was the third-choice goalkeeper for the national team and had been in the squad for the World Cup in 2010. His equivalent in Italy, England, Spain, Germany would be a millionaire, training at state of the art complexes. Among the throng was a young midfielder who had been hailed as 'the next big thing'. He had played Major League Soccer in America with Dallas. 'He was big news when he came back to Accra,' Samuel said. 'In all the papers. We thought he was the next Beckham but he was the next David Bentley. He doesn't know where his career is going.'

There was an air of desperation even at Liberty. In the corner of the training ground is a half-built mosque. 'The last owner of the club started to build it but then he died,' Samuel said. 'You would have thought they'd have finished it in his honour. But no.

Cruel, cruel, cruel. They have no money for that. They are dying. George knows that. It is a struggle to survive. Look in his eyes when you speak.'

George looked in his mid-fifties. He still had energy and passion when he spoke but there was more than a hint of panic at where the next pay cheque was coming from.

'It is a team that we started to develop young players,' he said. 'We have no programme for the Premier League, we don't need to win. We are having problems, we don't have the basics. I need to get two or three out to make some more money.'

The money would come from Fifa's Training Compensation Scheme. It is the lifeblood of Ghana football. A club like Liberty can fund itself for several years off the back of moving one player to Europe. The compensation, also known as a solidarity payment, is due to the team which develops a player from the club where he signed his first professional contract. A payment is due for every year the team honed the player from ages 12 to 23. Each player has a 'player passport' which records the clubs he has played for, and for how long, so compensation can be calculated. Often, however, academies have to waive their right to a payment, instead preferring to take a smaller lump sum, because they are not registered with a football association. At the lowest level, a roadside academy might take the money Liberty pay, or the offers of balls and kit. Liberty, operating in the middle ground, might instead agree a one-off transfer fee with a club. Agents have also been known to 'buy up' the economic rights of players on the cheap, exploiting an academy or club desperate for quick cash. 'A club might agree to that because they don't think they will get the payments,' Samuel said. 'They are just ordinary people without the expertise to fight the big clubs in the courts. So they take the easy option.'

Eby Emenike, the London-based Nigerian agent and lawyer, told me she had been working on five cases of European clubs not paying solidarity money due to Ghanaian clubs and academies. She said the clubs ignored the 'player passport' data.

The European Club Association said that according to Fifa's regulations, solidarity contribution paid by clubs for international transfers between 2011 and 2013 should have been 'approximately' $257 million, equal to five per cent of the overall transfer fee(s). The actual amount of money paid was $57.9 million (1.15 per cent of the transfer fees). That's a financial hole the size of $199 million. By contrast, in the same period $254 million was paid to agents. African clubs or academies received only 0.9 per cent of the five per cent rate due, lower than Oceania (4.6 per cent), Asia (1.9 per cent) and South America (1.5 per cent).

It was more than likely that due to the academies and clubs like Liberty giving up their right to training compensation, Africa was missing out on a greater chunk of monies, a sum that could be even bigger when one considered the possible impact of European clubs bankrolling academies in Africa. A former coach who used to work for a West African academy said: 'They fund some academies so they don't have to pay any compensation. Everyone is happy with the arrangement.'

Winning is not the be all and end all in Ghana but the anatomy of football in England, or other major European leagues, is matched in some regard. The rich clubs get richer and have the pick of the best players, leaving the sprats to scrap for survival. There is a three-tier system: at the bottom lie the 'roadside academies'; clubs like Liberty reside in the middle; at the top are academies with serious financial muscle provided by European clubs and corporate sponsors. This had led to a raft of academics and charities arguing that the European-style academy system in Ghana, which has been, by and large, replicated across Africa, is responsible for a new wave of neo-colonial exploitation. And it was these academies that incurred the wrath of Sepp Blatter in 2003 when he called the recruitment by European clubs of children in Africa 'despicable'. 'They are neo-colonialists who don't give a damn about heritage and culture but engage in social and economic rape by robbing the developing world of its best players,' he said.

One of the first such academies was Feyenoord Fetteh which was launched in 1999. It was a joint partnership between Feyenoord, the Dutch club, the Ghanaian Sports Ministry and tribal chiefs. In the article 'Football Academies and the Migration of African Football Labor to Europe', published in the *Journal of Sport and Social Issues* by three academics in 2007, Feyenoord were accused of adopting 'a classic neo-colonial industrial strategy by seeking where it could institute a facility that would provide a steady stream of raw talent'. Feyenoord had admitted as much on their website. They made no apologies. Feyenoord Fetteh no longer exists and has been subsumed, along with the Red Bull Academy (the same ilk as Red Bull Salzburg and Red Bull New York), by the West African Football Academy, or Wafa for short.

There have been other similar ventures: the Aldo Gentina academy in Senegal was a partnership between the Senegalese football federation and AS Monaco; Ajax bought 51 per cent of Cape Town Spurs in South Africa in 1999, renaming the club Ajax Cape Town, and the same year they bought the same stake in Obuasi Goldfields, a Ghanaian club, investing €5.8 million before selling up four years later.

Arsenal have been linked to an academy in Abidjan, the capital of Ivory Coast, called ASEC Mimosas. It was established by Jean-Marc Guillou, who was a close friend of Arsène Wenger, the Arsenal manager. Wenger was Guillou's assistant when he was in charge at Cannes and together they had signed players from Africa. When Wenger was manager of Monaco, the club invested money in ASEC. In the early years of 2000s, ASEC was essentially a feeder club for the Belgian side Beveren, which would field an all-African XI. The academy recruited 12-year-olds. Graduates included Salomon Kalou, who played for Chelsea, Kolo Touré and Emmanuel Eboué, who both played for Arsenal, and almost half the Ivory Coast squad. Yaya Touré, the younger brother of Kolo, also played for both the ASEC academy and later Beveren between 2001 and 2003.

In 2001 an investigation by the BBC's *Newsnight* programme found that Arsenal had made secret payments of £1 million to Beveren. It also found that Wenger was listed as investor in ASEC and had expected to make £100,000 from a £30,000 stake. ASEC's stated aim was to make money by selling players from their academy to Europe. Arsenal, under Wenger, bought Kolo Touré directly from the academy for £150,000 in 2002. He was sold to Manchester City for £16 million in 2013. Kolo was the perfect example of the money that could be made from the African talent pool by Europe's big clubs. He was stronger, faster and cheaper.

Fifa asked the Football Association to investigate Arsenal's relationship with Beveren with relation to conflict of interest and fair play rules. They were also asked to probe Arsenal's connections with ASEC. They found no evidence of any wrongdoing 'in relation to their dealings with Beveren' specifically to any breach of existing FA or Premier League rules. *Newsnight* responded by asking why the FA had not investigated the partnership with ASEC. The FA's position was clear. They did not have the power to probe that link as ASEC did not fall under their jurisdiction. The FA said it was Fifa's job to look into the relationship between the two.

Clubs in England have remained active with academies in Africa. Sunderland, in the lower reaches of the Premier League at the time of writing, has 'lent its expertise' to the creation of an academy in Tanzania. At the other end of the spectrum, Manchester City have 'an arrangement' with the Right to Dream Academy in Ghana. Its founder is Tom Vernon, a former Manchester United coach, who in 2000 started off with a handful of boys on a small dusty pitch. It has grown to be considered one of the most successful academies in the world and boasts a $2.5m purpose-built facility south of Akosombo in the east of the country. Its main backer is African oil giant, Tullow Oil. Vernon would not disclose the nature of Right to Dream's relationship with City: 'We have an arrangement with many clubs and partners but those arrangements are confidential. But if you look at where some of our players have gone it's not rocket science to work out.'

Manchester City admitted they were involved with Right to Dream and would not deny that they provided funding for the operation. By 2013 City had signed six Right to Dream graduates: Razak Nuhu, Dominic Oduro, Bismark Adjei-Boateng, Thomas Agyiri, Enock Kwakwa and Godsway Donyoh. Oduro, Adjei-Boateng and Donyoh are the only three still with City. All of them, however, had been loaned almost immediately to clubs in Scandinavia or Portugal. Those are notable destinations because of the looser visa and work-permit requirements for African nationals. The players, of course, had no chance of appearing for City because they had never played international football and would not have obtained a work permit. In 2012 Right to Dream commissioned a research paper into what effects the loosening of those work-permit restrictions might have on the coffers of the Ghana Football Association. 'Our research was quite interesting in highlighting huge financial losses made by the FA,' Vernon said.

Vernon was adamant that Right to Dream, Tullow, Manchester City – and whoever its other partners and investors were – were not guilty of neo-colonialism: 'I believe many academies have fallen down due to trying to impose European football systems, values, culture and structures in Africa that have failed. Could this be described as a neo-colonial approach to operating in Africa? Possibly, in terms of believing what works in Europe should simply work in Africa, and failing to tailor the model as we have – but I do not believe the wider business model is neo-colonial exploitation. The European clubs that have invested in setting up academies here, from what I understand, have had social objectives also, and the majority of clubs have been Dutch, where the minimum salary for a non-EU player is €250,000 per annum, so I'm not sure how the argument really holds up. These academies have also all offered a better standard of education to their pupils than the African FAs or professional clubs ever have.

'[Right to Dream] is an entirely different model and we were not set up by and do not belong to a European club, as the Feyenoords, Ajaxs and Red Bulls did/do; neither have we surrendered our executive power to any club or sponsor. We were born in Ghana and have built a culturally relevant school and academy.' Manchester City were asked for their view on neo-colonial exploitation but they failed to respond.

Ghana is one of the top five exporters of African players, which is an unsurprising statistic. Its society, culture and football structure could be said to provide the perfect ecosystem for the exploitation of minors. It would be no consolation to Blatter that Fifa bore its share of responsibility for the scourge. It was a pestilence which was Africa-wide as the conditions for it to thrive could be found in almost every nation on the continent.

It all began with poverty and desperate young men. For the fortunate few, like Michael Essien or Kolo Touré, football had been a route out. Their rags-to-riches stories had inspired and offered hope. A false hope, of course. The footballer who made it to the top was, literally, one in a million. Boys like Farook, fingers numb from splitting old laptops apart, and going slowly dumb from the acrid fumes, had little else to aspire to. An education was not a tangible dream. Football was. It was there, on the television sets, on the billboards. And it was easy to enroll in a club or roadside academy.

As we know, boys are easy, cheap prey to exploit. In a wider context, the very future of African children is under threat. Herbert Adika, a Ghana Football Association executive has said: 'Everybody wants to play football but all of us cannot be footballers.' Too many young men believe the future is at their feet, rather than their hands or minds. They believe their saviour will arrive one day by the side of the football pitch, holding a contract to a top club in Europe.

The men who run the roadside academies can be charged with the same naïvety. James Esson, a lecturer in human geography at Loughborough University, who has written extensively on football slavery, said that partly the problem is driven by either unemployed or 'precariously employed' men in their twenties who see themselves as entrepreneurs. It's an important point, which could easily be missed. 'They view owning a Colts team as more than a recreational activity or hobby,' Esson wrote in his paper, 'Modern Slavery, Child Trafficking, and the Rise of West African Football Academies'. 'It is a window of opportunity, a chance to be self-sufficient and economically active. They take financial risks and invest in colts football in the hope of making a profit.'

Profit. Those young boys, like Farook, are no longer seen as human beings. They are seen as capital. And for that Blatter and Fifa could be blamed. Although Blatter would argue the Training Compensation Scheme exists to prevent rich clubs exploiting poor, the average boy on the street had been monetised. With one, just one, capable of netting thousands of dollars, it is no wonder there has been a boom in youth football in Ghana.

Despite the 'do-gooder' intentions of the super academies, like Right to Dream, who get due credit for educating kids to a higher standard than is available in Ghana, it is hard not to believe investors want a return. European clubs are also using the academies as ways to circumnavigate transfer rules. In effect they are 'holding pens' where clubs come along, view and then brand the stock they want until they are mature enough to be transported.

The compensation scheme has also been responsible for negating competition, or stripping a continent of its talent. This, it could be argued, has hampered the development of a footballing continent, something hopelessly at odds with Fifa's ambition to develop the game globally. The majority of players need in Africa to be playing with the best standard available – as it is, only a minority are taken away to play at the highest level in Europe. Football in Ghana, as George, the coach of Liberty Professionals said, is no longer about winning matches or titles. It is about finding the next big star to sell.

That is a problem. That 'big star' can only shine at its brightest out of Africa. So players, coaches and academy managers all have a desperation to move, which puts them in contradiction with another Fifa ruling: Article 19. 'Problematically, this migratory disposition is accompanied by a realisation that obtaining a visa to enter a European country is easier said than done,' James Esson said.

But it is far from impossible. When these rules and regulations need to be broken so a kid can be trafficked, so a profit can be realised, help is at hand. And it is the criminal underworld and human trafficking gangs who offer it.

13

Out of Africa

About a 30-minute drive north of Old Fadama, opposite the navy hut of the local police headquarters and under the watchful eyes of a man holding a chicken and two tethered goats, waiting for the vet to open, was another 'illegal' roadside academy.

The 'pitch' was rutted and dusty and narrowed by mounds of earth on one side and trees, providing welcome shade, on the other. The goalposts were rickety and rusting. Despite the modest surroundings, the ebullience of the players was unconfined. The ball, leather missing and scarred from a thousand kicks, was almost as big as they were. It bounded away from them or bounced high up to their necks as if in harmony with their excitement. There were about 40 of them altogether, some as young as ten but most aged 16 to 20. They didn't all play at the same time. The rest waited in the shade, watching carefully as the dust from red-clay soil was whipped up to veil the ball and their friends' feet in a pink wisp.

The two coaches, Tino and Derek, stood under the trees also, offering a mixture of encouragement and rebukes. 'That's it! Good pass, Richard!' and 'Why are you not moving for the ball like I told you? Come on!' The skill and touch of each boy was surprisingly deft. Skinny legs trapped dead the weighty ball without so much as a wobble. Skipping feet manipulated it from toe to toe. There was a robustness to the play, too. The boys charged into one another and slid on the hard ground. Tino and Derek encouraged them to 'be strong!'

'What we do here is about preparing,' Derek said. 'We pick boys from various places but no monies change hands. We don't play in a league system. We train. We train six till nine every morning, Monday to Friday. We are helping those people who are good. We groom them in the basics and techniques. After that, you are a complete player. They can play in a league. Eighty per cent of the people we groom are 16 to 18. The 20 per cent are more senior and maybe have travelled to Malaysia, Vietnam.'

Tino, a former player who had only recently retired and claimed to have played all over the world, interjected, 'We have one guy who went to Malaysia, one to Thailand.' He was quieter than Derek and spoke with a hiss.

'They sign and play for one year, they come back,' said Derek. 'We only want them to go for a year so they can be seen by other clubs in Qatar, Oman. Clubs there have money. So if they don't get signed to there we say, "Come back." One of our boys has just signed in Kenya. We had a striker here who played for Kaiser Chiefs in South Africa.'

Like every other small academy, Tino explained that if he couldn't get clubs from abroad to take his players, he would try to sell them to Accra-based teams like Liberty Professionals. But this academy was not actually like every other. You might go to visit Tino to look at his players. But more likely you would go to see Tino because you needed his help. He has a notoriety in Accra. He is part of the city's underworld; part of a human trafficking network which was ultimately responsible for trying to smuggle almost 150,000 – mostly from Africa – across the Mediterranean in 2014. The migrant boats you read about in the newspapers being abandoned off the coast of Italy, or sinking and leaving their passengers in a watery grave, are the work of such gangs. Sometimes they carry wishful footballers. In photos, if you look past the women carrying babies, you can sometimes see the shirts of Argentina, Brazil or Spain on the backs of the migrants.

It is a long-standing problem. Disasters such as Lampedusa, the tragedy which William Swing, of the International Office for Migration (IOM), gravely reminded everyone of at the UN conference in Geneva, are now, sadly, commonplace. In May 2007 a fishing trawler abandoned by its captain washed up on the shore of a Tenerife beach. On board were 130 young African men, 15 of whom thought they were going for trials at Real Madrid and Marseille.

Tino is connected. If you want to get a boy on one of those boats from the coast of West Africa bound for the Canary Islands – a favoured route of the gangs – then he is your man. But he is far more valuable to the football community than that. He is a specialist. A documents man. Tino can get visas, passports and birth certificates. And that was why I wanted to talk to him.

'I need your help with documents,' I told him, having once again explained Scout Network's aims and ambitions. He didn't look at me, chewed his gum a little faster, and nodded to Derek. 'Let's talk over there.' The three of us walked to the other side of the pitch to sit on a blue bench, just in front of a crumbling basketball court where kids were throwing around a tennis ball. Tino had yellow eyes and he fixed me with them. He chewed his gum slowly, menacingly. I had been warned that this could be a potentially dangerous situation. Before travelling to Accra I had spoken about such a meeting with a Metropolitan Police chief superintendent who had investigated murder and witchcraft by gangs in the African community in the UK. He had not been encouraging. He said 'the risk was very high'. In the rather clipped and unemotive language that all officials of his type were prone to using, he added, 'I suggest that you would probably need to think through very carefully what you are doing. I'm not sure what you mean by undercover, but I suspect this would substantially increase the risks on a number of levels.'

I was also aware of the death threats that had been made to Jean-Claude Mbvoumin when he started to expose the issue. The risk, I reckoned, was worth taking. I thought my undercover story robust (it hadn't let me down so far) and I had taken the time before going to Accra to print Scout Network business cards and notebooks, both of which I flashed prodigiously at the earliest opportunity. Besides, I had a burly-looking driver provided by a friend at the BBC World Service. And then there was the police station just behind my left shoulder. I could sprint there if required.

I wanted to find out just what was possible on a continent where anyone who had spent time there said 'everything is possible'. Jean-Claude told me that humans could be purchased. How cheap could a player be bought and moved? I had already found out how much it would cost to buy a kid from the Accra slums. Now I wanted to know the prices to obtain the necessary documentation to move him to Europe. It was a cliché that the African footballer was not as young as he said he was, so could passports and visas really be fixed or produced out of thin air, with the right date of birth to enable them to bust transfer rules?

It had not been smart to sit down. It exposed the tape recorder in my breast pocket as my shirt slackened. Tino could have seen it if he chose to look. But those eyes, which I began to find terri-fying, did not budge. 'We don't know which country you need a visa or passport for,' Tino said dismissively. 'You tell me and then I will phone you and tell you.' He looked back to the pitch as if to suggest that the meeting was over.

'I need a regular passport and visa guy,' I blustered.

'That's his area,' said Derek. 'He has people on the inside. In the underground in Ghana he can get these deals done.'

'Of course,' Tino said, with nonchalance. 'This is what I do.'

'He personally has the links,' added Derek. 'He knows who he needs to call, who to call inside and make sure that [the player] is going to the UK so he needs a visa as soon as possible. [The player] is going to Mr John for football, so it is reputable.'

Tino began to thaw as I said I would need to move four or five underage boys a year. The stare had softened. It seemed he preferred to let Derek do his talking for him, perhaps because his English was not as good. Emboldened, and having started to chew my own stick of gum quickly and with the arrogance that 'blond' scouts were known for in this part of the world, I talked of a scenario. I thought of Frank, the boy who Lois had taken from her Accra academy to Cyprus and had impressed 'John' greatly in the illegal match.

'So there's this boy, from an academy run by a friend, Lois—'

Tino laughed. 'I know that team,' he said. 'The woman. Lois. I know her. I was in Dubai two to three years ago. An agent took me there and there was no team for me. So my manager called Lois and she called an agent in Cyprus to link me up. I know that lady. She is from Accra. She moved about three players to Cyprus. She will go to Egypt or Nigeria and get them a visa to Cyprus.'

Tino was right. That was exactly what Lois did. Inwardly, I was surprised at the 'small world' of Accra football. Outwardly, I gave away no hint and continued with my story about Frank. I said he was 16 and I wanted a passport and birth certificate to show that he was 18 so he could move to Europe to play football, thus sidestepping Fifa's Article 19.

'Ah, OK,' Tino said. 'You need the passport to say 18. You don't have a problem, my brother.'

It was $600 for a passport and a further $100 for a birth certificate. 'I take him to the passport office, they take his picture. On the passport it will not be stated he is a student. He will be a footballer.'

For the birth certificate, Tino said he would need the identity cards of the 'mother or father'. He would need assurance 'from the parents', something which would not be difficult for a bright young thing in Accra if he had been adopted by an academy manager. 'You need that assurance from the parents,' Tino said.

As Frank had been adopted by Lois, that would not be a problem.

Visas and work permits were also Tino's remit. 'The visa depends on the country. So many visas. My sister is a travel agent so we link together. Italy is not a problem with an invitation [from a club], as soon as you get me that we do a Schengen.' A Schengen visa allows the holder to move freely between 26 European countries, although not the UK and Ireland. They cost about €150 and are not easy to obtain. There are strict rules and regulations to follow to get one. Tino wanted $7,000 to grease the palms of the black market. That was cheap. In a previous communication with a Ghanaian agent through the Scout Network email, I was told it would cost $8,000 through contacts with the criminal underclass.

The Schengen visa has been exploited by traffickers since its creation in 1995. Gangs have bribed contacts in embassies to 'rubber-stamp' applications. In early 2015 there was concern by western intelligence agencies that jihadist groups were using them to smuggle sleeper cells or lone operatives to commit terrorist attacks in Europe.

More money would be needed for Tino to speak to his contacts 'inside' to get work permits. 'Italy, Portugal, Czech Republic,' he said. 'I can do work permits for those.' Tino explained that football clubs would get work permits for players by registering them for jobs as anything but footballers, and with a totally different company. 'Maybe computer analysts . . . whatever they wish,' he said. The club would then pay the player his salary through the company. 'It is fine so long as he is not employed by the club. You need to tell me the country, the charge is different for each one.' I asked whether I should budget for around $1,000. Tino seemed happy with that figure.

Once the money was paid it would take two weeks for the documents to be ready. They would, Tino said, arrive without fail. They would be legitimate, not fakes. That took me back to what Jake Marsh had said about such visas. They may be illegally obtained but they were genuine. 'No problem, brother,' Tino said again. So for as little as $8,700 it would be possible to obtain a passport and birth certificate with a fake age plus a visa and work permit to mainland Europe. Including the paltry fee to buy a kid footballer from his parents in the slums of Accra there would still be change from $9,000. That was the cost of a human being in Accra. To a football club, scouting company, agent, sex trafficker or human-organ harvester, it was nothing. I thought of poor Jay-Jay. Had his abuser visited a man like Tino? Had he paid a similar sum? Everything was possible in Africa.

Lois was not happy. She wore a scowl and her new Mohican-style haircut made her look rather fierce. 'Everyone I meet is screwing me up,' she said. 'It's annoying, tiring. I keep putting in money, putting in, putting in. I run this whole thing alone. I pay fees for so many boys. Fifteen! Trust me, I had saved a lot of money, I used to have a job. I'm jobless.' She managed a laugh at that.

We had spent the morning watching three matches, all of them involving her teams – under-12s, under-15s and under-17s. The pitch was dreadful, the standard of play was remarkably good, the boys were careful with the ball and wreckless in the tackle. It was exactly as I had come to expect. The only incongruity had been the boy at the back of the line for the water bottles. His peers were wearing Arsenal, Chelsea, Juventus, Real Madrid or Barcelona shirts. He wore the colours of Oldham Athletic.

'I used to work,' Lois continued as we sat in traffic on our route back to my hotel. 'I used to be a banquet manager for a hotel. I had a degree in hotel management. Maybe I need to go back to that . . .' She waved away a boy who could have been no more than ten who was walking between the bumper-to-bumper cars selling toilet bleach. 'I've been doing this five years. It is hard work,' she added.

In those five years, she claimed, she had managed to move ten players to European clubs. I asked her to write down their names, ages now and when they moved. Seven of them had left Accra before they were 18, one was as young as 15. For a small academy manager like Lois that was, despite the probable breach of transfer rules, success. Well, it would be if she had received training compensation for any of them. She hadn't. Nor was she likely to. Fifa gave clubs or academies two years after the transfer to claim the money they were owed and the time limit on seven of Lois's players had passed. Making a fuss would be a most foolish thing to do: Fifa would investigate and discover the ages when the players were transferred. So Lois had to rely on the trust and goodwill of clubs and agents paying outside of the system. It was not forthcoming. 'All these agents I deal with are all thieves,' Lois said. The 'h' in 'thieves' was silent.

No wonder Hamid had labelled her in Larnaca 'the most amateur president of an academy in the world'. She had laughed at that. But it was a laugh born from embarrassment and shyness. She told me she had only met Hamid the day before. Imari, Hamid's talent spotter and the former footballer from Ivory Coast, had been the conduit for that meeting. Months later Lois regretted ever meeting Hamid. She can hardly have been surprised. She regretted ever meeting Imari, too.

'Oh, that one,' she spat as I mentioned him. 'He was a friend of a friend of mine when I was at school in Cyprus. When one of my players was transferred to Cyprus, Imari and an agent helped with the transfer. They were paid some money, €50,000 and I never got my part. One stupid thing I did was thinking, "We're friends from school." I never had anything written down, no contract.' Hamid, she said, had 'played me'. She told me that she had sent three of 'her best boys', all over 18, to an agent Hamid had said could get them clubs in Greece. Almost six months later they had yet to play a single game.

'Did I ever tell you about the trial game Hamid staged?' I said. 'Twenty or so Africans all in this tiny town in Cyprus. All of them had come over to play football. None of them were playing at all. What was going on?'

'Something fishy,' Lois said.

Her 'best boys' had run out of time on their visas so Hamid had contacted her asking her to send €3,000 to renew them so the agent could continue a search for a club. She paid. 'I paid with my own money from my club,' she said with indignation. I didn't ask her why. I had begun to feel sorry for Lois. She had been outwitted by Hamid, although it was not a particularly canny manœuvre. Why would you hand over more money when the agent had failed to find a club in six months?

'I won't work with Hamid again,' she said. 'I told him that. I gave him a piece of my mind.' She wobbled in her seat at that, as if it had re-inflated her pride. 'He said, "Send me some papers saying you don't need training compensation, they weren't trained." Of course they were trained. I need the training compensation to run the academy. I said they should send them back or they should let them leave and I can take them to Sweden. I have contacts there. I told them I wanted to take them to Sweden and they intentionally delayed that . . . the agent said he had a plan and we should wait. "So send the money for a visa renewal," they said.

'Do you know what they are telling me now? The only option for the boys to play now is for me to declare that they have never played before, declare them first registration. They've never played in Ghana. That's so they can steal the players and so I can't demand anything. I was confident in the boys I was sending, I sent them with the help of my sister . . .'

Ah, yes. The sister who worked for the Ghanaian embassy in Egypt. She was Lois's Tino, it seemed. So if I wanted to move players for Scout Network, what could she do for me?

'Normally she gets me letters from the office of the president [who] has asked for the embassy to give the player the visa. There are too many scammers around so that's why I have to do that. Sometimes they would see a document and they think I'm moving a player for a scam. There'd be no problem moving a player under 18 so long as we have agreement with their parents. There is no problem with any of my team because I have adopted a lot of the boys. I get the rights from the parents, a letter signed by them. I say, "He is my son."'

Lois told me she had just 'adopted' a 12-year-old. He was her next big hope, and when she talked about his ability as a footballer it was clear her earlier wittering about going back to the hotel trade was all talk. 'They call him "Maestro",' she said. 'I pay all his school fees. His parents are dead, so the family who have him know I want him to be a footballer. I pay 300 Ghana cedis [£50] per term. I want to invest a lot in that boy. I'm not going to pay anything to the family because one thing about Ghana is if you keep paying, they keep asking. I'm telling you, if he doesn't listen to me he could end up selling stuff at the traffic lights.'

If Hamid and Imari had shown flashes of their true colours to Lois, I saw the full rainbow. Upon my return from Accra I thought it time to email them as myself, asking why they had discussed with John a scheme to move under-18s from Africa. Hamid, who ignored my question about why he was charging players for visas, threatened to hack my email so he could find out who, and presumably where, I was. Imari was more menacing. 'You should feel the weight of hands,' he wrote.

14

The Forsythe Saga

'My policy is not to get into a car that won't start,' Christopher Forsythe said as he shielded his eyes from a fierce Accra sun. 'It's a very good project and I'm happy to be involved.' I had been corresponding with Forsythe for almost a year. It was the first, and only time, we met. It was a meeting by chance. One which very nearly didn't happen. He was one of the first Fifa registered agents who had received Scout Network's email about looking for partners to bring under-18s to England. In a professional and detailed reply, Forsythe wrote: 'I would like to have the chance to explain in more detail the project that I have set up initially in Ghana to establish a steady pipeline of top level footballing talent into European clubs.' His focus was 'providing young (typically 16–23) players' to Europe.

Although Hamid, Imari and Lois had revealed how players were moved from continent to continent, I wanted to know more. Specifically, how people within football were ignoring Article 19. I wanted more details from an agent who was not afraid of skullduggery. More tricks, more scams, more cheats. Of course, I didn't ask Forsythe if he was that man, but I impressed upon him the need for an expert in moving underage players. 'I assure you that you have come to the right person,' he told me.

Indeed, I had. Almost two months later to the day he sent that email, Forsythe was the subject of a sting by the *Daily Telegraph* newspaper and the Channel 4 documentary programme, *Dispatches*. He had been exposed agreeing to fix Ghana's international fixtures by using corrupted referees. The investigation cast a shadow over the World Cup, which was taking place in Brazil at the time. The *Telegraph* labelled it a 'football match-fixing deal'. Its exclusive read:

Reporters from the *Telegraph* and a former Fifa investigator claimed they represented an investment company that wanted to 'sponsor' games. Christopher Forsythe, a registered Fifa agent, along with Obed Nketiah, a senior figure in the Ghanaian FA, boasted that they could employ corrupt officials who would rig matches played by Ghana.

The president of the country's football association then met the undercover reporter and investigator, along with Mr Forsythe and Mr Nketiah, and agreed a contract which would see the team play in the rigged matches, in return for payment.

The contract stated that it would cost $170,000 (£100,000) for each match organised by the fixers involving the Ghanaian team, and would allow a bogus investment firm to appoint match officials, in breach of Fifa rules. 'You [the company] will always have to come to us and say how you want it to go . . . the result,' said Mr Forsythe. 'That's why we will get the officials that we have greased their palms, so they will do it. If we bring in our own officials to do the match . . . You're making your money.'

Mr Forsythe said that match fixing was 'everywhere' in football and that he could even arrange rigged matches between Ghana and British teams. 'The referees can change the matches every time. Even in England it does happen,' he said. Following the meeting in London, the representative of the investment firm asked if his company could be sure their approach would work. Mr Forsythe replied: 'We will always choose associations/countries that we think we can corrupt their officials for all our matches.' He listed a number of African and European countries, adding 'we can look for match officials who will sing to our tune'.

I had contacted Forsythe by chance, deploying the method used by the fakes and the rogues mentioned by Jake Marsh and Eby Emenike: emailing as many agents as possible. Forsythe would go underground, I thought, after the *Telegraph* story broke. And he did, telling me on the telephone that he was suffering from malaria. However, there was something about Forsythe's demeanour in the *Dispatches* documentary that made me believe all was not lost. He was a showman. He loved to be the centre of attention. People were hanging on his every word as he 'educated' them about football corruption. So I kept emailing him as if the *Telegraph* sting had not happened, informing him of the progress of Scout Network; how we had established links with other football clubs and the successful scouting trip to Larnaca. Forsythe wrote back, 'I appreciate your interest in working with us and by this email I am introducing you to my colleague Ralph Gyambrah, who will be in charge coordinating with you for a successful program in Ghana. Please liaise with him as he is aware of all your plans.'

Before the year was out Gyambrah had been appointed as the general manager of Berekum Chelsea, the club whose chief executive, Obed Nketiah, was embarrassed with Forsythe in the *Telegraph* exposé. Gyambrah had founded DC United, a lower league Ghana team, with Forsythe and had suggested he had experience of taking players to Italy. That nugget of information gave me the opening I was after. 'We would like to scout players in Ghana and then eventually bring them to England to play in League Two football,' 'John' wrote. 'The younger the better. This will be easier if we can take them to Italy, or another European mainland destination first, as it will be then easier to move them on to England because of border controls. Where I will require your expertise is getting the players to Italy (passports and visas) and an agreement with a "holding" club.' This was the illegal 'bridge transfer', a move which Lois had taught me in Larnaca.

Gyambrah was on board. He wrote that he had 'drifted to the Portuguese market to see how best we can partner clubs since lots of new laws are being passed in Italy making it difficult to place players'. He added that the cost of moving one player from Ghana to Europe, and 'taking care' of him, would be about £1,000 for six months. We agreed to meet in Accra to discuss the fine detail.

The day before that meeting, Gyambrah emailed to say he had made an 'impromptu' trip to Italy. Instead, he suggested I spoke with his chief scout called 'the Major'. I was not interested in talking to a scout, so I emailed Forsythe, complaining that I had gone all the way to Ghana to talk about a partnership with his associate and he had let me down. Forsythe said he would step in. 'I am talking to Bruno, my new contact in Portugal, about the possibility of creating a partnership to place players from Ghana through there for onwards transfer to English League One and Two clubs,' he wrote. He asked for the full details of Scout Network's project. During some downtime by the hotel pool, 'John' got creative.

The plan

To identify young talent because it is an opportunity for English clubs to get ahead of the bigger clubs in the Premier league, who capture ALL the young talent in the UK. Our business plan focuses on finding young talent in other territories. We are looking at under-18s all over the world. But Ghana is a great place to start because of its reputation.

The clubs

We have agreements with League One and League Two clubs to search for players. Because of the number of clubs we are working for we have a pool of money to find the best players. This gives us an advantage over other scouts who are tasked by one club to look for one player, making scouting very expensive. We are tasked by four or five clubs looking for players in up to 20 positions. All the clubs we work for are go-ahead and ambitious. They recognise the need to look in new territories.

The talent
We would prefer to find under-17s as it is a sad, but true, fact that a lot of players if they are not scouted and signed by 18 may not be good enough. So we need to find players who have not been seen before. We are in it for the long term and plan to be visiting Ghana five or six times a year to watch a player progress.

The territories
We have agreements with partners in Larnaca, Cyprus, Sierra Leone, France (specifically Ligue 2) and Florida, USA.

Partners
We require partners who are able to help us solve issues. In this regard we are interested in a partnership with Portugal as discussed.

Forsythe was happy with what he had read. It was a 'very good idea to catch them young,' he replied. I stressed, once again, that it would be his job to 'assist us logistically, specifically with regard to the problem of finding a club in Italy or, as you alluded to following conversation with Bruno, Portugal. We need partners who can help us get players to territories where they will be able to come to the UK.'

In another email Forsythe said, 'This project requires hard work. I am a workaholic and would not get into a car that won't drive so [am] always clear on goals and objectives for end results. I will put my 100 per cent in so expect results at the end of the day.' The undercover *Telegraph* journalists were also promised '100 per cent'.

The next day, we met at the Mövenpick hotel in Accra. Forsythe had a roly-poly figure and small, squashed eyes in a chubby face. He was polite, softly spoken and after pleasantries sat by the pool wasted no time in telling me exactly how he thought it would operate. He drew diagrams in his notebook. He had it all worked out. He had done it before.

What followed was a precise guide to football's trade in kids. He revealed how to buy players for as little as £370 and not pay them a salary. 'We only need to feed them,' he said. Crucial to the project was setting up a 'ghost' club in Ghana, which would be owned by Scout Network, to circumnavigate Fifa's rules on transferring minors and third-party ownership. He boasted of a 'visa loophole' which would allow the movement of under-18s to the UK through his NGO, ForSports Foundation, in the guise of improving the lives of the underprivileged. 'We have the potential to bypass international transfer certificates and work permits,' he said proudly.

Forsythe's charity work had given him an air of respectability. He was born into poverty in Ghana before being adopted by a Belfast schoolteacher. He had supported Glentoran FC. When he returned to live in Ghana, in the Sunyani area in the west of the country, he set up an academy and named it after the Irish club. Supporters sponsored individual kids and raised funds to improve its facilities. The charity, which aimed to empower kids through football, was 'funded' by his football scouting and management agency, ForSports Management. In return, Forsythe had a potential pool of talent. It was this ethically vague arrangement which seemed to inspire the idea for his partnership with Scout Network.

'We get to help the kids,' he said. 'We get the player.' Naturally Forsythe wanted something for himself. He asked for a salary for his expertise of smoothing the paths for players to move abroad. And a bit more besides. 'I believe in not what I get now but the end resource so . . . in two years the players have been going for £1 million and £2 million. I want an agreement to have a percentage of any future transfers.'

From the outset, Forsythe assured me there would be no issue moving players under the age of 18 to Europe. 'There wouldn't be a problem, my other company is a travel consultancy. We are trying to move four or five players to Italy. There won't be a problem.'

There wouldn't be a problem finding the players, either. His plan was to scout for talent in the three northern regions of Ghana, the Ashanti region and the west of the country. His scouting team would identify '25 to 30 players' who would then be brought to a tournament to be attended by Scout Network, who would pick the best players 'to move to Portugal, Italy'. Then they would be moved to England.

Forsythe said that players could be bought from clubs – or academies similar to the size of Lois's – for 5,000 Ghana cedis or as little as 2,000 cedis (£370). Scout Network would 'own them 100 per cent' so there would be no need for those clubs or academies to receive training compensation in the future. 'We just feed them, give them somewhere to sleep,' Forsythe said. 'We don't have to pay a salary.'

Those players would then be signed to a club in the Ghana second division which had been specifically founded for our project. It was the ghost club, to be owned by Scout Network. The club would play in the league but it would be used primarily to groom players for Europe. It was a plan which brought out the showman in Forsythe and laid bare how, in Ghana, rules and regulations were to be disregarded when there was money to be made.

'Scout Network as a company cannot own the players,' he said. 'So we need to create something which 100 per cent has an agreement with Scout Network and will be the one to move players [to Europe]. It is owned by Scout Network. Scout Networks hides behind [the club] to move the players. Because if you go to a club in Italy and you, as a company, own the player, moving [the player] will be difficult. Fifa are trying to abolish third-party ownership. We can have a division two club with no intention of going up to any level in Ghana. Scout Network owns that club and will do all the transfers. If the player is scouted by Scout Network and they are [trying to] move them, Scout Network will not get [authorisation] from the Ghana FA because they don't know you. If they hide behind the club they can use the club to facilitate the transfer to Portugal or Italy. The club will then request an international transfer certificate from the Ghana FA.'

No player could move from one country to another without an international transfer certificate. They were issued by the 'selling' football association. So if a player was moving from Ghana to Portugal, it would be the Ghana FA who would be responsible for the certificate, or ITC as it is known in the industry.

'So this is a ghost club?' I said.

'Exactly. Every player coming from here is owned by Scout Network, they own the club and use that division two club in Ghana . . . to move [players] to Portugal, request the ITC from the Ghana FA because the club is affiliated to the Ghana FA.'

'To all intents and purposes they think the club owns the player but we are behind the curtain?' I asked.

'Yes,' Forsythe said, looking very pleased with himself. 'If it is called Scout FC [Forsythe decided this would be the name of the 'ghost' club], who are the owners? Scout Network. If Scout FC source a player the money goes to Scout Network, [who are] not breaching any third-party ownership.'

'This is the expertise I need.'

'There is no purpose of [the club] going to division one or the Premier League in Ghana,' Forsythe said. 'The purpose of the club is for the players to train. At the end of the day the players [have] to be ready for the next destination. We need to apply for visas to

Portugal, we need an introduction letter from the Ghana FA for the purpose of visas. It's very important we get Scout FC.'

'I leave all that to you?'

'Yeah, otherwise we breach Fifa rules.'

'Behind the curtain . . .'

'Yes.'

Forsythe told me DC United, the club he said he owned with Ralph Gyambrah, was 'behind the curtain', allowing them to move their players to Italy. He said he would run Scout Network's club for me. 'It's not expensive,' he said.

A conveyor belt of talent to Europe, having players ready to go every year, would be needed, according to Forsythe. He suggested keeping the small clubs and academies sweet by gifting sets of balls and kit so to have 'first refusal' on their players.

'My expertise is to manage this, prepare them for the move, do visa applications, do everything for you. I will start working for the first five players to go and when the first five are gone . . . you still have 20. The second batch. When the next five have gone I prepare to move the next five. You say to me, "Chris, we are moving one to three players from Portugal to League One and Two [in England], get the next batch ready."'

It was the mysterious Bruno who would be able to get the players into Portuguese clubs. 'He works with a company back in Mayfair,' Forsythe said. 'He knows somebody who has a division two club in Portugal.' He didn't disclose the name of the club. He showed me a memorandum of understanding with Bruno. 'He has to be involved as [we're] using him to take players to Portugal,' Forsythe said. 'We will be using the lower divisions a lot. Mostly the lower league clubs will be interested in such an agreement.'

There was, surely, a problem. As we know, Article 19 of Fifa's transfer regulations does not permit the international transfers of a player under the age of 18. That's why Fifa's Transfer Matching System (TMS) had been set up, specifically to counter transfer frauds. The TMS demands that the selling club has to provide all the details of a player, including his age, and this had to be 'matched' by the purchasing club otherwise the transfer would not be allowed to happen. Only if every piece of data 'matched' could an ITC be issued by the Ghana FA. Forsythe looked at me with pity, as if to say, 'This guy has no idea how things work here.'

'TMS over here?' he said dismissively. 'We are not into the system properly. We take care of them. Don't worry about those areas. Every player we move we can get ITCs.'

'Regardless of age?'

'Yeah. But not under-14, that is too young.'

Forsythe explained that he had been able to take under-18s to Italy on student, or temporary visas, and place them in the academy or youth set-ups of squads until they turned 18. He was then able to apply for an ITC through the Ghana FA. Failing that, he said it didn't matter if they were under 18 because 'most players in Ghana are not registered as professionals, they are amateur'.

In reality, there was no exemption under Article 19 for amateur under-18s being allowed to move.

'So, at 16 we take the player to Portugal with Bruno and on a student visa?' I asked.

'Then you apply for an ITC at 18,' Forsythe said. 'The Ghana FA will see that he played for Scout FC so he qualifies for an ITC.'

'Can he play?'

'Yes he can play, but not earn anything. Food and accommodation the club pays.'

That sounded like a slave contract. There was another trick up Forsythe's sleeve. It was the more notable ploy of how he could ignore visa and work-permit rules to get an under-18 into

England. By using an NGO as cover, it would be possible for Scout Network to take a player directly to one of its English clubs. Forget Italy. Forget Portugal. The only caveat, Forsythe said, was that one had to be careful not to try it too often as the authorities would become suspicious. In an earlier email he had described it as a 'loophole'. Once again he revelled in delivering a lesson: 'Yeah that one . . . to do with the foundation . . . that is the UK. You know I work with underprivileged children. Some are very good footballers. The League One club can say, "OK, look, we have seen a player from a project in Ghana and we think we can bring the player. The option is not for the player to play football, it is to continue his education and we are bringing him from a foundation in Ghana, a recognised NGO which trains underprivileged football players." So they know that in bringing the player from this area to the UK, they are trying to help the children. In future they will have a better life and, at the end of the day, they can help reduce the poverty, help the family. The League One club can pick the player straight from here. That can happen. We can say, "There is a player over here who is good and if you are interested we can bring you the player."'

'What about visa problems, Chris?'

'They have no issue because the papers are not to play football. But at the end of day they are glad they are bringing the player over, he has no future in Ghana. This player . . . educationally he is good and he knows how to play football, so the club picks the player, he goes to the academy, continues his education and plays football. So you have helped reduce poverty back here.'

'And we get our player.'

'Exactly.'

'Even though he is 16? And what about an ITC?'

'He can play because the club brought the player to the UK to give him a better life. He doesn't need an ITC because the club is taking care of the education. My NGO has this. We can make Scout FC an NGO in Ghana.'

So 'Scout FC' would not only be a ghost club purely set up to move players abroad (with no interest in winning matches) but an NGO which claimed to be helping kids out of poverty by sending them to the UK on 'scholarships'. The key was stating that they were moving to further their education. Football would be secondary.

'He is going as a student but he has the quality to play football,' Forsythe said. 'First it is to continue the education and at the same time he is playing. It's like students who are allowed to work 15 hours a week.'

I massaged Forsythe's ego a little: 'This is very impressive. This is expertise. This was my concern, how to move [under-]16s.'

'I have gone through the system and I know it works,' Forsythe said. 'They can go to sixth form in the UK. Education is the priority . . . after three years you can apply for residency.'

'So we have the potential to bypass ITC and work-permit rules?'

'If we have submitted the visa application they will need a letter from the club – they will sponsor the child for his education and there will be a letter from the school and a sponsor letter from the club and they will issue the visa.'

'We can move 14-, 15-, and 16-year-olds?'

'Yeah, as long as they are academically good, 'cos we're trying to give a better life.'

Forsythe made it sound almost noble. 'I knew there were ways to move players without ITCs,' I mused. 'I just didn't know how.'

There was a smug look on Forsythe's face. He sat back in his chair to either bask in the heat or his own glory. 'So,' he said, 'how soon can we start the car?'

Following Forsythe's meeting with John, I emailed him to offer him a right to reply to my allegations. He said he knew John was recording the conversation. 'I made sure I was careful in all discussions with him,' he wrote. 'I didn't say anything contrary to the rules of the transfers of minors in football.' Forsythe admitted planning to set a club in Ghana but denied it was a 'ghost' club. With regard to the NGO 'loophole', he argued that he would never 'sanction a move for a minor to travel for just football purposes'. He also revealed that the match-fixing exposé 'nearly led me to a suicide mission'.

In February 2015 Forsythe was banned by the Ghana FA for three years from all football-related activity and had his agent's licence revoked for his role in the match-fixing sting. The car, most definitely, was going nowhere.

15

Didier's Story

Didier had seen the world in his quest for footballing stardom: Qatar, Brazil, Argentina, Spain, Malta, Corsica and Paris. 'Football comes first,' he said. 'And then adventure.' He left his home, Yaoundé in Cameroon, at the age of 13. He was now 21. In those eight years he had been a slave, had been robbed, beaten, racially abused and homeless. An agent asked his mother to fake a death certificate for herself and his father so a club could sign him. When he was 17 he was woken on the floor of a bank ATM kiosk in Madrid by his mother calling to say his dad was dead. Misadventure sounded more appropriate.

'I was always excited to travel,' he said. 'Some things happened along the way which were not so good but they made me a man. I am a fighter because of those things and I will keep on with the fight until I get my chance to play.'

His journey had begun in the first year of his teens when he was one of hundreds of boys selected by the 'screening' process for talent run by the Aspire Dreams programme, at the Qatari academy in Doha. 'I was only there two weeks,' he said. 'It was luxurious but there were lots of cliques and if the trainers didn't like you, you didn't play. I came home.'

Within 12 months he was in Brazil, training at Cruzeiro, who were one of the biggest clubs in the country. 'It was just a training centre,' he said. 'They looked after me very well. They gave me a place to live, fed me, gave me pocket money, but in the end I had to come home. I was a minor and they couldn't sign me. I had the Brazilian rhythm, the Brazilian style. Yes, they liked me.'

These were mere blips compared to what would follow for Didier, a striker who was no more than 5 feet 9 inches. 'I came home and I heard that there were some trials for boys to go to Argentina. A white man was coming to see the trials and when you know a white man is involved lots of players come.'

Didier impressed. The agent – the white man – said he wanted to take him and four others. But first his parents would have to give consent. 'He was very charming when he spoke to my parents,' Didier said. 'They signed papers saying that he was in charge of me. Like he was my guardian. He had rights over me. He could do whatever he wanted with me concerning football, he made the decisions.' That was Didier's first mistake. The second was his family giving the agent $2,500 for 'visas and papers and things'. They had paid the airfare themselves, too.

Didier sighed. 'I will tell you what happened.' And then he began. 'I left Cameroon on the 24 December 2008. I was 15. When I got to Argentina my mother had given me some money, about €1,600, and he took all of that. He took my passport, my birth certificate and the return plane ticket. He took me to stay in a pension. I arrived at 3 a.m. and I tried to sleep. I couldn't. At 8 a.m. I had trials at Boca Juniors. My eyes were red. I was sleepy. So I didn't play well.

'I had a trial at Tigre FC and I was supposed to trial for one month. But they wanted me after three days. I succeeded in three days! I was so happy that I wanted to call my mother. But the agent, he refused. I wasn't allowed to talk to her. I went to live with the agent and his wife and children.'

Didier was used as a slave by the family. When he wasn't at football training he had to look after the couple's three children – aged eight months, two and four – for hours on end and was fed only 'chicken lungs and rice'. If he did something wrong he was punched or kicked. The agent would give him the equivalent of €1 pocket money and a return metro ticket on the weekend.

'I was very, very badly treated,' he said. 'I, uh, went through a very bad moment in my life.' He wiped tears from his eyes. 'I think I have never suffered so much. I couldn't tell my mother. When I called her he made me put it on speakerphone and he stayed in the room. His wife was a racist. I would be beaten. I was not allowed to eat with the family. I was not allowed to sit on the same chairs as them.'

Tigre FC wanted to sign Didier permanently but they couldn't because he was under 18 and his parents lived in Cameroon. 'If they moved to Argentina, it would be possible but they couldn't, so the agent had an idea.' The idea was for Didier's mother to provide false documents stating she and his father had passed away so the agent could claim he had adopted him. In short, to fake their own death.

'My mother said to me on the phone, "Are you crazy?" I told her to do it because he was listening and then, very quickly, in our language I told her not to.' When the agent's scheme failed, he was furious and told Didier that if he didn't tell the club that he had paid for his airfare he would not return his passport. 'The club reimbursed airfares so he got the money. But my mother had paid for that ticket. She had to pay again for me to fly home.'

After one year in Argentina, Didier returned to Cameroon. He said he was 'psychologically beaten' and gave up the game: 'I wanted to leave football because in Africa we say that if you go with the white people and you play well, you will stay. But I went to the white people and I showed them that I play well, and I was disappointed. I thought maybe I will just end up as a tramp or something. My father told me, "You're still young, there are still opportunities, you're going to continue, you're going to travel."'

Didier did travel. Tenerife FC wanted to sign him but, because he had 'signed away his rights' to the Argentinian agent, they 'didn't want any hassle'. With little money he survived on 'biscuits and juice' for €3 a day and slept on the streets. It was when he was resting his head on his suitcase by a cashpoint that his mother telephoned to tell him his father had died. 'I did not go to the funeral,' he said. 'My mother said I should keep looking, that after what happened in Argentina I was already a man. So I missed my father's funeral.'

He failed a trials at Atlético Madrid and at clubs in Malta and Corsica. Didier went home. But he came back, first to Madrid and then Paris. 'A friend told me about Jean-Claude, so I contacted him,' he said. 'He told me to come. I've been here one month. I am staying with my cousin. She said I should try in France because in Spain, the blacks don't have as much opportunity as in France.'

16

'We Don't Care Who You Are'

In 2010 the worldwide transfer market was described as a 'jungle', a lawless mass where money laundering, people trafficking, exploitation of minors, tax evasion, third-party ownership and pretty much every other brand of fraud and deception was rife. That portrayal came from Mark Goddard who, as the general manager of Fifa's Transfer Matching System (TMS), which ratified all international transfers, was akin to football's Tarzan. With a virtual machete, he had cut a swathe through the unregulated, unkempt undergrowth of a market which produced up to 30,000 transfer deals a year totalling more than $1 billion. Goddard, a no-nonsense Western Australian, was proud of his work. Via a Skype call he told me with all the chest-beating brio of a lord of the jungle that the TMS was the stellar registration tool for sportsmen: 'It's the best one on the planet . . . by a country mile.' He had elongated mile for emphasis.

On the face of it, the TMS, a web-based system, is impressive. It is responsible for one of the most stunning regulatory rebukes in football history. In December 2014 Barcelona were handed a 14-month transfer ban for signing six players (between 2009 and 2013) from overseas under the age of 18 to their La Masia academy, which had produced the likes of Lionel Messi, Andrés

Iniesta and Cesc Fàbregas. A breach of Article 19, trafficking of minors, a slave trade – call it what you want – Barcelona had been shamed.

Before Goddard and the TMS had finished with them, Barcelona were the behemoth which bestrode the game with apparent impunity. Thanks to their wealth, titles, vast global-support base and a carefully nurtured cultural and ideological superiority, the club was football royalty; keeping the proles in check with the outside of its left boot, gorging at the top table of the sport's establishment, an embodiment of the sort of pre-eminent sense of entitlement present at the biggest clubs or teams in most sports.

This was what made the carpeting of Barcelona so significant. It was proof, Fifa believed, that it did not fear reputation.

Barcelona reacted as one would have suspected. Before their match against Real Betis in April 2014, they unfurled a giant banner which stretched to cover the first two tiers of the mountainous Camp Nou. '*No Es Toca La Masia*', it read. Do not touch La Masia. The club president, Josep Maria Bartomeu, refused to recognise Barcelona had done anything wrong and insisted they would not be changing their policy. A statement read: 'With all respect for the sports authorities, the club has expressed its utter nonconformity with the resolution.'

A lack of responsibility was a theme. Unicef, the world's largest children's charity, would not condemn Barcelona's child-welfare policy either. But then again Unicef would receive \$2 million a year from its association with Barcelona until 2016, and was the first organisation to be carried on the famous *blaugrana* shirt.

'If you fail to follow the rules there should be consequences,' Goddard said. 'That's what we've done.'

The rules were quite simple. Article 19, in case you needed a reminder, prohibited the international transfers of players under the age of 18. In 2009, Fifa amended the small print of Article 19 to ensure that clubs used the Transfer Matching System. For the first time since the rule was drawn up, Fifa were able to police it. Until TMS was launched in 2010 – it took five years to design, build and test – there had been nothing to stop clubs and agents behaving as they wished. International transfers had been conducted by the light of the moon; clubs or agents did the deal and agreed the paperwork. This was sent to Fifa who checked it and then sent it, often by fax or post, to the national association of the buying club. The 'buying' association would request the national association of the selling club to send them the player's registration. Once it had been received, again by fax or post, the documentation would be sent back to Fifa, who would give the green light for an International Transfer Certificate (ITC) to be issued. It was during this arduous and chaotic process that corruption took hold. For example, a player might not actually exist and the transfer was purely to move money from one continent to another. Or a chunk of the transfer fee might disappear into the wrong bank account leading to disputes between clubs and agents which Fifa did not have the time, organisation or manpower to solve.

'Football was without a practical way to make sure regulations were being followed,' Goddard said. 'If you're asking other people to follow your rules but you have no way to check whether that's the case or not then things aren't working very well. That was realised when we went round the planet to roll the system out and started to see behaviour that was not actually allowed. But because there was no way of saying it was wrong or stopping it, they thought it was OK. It's not like many clubs or associations were deliberately breaking the rules. They would do things and no one would say, "You can't do that."

'Say you have a speed limit of 120 kilometres an hour and you put a sign up saying, "That's the speed limit." But if you have no way to check whether that's being broken, eventually you might go and sit on the freeway, start checking and see people driving at 160 kilometres an hour. Now the sign is up and we're checking. You now have an online real-time platform where both parties can see the status of the transfer at any point in time or anywhere they are on the planet. That's a huge jump in technology from fax machines and a courier service. We can now count the number of transfers. No one had an idea how much money was involved [before]. We can also see the number of clubs who were active. All of this was previously unknown as it was being handled in an unstructured fashion on a club-by-club basis.'

For a transfer to take place, the buying and selling club must log in to the TMS's online server and both input up to 30 pieces of data. These include the date of birth of the player, length of contract, bank details, the fee, how the fee will be structured, the currency, and who the agents or intermediaries are. If the data supplied by each club does not match, then the transfer does not go through. It can take as little as seven minutes.

'Our record is 371 in one day, I think,' Goddard said. 'Once the data is correct then it goes to the member association and they are responsible for handling the international transfer certificate (ITC) process, so the computer supports the stakeholders. In no way does it make the final decision or validate the final situation.'

So what the TMS does is give a green light to the member association to conduct a transfer, having ratified that both parties agree on who is being sold, for how much and for how long. What it cannot do during the seven-minute online process is check whether the information provided by the clubs is legitimate. It means that the system is potentially open to abuse by collusion on the part of clubs or member associations, particularly with regard to minors.

For example, there is little to prevent two clubs 'agreeing' that a player is over 18 when he is not. Granted, the TMS is robust enough to demand that a grand deception is one of the only ways to fool it, but it is a loophole none the less. And, as I had discovered, there are people more than willing to try to get away with it. Christopher Forsythe, sitting by the pool at the Mövenpick hotel in Accra, said the TMS was no impediment to moving minors. 'TMS over here?' he said. 'We are not into the system properly. We take care of them. Don't worry about those areas. Every player we move we can get ITCs.'

'Regardless of age?' I queried.

'Yeah.'

That offered a hint of collusion between the buying and selling clubs and the football association whose job it was to issue the transfer certificate. Nor could the TMS track transfers from the illegal academies who were not registered with an FA. The TMS did have a team of investigators who could demand to see any relevant paperwork or documents for players, such as birth certificate or passports, but when it is possible to employ people like Tino to get the documents required from his underworld connections, or Lois using her sister's embassy connections for visas and letters of support, it is easy to fear that little can actually be done.

'The lengths at which people will go to go round any system is extraordinary,' Goddard said. 'The options are endless. It's human nature. There's conflicting agendas, but the misrepresentation of information, forging of documents, these are the kind of things we encounter. We have a good success rate of determining whether the documents are accurate because we can follow up with the stakeholders. "Do you have this form? Is this your letterhead? Is this your signature?" That's what we try to determine.'

Goddard admitted, however, it was hard to envisage the TMS making sure that the incidents of trafficking, like those suffered by Sulley, Ben or Didier, would be a thing of the past. For a start, no regulations needed to be met to take a child for a trial. If that trial was successful, only then would they need to satisfy the system: 'Does it prevent it from happening completely? It would be naïve to think any system is perfect but over the last year we've proved we take things very seriously in using the platform to make sure the rules are being followed. It's a global situation. You are dealing with immigration topics, political instability in countries which are causing people to move, and nations that are dealing with the topic from a different angle. So it's much broader than saying an under-18 is moving for football only. Are they a refugee? Are they seeking political asylum? Are there wars going on? It's a big thing.'

As big a 'thing' is changing attitudes within football. Despite there being a better understanding of Article 19, clubs are still trying to sign minors, whether legally or illegally. The legal route involves asking Fifa for an exemption. There are three exceptions to the rule: when the player's parents move to the country where the club is located; when the transfer takes place within the European Union or European Economic Area; and when the player lives less than 100 kilometres away from the club. The TMS investigators might be called upon to ascertain whether documents are legitimate with reference to the first exemption: 'One of our messages was, "Please don't look past the current rule." If they're under 18 they're not meant to go anywhere. That's the rule. That was lost. There was always a want to not follow the rule so we really did reinforce Fifa's stance which is, "If you're under 18 stay with your family unit and when you reach 18 do what you want." I think those kind of principles had been lost and clubs and associations needed to be reminded of their responsibilities. You do realise that exceptions are, by definition, an exception. There's a very good reason why the exceptions are there, but there's a very good reason why football has the rules there in the first place. You don't want football being used to break up families, or under-18s moving to other parts of the planet because it can potentially go very wrong.'

There was evidence, however, that exemptions *were* encouraging clubs to try to sign minors, which rather contradicted Goddard's confident stance. Goddard said 'thousands' of applications were received every year, and there had been a marked increase in the number in recent years. In 2011 the TMS recorded that there were 1,500, rising to just under 1,800 in 2014. Most disconcerting is that the overwhelming majority of those cases involved moving amateur players; the naïve, the impressionable, the dreamers. The clubs, conversely, saw potential and profit. In 2014, amateurs accounted for 89.5 per cent of applications for exemptions. This was a consistent trend. In 2013 it was 89.3 per cent, 90.1 per cent in 2012 and 90.2 per cent in 2011.

The reason for clubs making so many applications for exemptions was simple: they were almost always granted. In 2014 only ten per cent were rejected, and since 2011 Fifa had never dismissed more than 12.5 per cent. Which heavily suggests that either Fifa are not as serious about the protection of minors as they said they were, or clubs and agents have been employing the tactics talked about by Forsythe or Didier's 'agent' in Argentina, who asked his mother to fake a death certificate so he could sign for a club. The majority of exemptions from 2011 to 2014 were granted because of parents moving to a country for other reasons than football. In 2014 that excuse was used in 42 per cent of successful applications for exemption from Article 19. In which case, how robust is that exemption? Call me a cynic but, given what I'd heard and seen from Geneva to Paris, Larnaca to Accra, what is there to stop a club who desperately want to sign a 16-year-old from West Africa – reckoning he is the next big thing – from making sure his parents have a job at one of the board of directors' firms? Absolutely nothing. It is, of course, a slightly dubious tactic, but it is the one exemption that makes a mockery of Article 19. It gives the clubs a get-out clause. All they need to do is pull strings, call in a favour and get the kids' parents a job. And if a club really, really want a player, it seems they would get him – as evidenced by the application statistics.

In 2014 Spain was the country that made the highest number of applications for exemptions to Article 19, a whopping 352 compared to the next best, Portugal, with 168. Only 48 failed, which was two fewer than the previous year. English clubs made 112 applications for exemptions, with 23 being rejected.

The numbers from Spain made Barcelona's failure to follow the rules even more extraordinary. Surely a club with such might, sway and resources would have been able to convince a Fifa transfer sub-committee that they satisfied the Article 19 exemption? The answer to that is hinted at by the nature of their defence against the charges. They blamed an 'administrative error', argued they had done nothing wrong under Spanish law, and suggested skulduggery. 'Why we got singled out first and not others is a question for Fifa,' said Josep Maria Bartomeu, the club president. 'It all came about from an anonymous complaint surrounding [a] player. We don't know who made this official complaint, they don't want to supply this information. But it's clear that there are other clubs involved.'

Furthermore it appeared Barcelona tried to convince the Court of Arbitration for Sport they were a special case because La Masia, their much-vaunted youth academy, was exactly that.

It had been a production line of talent, so why should Barcelona change it? Messi, the jewel in their crown, signed at La Masia at just 13 from Argentina. Students played football for only one hour and 45 minutes per day, spending the majority of their time at school. It was this claimed dedication to the education and development of children, some from impoverished backgrounds, that formed the foundation stone of their argument. The head-teacher of the school gave evidence, as did Fabrice Ondoa, an 18-year-old goalkeeper from Cameroon who had been at La Masia since he was 13, and Elohor Godswill, a 19-year-old right-back from Nigeria who arrived at the age of just six. The pair talked about the life-changing opportunity that La Masia had provided and how they had been rescued from a future of poverty and strife. Neither Ondoa or Godswill was on the list of players Barcelona had been accused of illegally signing.

As it happened, Barcelona were not 'singled out'. In 2014 Fifa announced that Real Madrid, Atlético de Madrid, Valencia CF and Rayo Vallecano were also under investigation for similar breaches. Emilio Butragueño, the Real Madrid director of institu-tional relations, said Fifa had asked for information about 51 underage players signed by the club since 2009. One was thought to be the Japanese player Takuhiro Nakai, who arrived from Tokyo in 2013 to play for Real Madrid's under-12 team. 'We will continue to work with Fifa in every aspect they ask of us. We are absolutely relaxed about the procedure involving Real Madrid,' said Butragueño.

Other clubs have been sanctioned too. The first was FC Midtjylland, the Danish side. In 2007, FifPro, the worldwide players' union, filed a case against them and the Danish FA for importing 17-year-olds from a feeder club in Nigeria, FC Ebedi. Midtjylland had also argued, unsuccessfully, that the players had gone to Denmark to study. Two years later Fifa banned Chelsea from signing players for two transfer windows for inducing Gaël Kakuta, a 16-year-old from RC Lens, the French club, to break his contract. Didier Roudet, the Lens general secretary, said Chelsea 'offered the player's family a lot of money to leave'. Chelsea's case was not a breach of Article 19, but it showed football's regard for the welfare of minors.

When a club – nay, an institution – the size of Barcelona deems itself to be above the law, or perhaps unaware of it, it highlights the challenge Fifa, and football, has in trying to effectively impose sanctions to protect children. So far, two attitudes have been all pervasive: first, that a club will sign players under 18 if they are good enough, at any cost; and, secondly, 'If we're big enough, we can do what we want.'

'That exists everywhere,' Mark Goddard said. 'Some people believe they're not subject to the rules, there are exceptions that should be granted, and they can do what they want.' He made clear at this point that he was not referring to Barcelona, but continued: 'We don't care who you are, you will use the system as it is intended, which is consistent with creating integrity and stability. You can have arrogance, humbleness, do the rules apply, do they not? It's everywhere. We're not that interested in what their personal opinions are. We're into communicating what the rules are, what they need to do and not do.'

It was tough talk from Goddard and taken in isolation one could be convinced by such combative soundbites. Fifa didn't care how big a club was or how powerful. If they broke the rules they would, as he said, 'face the consequences'. It all sounded very honourable. But there was a problem. What about the Qataris? What about the Aspire Academies in Doha and Senegal, which have been taking kids as young as 13 from their families since 2007? What about the 'screening' process they boasted about on their website and at that UN conference in Geneva?

'Aspire Academy,' Goddard said. 'What about them?' The Fifa press officer who sat in on our call then interrupted. He sounded panicked: 'Just one thing . . . we scheduled for this to last an hour so we can limit this to another ten minutes. And not to just go into specific examples because it's not in the scope of the conversation.'

'Aspire move kids at 13,' I said. 'Why are they allowed to do that?'

'Um . . . I . . . can't say . . . I'm gonna take your point and say that, that's what happened,' Goddard said, for the first time sounding unsure. 'If you're telling me that is what's happening then you could provide some information and we're more than happy to—'

'It's not a secret,' I interjected. 'It's on their website. It's well documented that that's what they do.'

'Right.'

'Are you uncomfortable about 13-year-olds going to Qatar?'

'Our compliance unit does visits with various member associations and in those visits we go through how to handle the minors' situation. But short of starting a formal investigation this is all speculative statements which, to be frank, I'm not sure the information you've provided is accurate or not.'

17

Aspire

The Aspire Academy, based in Doha, is a futuristic, state-of-the-art training centre meticulously designed to hone the sporting stars of tomorrow. The 'Aspire Dome' is the largest indoor sports venue in the world. There are seven outdoor football pitches. Its sports science department, including altitude and biomechanical laboratories, are the envy of the football world. Its dormitories, for 255 students, offer cable TV, Wifi and *en suite* facilities. Manchester United and Bayern Munich, among others, have used it for warm-weather training.

Once completed, in 2004, all it needed was some footballers of its own to do it justice. Proper footballers. Qatari professionals and amateurs used it to train, but that wasn't enough. So one of the most ambitious and controversial talent searches football has ever seen began three years later. The project was called Aspire Africa and targeted boys as young as 13 in Morocco, Cameroon, Ghana, Kenya, Nigeria, Senegal and South Africa. Pelé, the Brazil legend, was drafted in to announce the programme. The press release trumpeted: 'When testing starts at the end of May, six thousand staff will screen more than 500,000 boys born in 1994 in seven different countries across 700 locations. In the first phase the best 50 players from each country, identified in the selection process, will go for a week of trials in the capital city of their respective nations. The top three from each country will then come to Aspire for four weeks of trials and testing. From here, following a period of assessment and discussions with the families, the most talented players will be enrolled into the Aspire Academy.'

The Aspire programme actually screened 430,000. Three players were granted scholarships to Doha. The programme then expanded. The name was changed to Aspire Football Dreams. By 2014 the number of players that Aspire had 'screened' had risen to 3.5 million. Twelve countries in Africa have participated, but the continent has proved not to be big enough. So Aspire have branched out to Asia – scouting 13-year-olds in Vietnam and Thailand – and the Americas, in Guatemala, Costa Rica and Paraguay. Initially three scholarships to the academy in Doha per year were offered to the best of the best. But that has also proved not to be enough. A second facility was built in Senegal in 2007 which allowed the number of scholarships to rise to between 16 and 18 per year. When it opened all scholars went there instead of Doha. The scholarships lasted five years. In 2014 up to 70 boys were living and training there. It is understood that the families of the boys were paid up to £3,500 per year.

The aim was twofold: to give underprivileged youngsters an education that they could otherwise only dream of; and to produce professional footballers. Aspire, stated the website, was 'the perfect bridge to professional football'. To that end in 2012 Aspire had brokered a deal to effectively buy the Belgian second division club, KAS Eupen. From the dusty fields of the 'screening' process, to final trials at the out-of-this-world Doha academy, to a full-time scholarship and then to Eupen, there was a clear route to stardom.

There was nothing secretive or mysterious about the Aspire programme. Nor was there anything 'speculative', as Mark

Goddard, the TMS manager, told me. Most of the detail could be found on the Aspire website. The rest had been reported widely since the programme's inception, with journalists freely given access to the academy itself and its operation. Indeed, Aspire were proud of their 'humanitarian project'. Bora Milutinović, the Aspire ambassador, informed the UN conference in Geneva, with relish, of the number of kids who had been 'screened' to 'give opportunities to young players from developing countries to reach the height of football'. Some might say they were brazen. It was wholly, apparently unashamedly, at odds with Article 19.

In 2007 five European MPs wrote to Sepp Blatter, the Fifa president, to express concerns about Aspire's talent search. They called it 'trafficking and exploitation of children'. 'We seriously doubt that children under 13 years can make autonomous choices that have such an impact on their lives,' they wrote. 'The protection of children against commercial [interests] and football clubs is absolutely vital. We would ask you to do a thorough investigation of this case, to check the practice is compatible with the existing rules and to apply, if need be, appropriate sanctions.'

Blatter agreed. In reply, he wrote, 'It [Aspire] is a good example of the exploitation of individual dreams and gives a misleading impression of providing access to education.'

A year later he had changed his mind. He had visited Aspire and was hosted by Sheikh Hamad bin Khalifa Al Thani, the emir. The Al Thani royal family, which funded Aspire, had put sport or, more specifically, football at the centre of a plan to prepare Qatar for a post-gas economy. The Qatar National Vision 2030 policy document explained how football could help Qatar become an 'advanced society'. The Aspire Academy and Aspire Dreams programme were early signs of Qatar's ambition to colonise the game and realise the 'Vision'. They also funded the International Centre for Sport and Security (ICSS), the self-proclaimed police force of world sport, who Jake Marsh worked for. These were considered 'soft' plays. Much harder was the power grab at Paris Saint-Germain: the club was bought by the state-owned Qatar Sports Investments in May 2011. Even Barcelona had received massive cash injections from state-owned companies in the form of corporate sponsorship. Then came the most formidable, and stunning, coup by the Al Thanis: the successful bid to stage the 2022 World Cup. It has, of course, since been sullied by allegations of corruption and bribery. Blatter, when he visited the Aspire Academy, had also been received by Qatari Mohamed bin Hammam, a member of the Fifa executive committee at the time. Hammam was the subject of an exposé by the *Sunday Times* in June 2014. It showed he had paid members of other football associations prior to the 2022 World Cup bid decision.

'This was a wonderful opportunity to see Aspire and to discuss the important role of sport in youth development and education,' Blatter backtracked. 'The essence of football is education, because it teaches team-work, discipline and respect for your peers and your competitors. The fact that Aspire has been able to combine both education and sport in one insti-tution is remarkable.'

One might argue that all that was truly remarkable was Blatter's volte-face. The *Sunday Times* reported that Blatter had made a pact with the Qatari royal family to protect his own presi-dency from bin Hammam, who lauched a failed bid to usurp him, in return for ensuring they would not be stripped of the World Cup. It was, therefore, worth examining Aspire Dreams' role in Qatar's World Cup aspirations. Did it only exist to discover talent young enough to be naturalised to play in Qatar's World

Cup team, and thus improve their chances of not being humiliated? Such on-field humiliation would make a mockery of plans to see the country recognised as a centre of sporting excellence, and not least cause them acute embarrassment with their Arab neighbours. There was nothing new about that criticism. But what if their search for young footballers, which had been described as 'child trafficking', had been used to curry favour and win World Cup votes? And why had Aspire Dreams been allowed to essentially transfer minors from continent to continent despite it being against the rules? Both were damning accusations.

The small, sleepy Belgian city of Eupen, 15 kilometres from the German border, was a good place to start. It had a football team with a reputation for mediocrity, a stadium which could hold almost half the population, and a reported €2 million debt which threatened KAS Eupen's existence. Most investors wouldn't have touched the club. But for the Al Thani family and Aspire, KAS Eupen was perfect. They wiped out the club's debt and pumped in a reported €4 million, including €200,000 a year for the youth team alone. In return, all they asked for was to run the professional part of the club, nothing else.

Aspire had a foothold in European football, a club where their most promising youngsters could gain first-team experience, improve and, eventually, perhaps excel enough to be spotted by bigger European clubs. In the 2014–15 season, Eupen had 12 players from the Aspire Dreams programme in their squad alongside six Qataris.

The head of the Aspire Dreams project, Andreas Bleicher, who had formerly worked for the German Olympic team, had originated the idea of controlling a European club in 2010, the same year that Qatar recorded its lowest ever Fifa ranking of 114.

Bleicher hired Josep Colomer, the scout who was responsible for taking a 13-year-old Lionel Messi from Argentina to Barcelona. Together they recognised that after players left the academy, they could go anywhere in the world to play football, and they would have no say, or control, in their development. 'We want our players to become the best in the world,' Bleicher told the *New York Times*. 'To do that, we needed a club of our own.'

The Aspire vision, from its 2007 origins, suddenly looked different. It had taken kids away from their families, something Article 19 had been written to prevent, but now it was actively looking to benefit from producing star players. It sounded very much like the 'neo-colonial' approach which had so enraged Blatter in 2003. Let's remind ourselves of that quote: 'Neo-colonialists who don't give a damn about heritage and culture but engage in social and economic rape by robbing the developing world of its best players.'

Bleicher wanted a tight grip on the players. Each Aspire player had to sign a contract which included strict image-rights provision. 'If a player gets really good, we can freely use his picture,' Bleicher said. All players also had to use the same agent. His name was Lamine Savane. Savane had been the Africa director for Aspire since 2007 and had been responsible for setting up the academy in Senegal. It is worth repeating. A player was not free to choose the agent he wanted to represent him. He had to sign with an Aspire employee. Players were paid the minimum wage (just under €70,000) for a foreign footballer in Belgium. A proportion of this was paid to the academy to cover their accommodation.

Critics of Aspire argued that the control they exerted over the players, and the Eupen project, was evidence of a grand plan to naturalise players in time for the World Cup. A 13-year-old from Paraguay offered a scholarship in 2010 would be 25 and approaching the peak of his footballing lifespan in 2022. In reality, though, for a player to obtain citizenship he would have to live in Qatar for five years after the age of 18.

Dr Paul Darby, a senior lecturer in sport and exercise at the University of Ulster, who had researched African football labour migration exhaustively, publicly denounced Aspire Dreams. In 2008 he said he felt 'very uncomfortable by the whole exercise' and argued there was a moral problem with seeking to build a sports culture in one country by under-developing the sports culture of another. 'I have a bit of an issue that the project is framed as humanitarian, rooted in a sense of altruism, helping kids in developing nations, and I think they use the term "empowering youth" on their website,' he told me. 'That's, to be frank, bullshit and bluster. Ultimately they're looking for athletes who can be naturalised and play for their national teams. And, if they get success in the game, that has all sorts of benefits in terms of Qatar's place in the Middle East. That's really what they're at.'

Aspire had always strenuously denied that a stronger national team was the point. Bleicher, however, appeared to be more malleable in his *New York Times* interview. 'Could it happen?' Bleicher said. 'I suppose maybe some of the players feel like they would want to represent Qatar, because Qatar helped them when their home countries did not.'

A former Aspire employee, who was part of the management team when Aspire Africa was launched, revealed to me (on condition of anonymity) that the project was not wholly philanthropic. We'll call him 'Mehdi'. He said, 'The message was "we're doing our bit". The reality was that, when I was having off-the-record conversations with the other senior management team, it was all about a fear that the Arab children are much smaller, they don't have the physical attributes that African players have. What they wanted to do was bring up the Qatari players by making them play against, and with, bigger, stronger, faster and better players because that would improve them.'

'Was it spoken about that the Africans could play in the national team?' I asked.

'Yes, it was. But that was not unusual. We had Kenyan runners who had been naturalised. So it was there in Olympic sports, and Aspire was also an Olympic academy. It wasn't just football.'

Qatar had form for the naturalisation of other countries' sports stars. One of the first imports was a Bulgarian weightlifter, Angel Popov, who won a bronze medal in the 2000 Olympics under his Arab name, Said Saif Asaad. In a scheme that had been lampooned as 'cash-for-gold', eight track athletes had switched to Qatar between 2003 and 2015. Foreign-born players who held Qatari citizenship made up more than two-thirds of the country's 16-man handball squad that won its first ever medal in the 2015 world championships, losing the final to France. What was interesting was that the tournament was staged in Qatar. Was that a precursor for the World Cup?

'What you see happening in handball, you just feel it will happen in football as well,' Mehdi said. 'The ultimate goal is the 2022 World Cup.' It has, to an extent, already started. Qatar won the 2014 West Asian Cup with a team that included Karim Boudiaf, of Algerian–Moroccan descent, and Boualem Khoukhi, of Algerian descent. Both had taken Qatari citizenship. In a friendly match against Algeria in March 2015, six of the starting XI were not born in Qatar. Mehdi said that naturalising players in time for the World Cup was not Aspire's only ulterior motive. They wanted to produce a Messi, a superstar who could be sold for millions. A 'best player in the world', as Bleicher had admitted. It left Mehdi feeling 'uncomfortable'. 'There's a lot more to it,' he said. 'Absolutely they wanted a Messi. That's exactly it. The whole idea was there would be a return investment in the future, but that might take ten or 15 years [from now].' It is understood that the Africa arm of the project had a budget of $4 million a year.

'I thought it was unethical,' Mehdi added. 'Totally wrong. There was the educational aspect. The boys were being taught English and Arabic. But I think they struggled. They had not been to school much. And what happened to them when they were deemed not good enough? They were sent back. There was no support network. They were on their own again.'

Another fierce critic of Aspire was Phaedra Al-Majid. Al-Majid was the 'Fifa whistleblower' who revealed that Qatar had paid Fifa members to vote for them to host the 2022 World Cup. Al-Majid worked as an international media officer for the Qatar 2022 bid team before losing her job in 2010. She had retracted the allegations in a signed affidavit in 2011 but she insisted she was 'coerced' into changing her statement. The FBI had offered her protection after she said 'threats' were made against her and her family. 'I'm convinced my phone's bugged,' she said, as an excuse for talking on Skype. Like Mehdi, Al-Majid said that Aspire Dreams was 'disgusting and heart-breaking' and 'absolutely' about naturalising talent. But her claim that the programme was used to gain votes for the bid cast it in a different light. 'One of the things we promised Thailand was was a Dreams programme,' she said. 'That was a huge thing.'

Worawi Makudi, president of the Thai FA, was an influential member of Fifa's executive committee – the same committee that decided where a World Cup would be staged. It has been widely reported that Makudi was under investigation by Fifa's ethics committee for his conduct during the Qatar bid. In May 2011, Lord Triesman, the former chairman of the FA, gave evidence in Parliament that Makudi had demanded the television rights to a friendly between England and the Thai national team in return for voting for England to host the 2018 FIFA World Cup. Makudi tried to sue Triesman but failed because of immunity given to speakers. In July 2015 Makudi was given a suspended jail term by a Bangkok court for forgery in his 2013 election to lead his country's FA.

'There had also been criticism in Africa with what Qatar is doing with Dreams,' Al-Majid continued. 'They take the best, and the rest they leave. One of the things that was promised to African Fifa executive committee members by Aspire was that not only will we take the best players, train them for ourselves, but train them to play on their own teams.'

Al-Majid's assertion that Thailand was offered an Aspire Dreams programme was backed up by a 'corporate and social responsibility' World Cup bid document that I obtained a copy of. It clearly stated that Aspire would 'build a football academy in Thailand emulating the Aspire Football Dreams academy in Senegal'. It also suggested developing 'a nationwide grassroots programme in Nigeria through Aspire expertise and local Nigerian organisations'. That is significant because Nigeria also had a vote on the Fifa executive committee.

It should be pointed out that of the 24 nations with delegates on the Fifa executive committee, Aspire Football Dreams operated in five of them. This was not lost on the Aspire Academy's marketing and communications department which, reported the *New York Times*, produced a document that detailed how it could help Qatar's World Cup bid. 'Every country where projects are conducted should vote for Qatar,' the proposal read. 'Five votes could be directly rendered favorable via an influence from Football Dreams.'

The role of Aspire in offering incentives to voters was raised as a concern in a 430-page report by Michael Garcia, the former attorney for the southern district of New York, into the bidding process for the 2018 and 2022 World Cups. It also found that Harold Mayne-Nicholls, Fifa's then chief bid inspector, had asked in an email to Andreas Bleicher, head of Aspire, whether the programme could 'evaluate and train' his son and nephew. Aspire offered to cover the cost of Mayne-Nicholls's son and nephew before having a change of heart. Garcia resigned after Fifa said the probe should be closed because of a lack of evidence of wrongdoing, refused to make public his investigation and then released a summary of his findings which he said were inaccurate.

Aspire were prickly, to say the least, when challenged about their project. Ward Abdallah, a media officer, wrote in an email to me: 'From the questions you have addressed, [it] seems you have your pre-judgement already. To be more precise, we are not that interested . . . as it really appeared you don't have any knowledge about our project although it is very transparent and published on our websites. I am sure you will not find any headlines here unless you really care about CSR [corporate and social responsibility] and helping young footballers.'

Aspire were invited to comment on the following allegations: the project gives a misleading impression of access to education (as initially alleged by Blatter), it was used to curry favour and win votes from Fifa members (in particular from Thailand), the ambition of naturalising players to represent Qatar was the reason for its philanthropic aims and, finally, there was no support network for boys who are returned to Africa. They did not respond to any of them. Qatari officials and Aspire executives have, however, consistently denied Football Dreams had any influence over votes, emphasising that it was a programme to help poorer nations and it provided limited benefit to Qatar.

Who benefits isn't actually that important – be it the Qatari national team, KAS Eupen, the boys themselves or their families – what is crucial is that Aspire Dreams has paid no heed to Fifa's Article 19, which has no exemption for registering foreign minors to an academy or amateur players. Aspire did respond to the allegation that they were involved with the trafficking of minors. They rejected any suggestion of wrongdoing. Abdallah wrote: 'We have open books, you should have changed your angle but seems you don't want to. There is simply no transfer of minors.' He also said that, because they are an educational facility and the boys 'don't play organised football', the rule does not apply. In other words, they are not affiliated with Fifa. From a strict regulation point of view that is correct. It appears a flimsy argument in the context of an ethical and moral debate.

But surely, in the case of strict regulation, the goalposts had been moved as soon as they bought KAS Eupen, who were, obviously, affiliated with Fifa? What Aspire was doing as soon as that arrangement was made was no different to Barcelona. Both were trying to produce players for their respective clubs. Aspire also use the same argument that Barcelona put forward in their case at the Court of Arbitration for Sport. The Spanish club said they were, first and foremost, educating boys in their La Masia academy: they were providing them with opportunities that they would have otherwise gone without. And if they became professional footballers and played for Barcelona, all well and good. The attitude was mirrored by Aspire with the 'bullshit and bluster' approach to humanitarianism. Article 19 has no exemption for education or humanitarianism. Aspire were asked whether their 'bridge to professional football' with Eupen was evidence that they held the rule in 'low regard'. They did not respond.

What also intrigues is the link between the Al Thanis, the Qatari royal family, and therefore Aspire, and Barcelona. Lionel Messi is an Aspire ambassador. An Aspire Dreams XI plays Barcelona's youth team every year. Senegalese Diawandou Diagne, who joined Aspire at 13 and went on to play two seasons at Eupen, signed for Barcelona's B team in 2014. And the association runs much deeper. In 2011 the Qatar Foundation, the country's charitable arm, paid €150 million to become the first sponsor of the hitherto sacred Barcelona shirt for five years. Then Qatar Airways paid just under €100 million for shirt sponsorship, as the Foundation's agreement was converted to a more general corporate sponsorship. There should be no real reason, therefore, why Aspire and Barcelona appear to have been treated differently with regard to Article 19. Their academies have operated in the same way, extolling the same virtues and professing the same aims. To all intents and purposes, both are bankrolled by the emir. Yet Barcelona, of course, have not won a bid to stage the World Cup at the Camp Nou in 2022.

When trying to fathom why Aspire have not faced scrutiny by Fifa, it is hard not to come to the conclusion that the governing body could not possibly tolerate another scandal involving Qatar. It will do nothing but further damage the credibility of the tournament if the host nation's flagship sporting academy is charged, or investigated, with illegally transferring minors. Perhaps that's why the Fifa press officer sounded panicked when I asked Goddard about Aspire.

Such an argument was given credence by Fifa's reaction to another sordid encounter involving the Qataris. A report by Amnesty International found that migrant workers building Qatar's 2022 stadia were 'treated like cattle'. It found workers were victims of forced labour and lived in overcrowded conditions exposed to raw sewage and no running water. There was, as one would expect, worldwide condemnation. Except at Fifa. Sepp Blatter said, 'It's not Fifa's responsibility.'

Article 19 was Fifa's responsibility, however, specifically the Transfer Matching System. It is understood that despite

Goddard's protestations, the TMS team are well aware of the numbers of children Aspire has moved across continents to Qatar and Senegal since the launch of Aspire Africa. Fifa reject any suggestion that a blind eye has been turned to Aspire's trade. A spokesman, when asked for a defence to the allegation, repeated that they did not have jurisdiction over Aspire which 'is not affiliated to any of Fifa's member associations … Fifa can only regulate activities within the scope of organised football.' How long does it take to confirm Eupen operate within that scope? Slightly less time than to discover the link between the Belgian club's owners and Aspire?

Still, it would be a surprise if the TMS were to file a case against them like they did Barcelona. 'We don't care who you are,' said Goddard. On the contrary, Fifa appear to care very much.

18

'Please Help Me'

Those were the only three words in the email. There were two exclamation marks. It was from Shinji, the Japanese boy I had met at the conference in Geneva. I had forgotten all about him. When I saw him last, he looked set to burst into tears when informed that the charity match in Geneva, touted as involving Samuel Eto'o and Yaya Touré, had been cancelled. He had brought his boots. He had expected to play. He was heartbroken. When I read it, I remembered how that bottom lip of his had wobbled. I wondered how his face looked when he wrote the email? Shinji seemed desperate. He was alone in Paris and had nowhere to stay. He had, it would transpire, fallen victim to a con. It appeared to be a typical case of football trafficking. A man, acting as an agent, who said he could find the young hopeful a football club had told him to go to Paris. He had paid money. And when he arrived the 'agent' was nowhere to be seen. It did at least provide an answer to the question Shinji was unable to articulate when I met him. He was a wannabe footballer, after all.

There were other questions to find answers to. Had he returned to Japan and been scammed there? Had he been trafficked before? That might answer my next query: what exactly had he been doing in Geneva when I'd met him? Also, why had he been tricked when, presumably, Jean-Claude Mbvoumin and his Foot Solidaire cohorts had warned him of the danger? He had sat and listened dutifully to the conference that day. He was well aware of the problem.

I replied immediately. Was he in trouble? Was he safe? What could I do to help? He didn't reply. So I wrote again. Nothing. It was several weeks before I heard from him again. Another email arrived. It was less panicked in tone. No exclamation marks. 'Can you help me?' I got an almost immediate response. He was in no danger – he was just about capable of reading and writing basic English – and this time he was in Orléans, 130 kilometres south of Paris, for a trial at a local club. He was alone. The 'contact' he had been given had not turned up. He had nowhere to stay. He described this as the 'problem encore'. He was emailing from a McDonald's restaurant but ended communication when he found a hotel room.

Shinji was, however, deeply troubled. He kept mentioning sums of money he had paid the 'agent'. Following several emails over several weeks Shinji's predicament became clearer. He had left Paris for good and had a place studying French at the university in Orléans. Over the course of 11 months, from September 2013 to July 2014, Shinji had paid the 'agent' €3,080. What was notable about the time period was when it started. Shinji had been giving money to the 'agent' before the Geneva conference. My initial reaction was that Jean-Claude and Foot Solidaire had picked up Shinji and tried to help him but he had fallen back into the wrong hands. He had, it seemed, been used as a personal cash point with his deceiver pushing Shinji's buttons whenever he was short. It seemed an enormous sum for someone so young and so far away from home. Hell, I couldn't afford to hand over that sort of wad. How many of us could? I presumed he hailed from a well-heeled Japanese family. I presumed his 'agent' thought the same.

The money paid to the 'agent' was for accommodation, trials at football clubs in France and travel for the 'agent' to visit the club where the trials would be held. Most of the time, it seemed from his limited written English, the trials and the accommodation had failed to materialise. Shinji was angry. He knew it wasn't right. He knew he had been scammed but, like the thousands of boys before him, his dream was too big. He was too desperate to be a footballer. He pleaded with me not to tell anyone, clearly ashamed that, time after time, this 'agent' had kept returning to milk him for money over so many months. Indeed, instead of answering my many questions, he mostly repeated the wish that it was all to be kept secret.

It was clear I needed to meet Shinji face-to-face to understand how he had been such easy prey. From the limited time I spent with him, it was true he had seemed a malleable target. He was too trusting, too polite, too deferential. 'Too Japanese,' said Miyu Mitake-Leroy, the translator I had hired to help me interview him. 'Those are our national characteristics and people take advantage.'

Miyu also said that the Japanese had another trait for which they were known. They were organised. It was a stereotype that I would not have had the gall to suggest but, given it came from Miyu's mouth, it had some legitimacy. They kept records. Shinji had indeed kept records. Perhaps Shinji's 'agent' had not bargained on that. He had receipts of the transactions he had paid to the 'agent'. He had SMS messages, the email address, the telephone number. In my experience of interviewing these kids, that was rare. Jay-Jay, for example, had nothing. Just a first name. Shinji had the full name. I hadn't expected to recognise it immediately. Let alone know the 'agent'. It was Jean-Claude Mbvoumin, the founder of Foot Solidaire.

Shinji had started playing football when he was ten. His hero was Zinedine Zidane. 'He was just fascinating,' he said. From the moment he first saw him play on television, Shinji wanted to emulate his hero and play in Europe. Like Zidane, Shinji was a midfielder. 'Technically I am good but not so physical. The coaches say I need to be better at the physical.' His parents were supportive of his ambition. 'It's the reason I can be here now,' he said, sipping a glass of water in an Orléans square in the shadow of the spectacular cathedral. 'They send money.' Shinji did not come from a middle-class family, however. His parents were cleaners. 'When a new house is built, for example, a cleaner goes in the rooms, and cleans them up. My parents did that together.' He has four siblings and said that he had been happy in Japan, living in the city of Nishio-shi, on the coast of the Pacific Ocean. 'It's where they make all the green tea.'

To help fund his European travels, outside of high-school hours – where he was studying sports science, which explained the initial confusion about him being a 'football student' – Shinji had undertaken part-time jobs. He had been a lifeguard and worked on a construction site. 'When I wasn't studying or playing football I worked from eight in the morning to seven at night.'

I found it difficult to imagine Shinji being much use as a labourer. A puff of wind could have blown him over, and it was easy to see why his football coaches had worried about his strength. He didn't seem to have any. He was a slip of a lad and, at 21, a year older than when I first met him, he had the look of someone much younger. He was delicate. In fact, with his slightly buck teeth and an expression which flitted between hopeful and hopeless, every inch of Shinji screamed vulnerability.

It was at school where Shinji's journey had begun. His tutor knew of his ambition and talent. He wanted to help, believing that the young man had the ability to make it professionally. By chance, he had a friend who was a professor at a university in Osaka who had spoken of a graduate who had played football in

France. His tutor phoned his contact, who spoke to the former student. A route to France emerged. The student knew someone who could help, a man with experience in finding trials, or 'tests' as Shinji called them, for hopefuls. It was Jean-Claude.

'Jean-Claude said he was planning to go to Japan, and so we [the university professor and the graduate] went to meet him when he came. And that's where I met him for the first time. At that time I thought all these people could be trusted . . .'

A plan was hatched. Shinji would travel to France to have a trial with a French club, Angers of the second division: 'I graduated from high school and was 18. It was March 2011, I came to France just for two weeks to take a test. And Jean-Claude is the one who took care of the co-ordination. I passed the test to be in the Angers reserve team. So, I went home to Japan to get my visa and prepared to live in Angers.

'There were three people who were organising the contract for me. The two Japanese people I told you about and one French man, who would be the agent. He was an acquaintance of Jean-Claude. That person was a lawyer. So he didn't have a real licence as an agent. So when I came to France with the idea that I would be playing for Angers I found out the contract was annulled. I couldn't join the team at all. And I didn't speak a word of French, either. There was nothing I could do, so I called the Japanese people, they told me that it wasn't their problem, and that I should sort it out by myself.

'When I was in Japan, I was told that when I got to Angers, I [would] get paid and that there was already a place I could live. But then, I had no place at all to live, and no income at all. I wondered how I was going to live. And that's where my parents helped me out with money.'

So Shinji had travelled from Japan to Angers believing he was going to sign a professional contract to play football and there would be somewhere to stay. Neither materialised. Let's just remind ourselves at this point that Jean-Claude's Mbvoumin's charity, Foot Solidaire, was supposed to try to prevent young footballers ending up thousands of miles away in that exact situation. And here was its founder facilitating such an occurrence. Shinji may have been over 18, but it was a severe conflict of interest.

Shinji had also been told that three per cent of his salary would go to the two Japanese. A further seven per cent would go to the agent-cum-lawyer that Jean-Claude had recommended. Later Shinji contacted the French football federation to find out whether the lawyer was a licensed agent. They wrote to him informing him that he was not. Why had Jean-Claude recommended an unlicensed agent?

Shinji's parents decided it would be better for Shinji to remain in Angers. He had a visa for a year and they had the money to support him. So he enrolled at the university. But did Jean-Claude help him?

'I think he contacted the lawyer guy, and he said he would come to Angers once. I said I would be waiting for him. He came but he said he went back home because I wasn't home. But that's improbable, right? So I think it was just a lie.'

At that stage Shinji had not paid any money. Not to Jean-Claude, the two Japanese or the lawyer. He returned to Japan after his year in Angers. Undettered, he emailed Jean-Claude for help to return to France. He said he had no reason to believe Jean-Claude was not trustworthy, instead blaming the two Japanese and the lawyer for the Angers débâcle. It would prove to be a foolish mistake. He looked wounded when I said, 'But you knew those three men were all connected to Jean-Claude?' It was February 2013. Jean-Claude said a 'solid plan' was needed.

'I had turned 20,' Shinji said. 'I wanted to come back to France right away. And I told him that. He said to wait and that it wasn't the right moment. He said to wait until August. But when we were in August he said it still wasn't the right timing. Then there was this story about going to Switzerland. I wanted to come much earlier in France but he told me that there would be this match in Switzerland, and that's how he convinced me [to wait].'

So Jean-Claude had told Shinji to delay his return to France until the time of the UN conference in Geneva, when the charity match would be played? 'Yes,' Shinji said. 'There would be a lot of famous people invited and that I would be able to play at that match. And that convinced me and I said that I'll go. He didn't say it would be a good opportunity for me to be scouted but it was implied. Of course, I was told I could play with those people and that TV would be present as well. And I thought that it was my chance, that I had an opportunity. If I could play at the match, it was a chance. And if I could get into a club by that way, well, it was worth going to Switzerland.'

I asked Shinji when Jean-Claude had started to ask him for money. He searched through his smart phone. 'Is he looking for the receipts?' I said to Miyu, the translator. 'Yes,' she said. Shinji emailed them to me, one by one. There were six altogether. 'The first time . . . I think it dates back a long time ago. It was for him to seek for clubs. I don't recall clearly when was the first time he asked for money, but he asked me many, many times.'

The first receipt was for a transaction via Western Union. It was dated 5 September 2013, more than six months before the Geneva conference. The total amount was €700. It clearly stated in bold type at the top of the 'customer receipt' that the 'sender' was Shinji Yoshida and the 'receiver' was Jean-Claude Mbvoumin. Shinji said this money was to get him trials at clubs: 'He told me he had a lot of connections and a network. He had connections with Évian, but also Angers. So the €700 mentioned was intended for seeking a club. One club was Tours, another was Chateauroux and two other clubs as well. In the end, I paid money for [trials] in those four clubs. But even these four teams, I never had any trials and never went there. It was a complete waste.'

On 2 November 2013, Shinji sent €250 for accommodation at another trial at Angers. It was a sign of his desperation that he would consider a return. But he did not go. He did not receive the money back. Shinji showed me an email exchange between him, Jean-Claude and a middle man who was arranging the trial. The middle man had written to Jean-Claude saying he had received Shinji's photo and he needed the money by Saturday. The date was 1 November. Intriguingly, he also wrote 'here are the invitations [for the] young Cameroonians that we brought [to] Angers'. This suggested Jean-Claude had sent other boys to Angers for trial but there was no evidence they had paid money.

The next payment was for €400 on 27 March 2014, a few weeks before the Geneva conference. The money was for a hotel in Geneva. In an email Jean-Claude wrote to Shinji: 'You can send 400 euros on Thursday for your extra hotel? This is a five-star hotel. It's called Hotel President Wilson in Geneva.' Ten hours later, Shinji wired the money. Shinji did not stay at the Hotel President Wilson. He stayed at Best Western's Hotel Century. I told you that was important, right back at the start of this story. Jean-Claude, Mathieu, the Foot Solidaire volunteer, and Amane, Foot Solidaire's poster boy, and myself stayed at the Best Western. A room for the night cost me €120. What happened to the difference? The next day Shinji was asked for a further €230. He paid using Western Union. 'I paid on the basis that I was staying at Hotel President Wilson,' said Shinji. 'But we stayed one night at this other place. One night.' He said he did not even have his own room. 'Mathieu, Amane and I shared a room. There were only two beds. Amane said he would sleep on the floor as he was the youngest.'

Shinji had flown from Japan to France and then on to Geneva to play in the trial match. It was a match which was extremely unlikely to ever take place. Yet Jean-Claude did not tell Shinji. 'He could've just told me, and then I wouldn't have had to go all the way to Switzerland. Even the plane ticket fee was a waste. I just don't understand why he didn't tell me.'

I didn't have the heart to suggest to Shinji that Jean-Claude might have wanted him there as a cash machine. Even in Geneva, Shinji claimed he had kept pumping him for more. In the hotel Shinji said that Jean-Claude told him he could get him a trial with Évian for €200. Shinji compliantly handed it over in cash. There was no record or receipt of the transaction. The trial never happened.

'Once the conference finished, we went out to eat,' said Shinji. 'I talked to Jean-Claude about the fact that I paid up to €630 for the hotel, that we stayed only one night, that it wasn't five-star. I told him. And so I believe that the meal we had after the conference was at my expense as well. He said it was included in the €630 I paid. But everybody was there. There were maybe ten of them. Ten grown-ups. And when I think I was the one that had to pay all of it, I don't understand the reason why I had to pay. I don't get it at all.'

I remembered when they had all left for the restaurant. I had been invited but had a plane to catch. Jean-Claude, Mathieu and the other Foot Solidaire volunteers looked very pleased with themselves. And then there was Shinji. Confused, angry, sad. 'Of course I was upset,' he said. 'It was incomprehensible.'

However, it was incomprehensible that Shinji had remained in contact with Jean-Claude. Not only that, he gave him more money. 'I trusted him,' he said. 'He was the top person at Foot

Solidaire, the charity which would help young people. My parents have told me not to speak with him again. I thought he could really help me.'

There were two further payments to Jean-Claude. The penultimate one (dated 27 June 2014) was the biggest of all. It was for €1,000 for a trial at Brest. This did take place. Shinji was not offered a contract by the club. 'It didn't go well,' he said. 'I had a fever, a migraine.'

Soon after that transaction, made via the French post office, with Jean-Claude clearly marked as the recipient, Shinji emailed me in desperation for the first time. He had returned to Japan to renew his visa and was back in France to continue looking for a football club. It was at this point where it was difficult to feel sympathy for Shinji. Why did he not cut his losses? Why did his family allow him to go back? Jean-Claude had proved again and again that he was unreliable. 'I don't know,' Shinji said. 'I just wanted . . . he said he had a network.' That bottom lip had begun to go again.

When he landed in Paris Jean-Claude was nowhere to be seen. Shinji had missed a connecting flight so was delayed but he had warned Jean-Claude via SMS. It was a story which, for the first time, elicited a laugh from Shinji: 'He was supposed to have brought a host family to the airport that day. But he said he didn't get my message that I was late and he was waiting, waiting at the airport and I didn't show up. I thought, "It's fine, because he will just contact the host family and it'll be fine." But then he said he had to search for a host family for me. He could've simply introduced me to the first family. But he didn't do that, so what happened to the host family he was supposed to have brought to the airport? In the end I stayed with a friend in Paris.'

Shinji paid Jean-Claude for the final time on 18 July 2014. It was €300 for travel expenses for Jean-Claude to arrange a trial in

Orléans. When Shinji arrived in Orléans he discovered Jean-Claude had given him the wrong time. The match was over. 'He told me to go there. It was clearly too late to be on time for the match. So, in the end, I wasn't able to participate. I had no place to sleep. It was 9 p.m., and I was alone. That was when I emailed you again.'

On Foot Solidaire's website there is a list of 'types of abuse suffered by young players'. They include abandonment, payments for trials, the false promise of a contract with a club, economic exploitation, lack of transparency in negotiating a contract, incitement to play competitions abroad and trafficking in human beings. According to Shinji he had suffered each of these at the hands of Foot Solidaire and Jean-Claude Mbvoumin. He was left stranded at airports, he paid exorbitant monies for trials, was told he would find a club, was charged false accommodation and travel expenses, had a playing contract annulled and was encouraged to leave Japan to try his luck in France.

If Shinji's story was true, and his receipts suggested it was, it discredits Foot Solidaire as an organisation, one which claims to provide a solution to football trafficking yet in the example of Shinji actively promoted it. There are few more grievous charges than a charity exploiting the victims it is supposed to be helping. Adding to their number is beyond the pale. Had Jean-Claude only 'co-ordinated' Shinji's move from Japan to take trials in France, that in itself would have been enough to ensure Foot Solidaire's reputation was in tatters. They would once again be starved of credibility and funding.

When football stakeholders raised concerns previously to Jake Marsh, head of youth protection at the International Centre for Sport and Security, of being unaware of what Foot Solidaire actually did, no one would have believed that they would have encouraged a Japanese player to come to Europe.

They might have thought they were disorganised in the failure to provide names of rogue agents to Fifa. They might have thought they were misguided in a partnership with Top Spot Ltd, a football talent search company. They would certainly not have guessed that they took money off a player.

If the incitement to travel was bad enough, then the alleged demands for money made to Shinji turn the stomach. Here was a wide-eyed and weak individual, exposed in a foreign country. A sucker. An easy target who fell for the methods used by the fake agents and conmen, the methods which Jean-Claude had sermonised against.

What had happened to Shinji was exactly what had happened to thousands of young boys elsewhere. Foot Solidaire had recorded their testimonies. They were blueprints for a fraud. It is worth repeating: Shinji had a dream of playing professionally in Europe. He paid money to an 'agent' for a trial in a foreign country. The agent abandoned him when he arrived. It's the classic tale and one known well thanks to the storytelling skills of Jean-Claude.

A few months after my meeting with Shinji, Jean-Claude was once more in the pulpit. The *Daily Telegraph* in London published a feature about Jean-Claude and Foot Solidaire. The article bemoaned 'chancers and criminals' and hailed Jean-Claude as a 'lone crusader against the game's endemic corruption'.

Jean-Claude, of course, is no hero if Shinji is to be believed. But let's forget the money for a moment. That Jean-Claude advised Shinji to leave Japan for France to take tests at various clubs makes him part of the trafficking problem. At the risk of repeating myself, it was what his charity was supposed to rail against. The question one cannot help but ask having listened to Shinji is: how many more?

Shinji was sure there were others. 'It is true that he operates that kind of business,' he said. 'He also said that he had some similar business with some people [in] Portugal. The taking a bit of money from young people, and helping them get into a club. That kind of stuff.'

There was no evidence of others. A test email from the imaginary Som Kalou, the 17-year-old Nigerian who was desperate to find a club in Europe, was sent to Jean-Claude. Som asked for help in getting trials with clubs and he offered to pay money. The response returned some credit to Jean-Claude and Foot Solidaire: 'Our organisation's first goal is to protect the young players, particularly, the minors (under 18). We can advise you to continue your training in Nigeria, in a local team and avoid fake agents. I would like to emphasise the fact that you are too young for an international recruitment (FIFA Regulation, Article 19 'Protection of Minors').'

It hardly rescued Jean-Claude's reputation, however. Shinji's records and receipts were enough to ensure that faith in his work and that of his charity was sorely tested. Re-reading the transcript of my interview with Jean-Claude in the light of Shinji's revelations, it was noticeable that he frequently spoke about money. He talked about how poor he was after retiring from football, the crippling costs he incurred when setting up Foot Solidaire, the phone bills, the loss of personal items, the cost of his website, the need for funding so he could have a full-time salary, the money he would charge boys for his Foot Solidaire passport.

My final question to Shinji before I left him in that pretty Orléans square was: is Jean-Claude playing on youngsters' hopes and dreams?

'He's mocking them, yes. It's one of the most sneaky, under-handed . . . We really want it to come true, so we're ready to pay a bit of money for it. And he knows. Jean-Claude knows that. That's why he's doing what he does.'

I emailed Jean-Claude in May 2015 asking one simple question. 'Why has Shinji been paying you money from September 2013 for trials, accommodation and your travel expenses?' He responded the same day, accusing me of conducting a 'sly destabilisation campaign' against his charity. The email was threatening in tone: 'If you're one of those people who try to weaken Foot Solidaire for political reasons or to continue [to] exploit the cause of African children under the pretext of protection of young athletes, we are waiting. And we know who you work for.' I replied detailing each of the allegations Shinji had made, including being left at an airport and the payment for Hotel President Wilson. He chose not to answer these.

'What Shinji forgot to tell you is that these sums are actually reimbursements,' he continued, 'and I can provide the proof of such trips and other expenses in Tours, Angers, Brest, Évian, Orléans, Beauvais and Châteauroux.

'The family of Shinji asked me to make these services [available to] Shinji in France since 2011 and not 2013, it was clearly understood that all services that require costs will be reimbursed [to] me consistently. Some were, most not. The reason is simple: Shinji [is] not part of [the] young people supported by Foot Solidaire, so I have to do it personally. This is what I explained to his family.

'These services include steps to find a small job, enrol in college, leisure, find a hotel room, and many other services menu, in fact, I was a concierge for Shinji.

'I am clear in this regard and I have nothing to reproach myself. What Shinji does not say is that the purpose of his visit to France was not football, but to learn French and French culture. But it changed *en route* and [he] decided to [become] a professional footballer and it took me to find a club that wants to welcome him knowing that he has not the level.

'Shinji should also tell you that he has not the sporting [ability], everyone who knows football made him remark. He did an internship (paid) last April in Nantes and could not be selected, but he insists.

'I am always there to explain to Shinji [the] reality [of] football and I told him not to move to Portugal where he recently paid €3,000 or €4,000 to be recruited [by] Marítimo but he does not listen.'

Despite Jean-Claude's defence, the contradiction not only remains but is strengthened. He supported Shinji's quest and even though he knew he wasn't good enough to play professional football, he kept taking the money.

My confidence in Foot Solidaire, not that it had been exactly high previously, had disappeared. 'I have integrity,' Jean-Claude told me. I snorted with derision as I recalled that quote. More pertinently, my confidence in understanding what football trafficking actually was had taken a hit. If I couldn't trust the anti-trafficking charity, who could I trust? What was true? What was a lie? What had been embellished? Foot Solidaire had been responsible for exposing the problem in the first place, yet, on closer examination, they had now been exposed as being part of the problem. I doubted them. So, suddenly, I was unsure about the tales of the boys they had helped. Boys like Ben, Sulley and Didier. Jean-Claude had introduced me to each of them. It was time to try to look past the emotion, the sob stories. It was time to ask questions of the victims themselves.

19

Lost Boys

Sulley, Ben and Didier looked fit and healthy. In fact, they looked every inch the powerful athletes they aspired to be. Sulley, a gentle giant of more than six foot, strode purposefully through the pizza restaurant in Paris's 17th *arrondissement*, Ben was lean and stroked his goatee beard in a cocksure manner, while Didier, short and stocky, bounced to the table, bursting with energy. They were in good spirits. Didier, wearing a natty sports jacket, was playing jester. He regaled the other two with stories about going clubbing with Real Madrid's stars when he was living in the Spanish capital two years ago: 'I saw Arbeloa, Ramos . . . the Brazilian guy, what's he called? Marcelo. Benzema's girlfriend,' he said, 'had tits as big as my head! All the girls did. Just to say hello to one of them would cost €5,000 . . .'

Girls were the main talking point, in particular how to avoid being 'tied down' by one when she found out you were a footballer with the potential to make big money. 'I would hang myself if I was made to marry my girlfriend,' said Didier. 'She's crazy.' They all laughed. They fell about again at Didier's bemused face when Sulley suggested that he didn't have to sleep with a woman if she had told him he was handsome. Didier then passed round a picture of his girlfriend, reclining, blonde and buxom on a beach.

'Well,' I said, 'she looks lovely. You should marry her.'

'This means you don't like me,' Didier deadpanned. They roared again.

When the hilarity ceased, they all took out their smartphones and tapped away with fierce concentration. They looked like footballers, they spoke like footballers, they behaved like footballers. But these three were football's underclass, not the sport's playboy millionaires. As described earlier, Sulley had been abandoned by an agent in Portugal, Ben had been conned out of €3,000 and left in a Paris hotel room, while Didier had been treated like a slave in Argentina. They'd all had it tough. But sitting around, waiting for the lunch I had arranged, they seemed happy and content.

It wasn't exactly what you would expect from victims of trafficking. Only a few of the thousands of boys running around European cities, Jean-Claude Mbvoumin would have told you, would dare to go home because, in most cases, the players were too ashamed that they had failed to make it as a professional or embarrassed that they had fallen for a scam. Since Foot Solidaire's inception, the charity had said that the 'shame' prevented boys like these from returning to their families. In almost every interview Jean-Claude had done he talked of this 'dramatic situation'. I had asked him myself, why don't these kids just go home? 'Yes, we advised them to go home,' he said. 'At the beginning. But how? The family pay the money. If they go home there is shame. It is a problem. You have persecution and I cannot advise that.'

Sulley, Ben and Didier did not want to go home. But they were not afraid of returning. They wanted to stay because life was good. They wanted to stay to pursue their football careers. None of them mentioned shame or embarrassment. Indeed, Didier had gone home. But he had come back for more. Remember, he had travelled to Qatar, Brazil, Argentina, Spain, Malta and Corsica in the hope of a football career.

Sulley had also been nomadic. After Portugal and Belgium, France was his third country. The pair might have been lost initially in a city they didn't know. It was their choice to be lost in subsequent cities. Sulley positively baulked at the suggestion that he might go back to Burkina Faso, shooting a look of astonishment at me as he ate his pizza.

'But do you accept that you will have to go home one day?' I asked again.

'Go home? Well, not really. One day I will find a club, that's for sure.'

Ben, who was from Cameroon, had laughed at the question. He still spoke in that whisper of his, and explained that 'life was better here'.

'Why?' I asked.

'Because here we live better than in Africa, we are very poor there.'

Didier's frown had creased so that his eyebrows met in the middle and formed a v. 'Go home? To do what?' he said. 'If I'm here it's because I decided to play. So if it wasn't for football I never would have left Cameroon. But I think if I abandon it now that would have been a waste of time. I would have wasted, I think, ten years of my life.'

'So, basically, you don't want to go home?' I asked.

'If I go home, the problem is what will I do?'

'You don't want to work there?'

'In Cameroon? If we see that I'm abroad it's because there isn't much work in Cameroon.'

'People will say that the prospects here are not much better, though,' I said.

'I think that's for those to say who haven't got out very much so they can't understand these things. For example, the rhythm of life in Argentina is different to the rhythm of life in France.'

Didier had a point: all things are relative. Why would you go back to Africa if you were playing football in a foreign country? It was, as Imari had said in Larnaca, speaking for the African footballer: 'I will kill myself to play here because I don't want to go back.' The problem was, none of these three boys was actually playing football. Sulley told me he had refused to play for a lower league club because 'the salary was not enough'. It was 'only' €100 if the team won. He would get nothing for a defeat or a draw. Ben said he was not playing because he had been recovering from injury, while Didier claimed he had turned down a contract offered by a club in the United Arab Emirates for €1,000 a month. He said he was 'searching every day for a club, sending his CV'.

It was peculiar. Where was the drive to do their time at a lower level and prove themselves? Did they honestly expect a big club, like Paris Saint-Germain, to come and offer them a deal?

And in the meantime, they were not working. None of them. And none of them were receiving benefit from the French social services. So where did they get their money from?

'Why don't you just get a job, Ben?' I asked.

'No,' he said.

'Because?'

'Because I don't have papers.'

'You don't have a visa?'

'It's gone . . . run out.'

Sulley reminded me that looking for a club was 'his job'. Didier laughed at my enquiry to him why he was not working, as if to say: 'Work? We're footballers! We don't work!'

So I bought the three Lost Boys their lunch. Lost Boys who would not go home, were not playing football and, apparently, had no income – yet could afford smartphones and nights out clubbing. I remembered Jean-Claude telling me how many boys ended up working on the black market. Before this visit, I had spoken to a former anti-corruption director of Interpol who, through Jean-Claude, had visited trafficked footballers in the city the previous year. He had said, 'Well dressed young men and fancy mobile phones? I was concerned that many of them would have been involved in some sort of criminal activity. In my experience, it was obvious.'

Sulley, Ben and Didier were finishing their desserts. They had reverted to talking about what they thought were the sweeter things in life. Sulley tried to convince Didier to go to a nightclub with him. 'I can't,' Didier sniggered. 'A girl might get pregnant.'

Since Jay-Jay had been in England, the nearest town to his village in Guinea had descended into ethnic-religious violence between Christians and Muslims. There had been hundreds of deaths. People had been burned alive in churches or hacked to death with machetes. Tensions had been stoked by politicians – cravenly so, in a quest for votes – who wanted to powwow with the mining companies eyeing one of the largest iron ore deposits in West Africa. Jay-Jay's abuser and trafficker had worked for one of those mining companies. Workers had engulfed the region, in some cases quadrupling the population of outlying villages. Food had been scarce. Tensions had risen again. Two tribes had gone to war. More death. Then Ebola had arrived.

Jay-Jay had never said, 'I want to go home.' Who could blame him? If death had not come from the hand of a religious extremist, partisan tribesman or indiscriminate Ebola, then it could have come from the hand of his own family. I had asked him if he wanted to return. 'Ooof, it is not possible,' he said. 'My father's family, the death threat . . .' Yet he pined for his father, mother and siblings. He had no idea whether they were alive.

I had not seen him since the trial at Cheltenham more than six months previously. He had seemed a disconsolate soul on the drive back to London that day. And today his mood appeared dark once again as he showed me into the sparse living room. There was no *Football Focus* on the television this time, instead a programme about immigration smugglers. He switched it off. There was a football in the middle of the room. Jay-Jay absently minded passed it back and forth against the sofa before collapsing into it, letting out a groan as he did so. 'Sometimes I think about my past, and I think about how I'm living here and alone, no family,' he said. 'That makes me think sad things about my life. My life now is very complicated. I don't know what I should do. Have you heard from Cheltenham?'

I hadn't. If my question about whether he'd heard from his family was my stock enquiry, this was his. He had asked that question a lot in the weeks that had followed the trial, either over the telephone, by email or text message. Jay-Jay claimed he had not heard back from the League Two club. There had been no email, no phone call. No feedback. Given his performance, it was not surprising that they had not been pestering him. So surely he couldn't be surprised? Surely he didn't think that they had 'forgotten' to call and ask him to return for another trial, to examine him more closely? I told him to forget about Cheltenham. 'They would have been in touch by now,' I said. Jay-Jay looked a little wounded. He shrugged his shoulders. 'Yes, maybe you are right.'

It was wrong of Cheltenham not to have sent an email or made a call, just as the fee Jay-Jay paid had promised. It wouldn't have taken much to send a standard note thanking him for his attendance, informing that 'on this occasion you have been unsuccessful'. I suspected that would have appeased Jay-Jay somewhat. Of course, he wanted to be told that he had won a contract, but a letter or email would have been something tangible, something to prove that he was still participating in the world of football, that he was still in with a chance. A long way from home and without a sense of belonging, Jay-Jay needed to feel part of something. Part of a community. Without a family he just wanted acknowledgement from a different one, the football variety. It would have been like receiving a letter from his mum, perhaps. I remembered how proud he was when he showed me the trial letters from Cambridge and Brentford, safely pouched in a plastic wallet. Did all the trafficked boys feel that way? Was it what kept them going?

'I don't have best friend or good friend after college,' he said with the sad face that I felt had become his trademark. 'I am always here. On my own. I go training on my own. I think about my family. I need to have a better way for my life. Football or family. Maybe one day that will be good. I am always thinking about them and I don't know what I'm going to be.'

Maybe Jay-Jay knew, deep down, that his dream was hopeless, but he was wedded to the sport by how his horrible, heartbreaking story had begun. Football had got him into this mess and it was going to get him out of it. In that regard, football was something of a captor.

There was, though, another side to Jay-Jay. Since I had seen him last, he had played for another three different amateur teams, either in the Saturday or Sunday leagues. 'I don't have a regular team.' He spoke as if he genuinely believed he was a fine football player and he couldn't understand why his ambition had not been realised. What jarred most was his assertion that it wasn't his fault. It was everyone else's. This was wholly at odds with my belief that he just needed to be loved.

'I tried to explain to my social worker,' he said. 'For me, I don't have a team which can do training. I ask again my social worker, "I don't have a team. I need to do training."'

The complaining continued: 'They need to help me to go and train regularly in a gym because it's too cold outside. Yeah, it's too cold. If I do my training properly, I will get a better team because I know my capacity. As soon as I came here I don't do training, I never go to a team which does training. My football is going down, down, down.'

After Cheltenham, he had gone to a soccer school in Warwick. He said all the other players were 'too lazy' in response to a coach asking why he did not pass the ball more. 'They don't run, they just stand . . . so I do it myself.' He told me he didn't even know the name of the coach of one of the teams he had played for. 'I can't pronounce it.' He said he failed the trial at Brentford because there had been no 'proper warm-up'. Yes, I was starting to think Jay-Jay blamed everyone but himself.

There had always been a confidence about Jay-Jay. Most of the African boys I had met were the same. They were without modesty, and if you were to meet one, just one, for the first time, you might be fooled into thinking you had just shaken hands with the next Maradona. But considering I had seen Jay-Jay with a ball at his feet, it was arrogance bordering on delusion. He sounded ungrateful and bitter. He had little reason to think the former, more so the latter. I explained to him that if he really wanted to play football professionally, he needed to pick a team, play every week and score lots of goals. Only then would he stand the chance of getting talent-scouted. He nodded, but I wasn't sure he understood.

What Jay-Jay lacked was an understanding of how football worked in England. He thought he could rock up to a trial, dazzle the coaches with his skill, be offered a contract, receive the adulation of the club's supporters and then live the good life. It wasn't like that. You had to work much harder than that. First he would have to prove he was far too good a player for the Saturday or Sunday league teams that he played for. His commitment and fitness would have to be vastly superior. His tactical awareness, too. Then he would have to prove it all over again at the next level up, then the next level and so on. No one had told him he would have to 'do his time' at a low level, playing in front of one man and his dog. That was the feedback that Cheltenham should have given. The money he paid for that trial should have meant he received some wisdom in return. After all, what did he know? He was just a kid from Guinea. He needed to be told what his strengths were, what his weaknesses were. Whether he had a future in football. I was sure he didn't, but I was not qualified to offer that hard but fair advice. 'What if you can't be a footballer?' I asked.

'I want to be footballer . . . sorry, say the question again.'

'What other job would you like to do?'

'If I can't be footballer I would like to do mechanic or electricity [electrician], so, yeah . . . I applied to do mechanic courses and they said my English needs to be better because it's very complicated. They said I need to be level two English. I am level three. That's what the college said to me.'

I was surprised that Jay-Jay had given any thought to a career outside of football. I thought he was single-minded in the pursuit of his dream but the fact he had considered becoming a mechanic or electrician was positive. It made me think Jay-Jay's story could still have a happy ending. If he could learn a skill or a trade then he had a future. He could earn a living. He could put the past behind him. But for that to happen, he would have to break free from football.

I had a plan. 'My idea is to get a one-on-one trial, a really hard test so you can get a better idea of your chances of being footballer,' I said. 'No one has told you what type of player you are – your strengths, your weaknesses, and if you are any good. Is that right? When you've gone for your trials, no one has given you feedback?'

'Yeah . . . yeah . . . a trial for me is excellent,' said Jay-Jay, as if the idea had grown on him.

'That's what you need. I will try to organise it. You need to know so you can move on with your life and try to be something else if need be. OK?'

'That would be good.' Jay-Jay smiled and leapt from the sofa. 'You want tea?' he said. I nodded. He dribbled the football into the kitchen, shimmying this way and that, as if trying to avoid an imaginary defender.

20

Run

'Are you one of these people who thinks it's a story about poor African kids? They run. They get to Europe and they run.'

It was an unequivocal answer to a question which, with unerring frequency, had demanded to be answered from the start of this journey. It had been the juggernaut on the horizon of a one-track road; a speck at first, clouded in the dust of the road, but over time growing menacingly bigger, the distant hum of the engine getting louder. My time in Accra had made it more prescient; the slums, the poverty, the desperation in the boys' eyes, the rutted pitches, the willingness to break the rules. Seeing the West African football industry at its limp, faltering grassroots had brought a clarity. Then, of course, there had been Hamid's boys, a platoon of them turning up in a small town in Larnaca for a trial game. Hamid had said all of them had overstayed their visas. The shenanigans with Jean-Claude Mbvoumin, his dubious relationship with Shinji, the lunch with the Lost Boys in Paris – fiddling with their expensive smartphones – and none of them prepared to play football at a level they considered beneath them . . . all had made an impression. After months on the road, cynicism and mistrust had taken hold. The juggernaut was unmissable. It was blasting its horn, bearing down.

At the outset, the intention had been for the story to be all about those 'poor African boys'. They were victims who had compelling tales to tell. So the perpetrators had to be found, dissected and exposed to give those stories the context which they deserved. It was why Scout Network had been set up: to try to uncover the football people who had left this collection of disaffected young boys to rot. I got caught up in the emotion of it all at the beginning. I was on a quest to find the truth. I had tunnel vision. I was single-minded in the pursuit of vanquishing the traffickers.

It was inevitable, however, that the focus would have to turn on to some of the victims themselves. That juggernaut had just kept on coming. From Geneva to Larnaca, Paris to Accra, a faith had been slowly eroded. Cruelly, empathy, too, had taken a hit. Cold-hearted reason had taken its place. 'Hang on a second,' I thought, 'a major part of this whole story is not right.' The juggernaut was doubt. The question was: were these boys telling the truth?

Chief among my concerns was the actual explanation behind the football trafficking. There were two types, remember. The first saw an agent jettison the player after a failed trial. Understood. But the second made no sense. An agent asked families for thousands of pounds so he could buy the player an airfare, visa and passport and take him for trials to Europe. As soon as the boy left the departure gate, the agent was not seen again

Eby Emenike, the London-based football agent, admitted she was 'puzzled' by the scam. Jake Marsh, head of youth protection at the ICSS, could not fathom it, either. There was no logic. Why would an agent con a boy and his family for several thousand pounds, selling a false dream of footballing stardom, take him to Europe and then abandon him in a hotel room or at the airport? And never actually take him to trial at a club?

Think about it. Think about it in the context of Ben from Cameroon. He paid £3,000 to go to trials. From that £3,000 the 'agent' would have had to pay for his own airfare, Ben's airfare, visa and get him a passport. He would have made, what, £500? Why not just take all the money and run?

After all, that is what happens with the 'online scam'. Boys are made promises via email and harassed until they pay up. They don't receive a visa or a passport. They don't receive an air ticket. They don't get on a plane. They don't go anywhere. That, as a con, makes perfect sense. As does the first type of trafficking: a player has paid money for a trial but is cut loose when he fails. The second version was a contradiction. It also happens to be the most prevalent, the one a media hungry for injustice has devoured. And why not? It's a classic yarn. Good versus evil. Weak versus strong. Poor versus rich. But could it be that the truth was stranger than the fiction?

Let's change the context for a moment. Most of us have received emails, at one time or another, from someone claiming we have won the lottery in a foreign country. Nigeria, for example. Now, the anatomy of that scam might have been: to collect your prize, you need to send, say, £1,000 to release the funds. Misguided folks wire the money and never hear anything again. The equivalent in the example of the second 'type' of football trafficking is Mrs Smith sending the £1,000 and then the conman buying her an air ticket and visa and flying her to Nigeria. Then she hears nothing. What could the con artist possibly gain from spending all that money taking her to Nigeria? Nothing.

Yet it is that type of fraud we hear so much about – it's the story repeatedly told by newspapers, magazines and television channels. And it was the main one Jean-Claude Mbvoumin had highlighted, earning exposure for his charity. The one boys all over Europe had told various social services.

'They run. They get to Europe and they run.' Those were the words of Darragh McGee. 'That line about being "one of those people" and "poor African kids"? Someone said that to me when I started out looking into it. Your perceptions change. They run. It happens.' He had lived in Accra and had worked as a football coach at academies in the city, including Feyenoord Fetteh, which would later become the West African Football Academy. He was an academic, a faculty member of the School for Health at the University of Bath, and had authored a paper on child trafficking in sport.

'Of course it doesn't make any sense,' McGee said. 'What sort of criminal operates that scheme? Not a very bright one. Not a very rich one, either. The fantasy of exile underpins the game of football in West Africa. You'll hear of agents complaining they've had boys over with them and they've run. There were two boys last year. A French agent working in Cameroon went public, lamenting that they ran and they destroyed his reputation and he can't do anything about it.

'Stories abound about youth tournaments across Europe, even in England. Just recently, six members of a youth team from Cameroon bolted out of a hotel window the night before a tournament in Belgium, jumping into cars with Belgian plates on them. Did they turn up somewhere saying they'd been trafficked? Almost certainly.'

What McGee was saying was that, at the very least, some of the boys who had told Foot Solidaire or social services that they had been victims of the second type of trafficking – abandoned at a hotel or airport – may have been complicit. He was also suggesting that it was the supposed villains of the piece – the agents – who were victims. They were having their supposedly good names sullied.

McGee was not the only academic to have raised suspicions that not all was as it seemed. James Esson, a lecturer in human geography at Loughborough University, had explored the subject in a paper ('Better Off at Home? Rethinking Responses to Trafficked West African Footballers in Europe') following nearly a year of research. He spoke to 20 boys in Paris who had been trafficked. Most of them he found through Foot Solidaire. One of them was Richard from Guinea who had given an agent €4,500 for 'plane tickets and everything'. When he got to Paris the agent disappeared. Just like Ben had said, the agent had taken away his passport and visa. That is exactly what trafficking gangs do who want you to earn back money in the black market.

Esson made the point that it was wrong to assume that people who had been 'football trafficked' were 'passive victims' whose decision-making skills had been rendered 'null and void'. He argued that because they had undertaken immigration independently of their parents they didn't match the stereotype of a trafficked victim at all (Esson found that it was accepted for children to be moved from country to country within Africa on the say-so of their parents for schooling, to stay with relatives, to work). In addition, football trafficking victims had overstayed their visas and had no way of verifying their status as a child. 'In the eyes of French immigration, they were simply male adults staying illegally in Paris,' Esson wrote.

Another characteristic of an illegal immigrant at odds with a trafficked victim is one that did not want to go home. The boys Esson met, just like Ben, Sulley and Didier, did not want to return to Africa. If what had happened to them had been so terrible and life had become so intolerable, why not go back? In France, and the UK, government assistance was available for displaced people to be returned. In the case of football's trafficked boys, the phrase 'there was no place like home' is taken literally. Esson found that they spoke of Europe as a 'paradise' in comparison to where they grew up. Indeed, Old Fadama, Accra's slum city, is a hell on earth compared to the streets of Paris. Choose: broke and hungry in Old Fadama or Paris? There was always a possibility of 'upward social mobility', Esson stated, in Europe whereas the prospects at home were bleak and getting bleaker. 'Life as an undocumented migrant in Europe is more preferable than returning to their country of origin.'

Still, few of the boys would readily admit that was the reason they were still in Europe. They instead preferred to talk about the 'shame' of going home, the 'embarrassment' at being seen as a failure or as someone who had been fooled. 'Dominant accounts of football trafficking frequently attribute irregular football migrants' disinclination to return to their origin countries to the shame their situation will bring in their country of origin, particularly as family members and the wider community often financed their trip,' Esson wrote. 'There is some truth to this claim, as all of the irregular migrants I spoke to in Paris had at one point or another felt ashamed and embarrassed by their situation. Many also suffered from bouts of guilt tied to a belief they had destroyed the lives of family members in their country of origin who had sacrificed to fund their passage abroad.' Ben, Sulley and Didier, of course, insisted they did not subscribe to that view.

So, add the boys Esson interviewed to Ben, Sulley and Didier and you have a contradiction. Here's another: the victim and the victim's family believed that leaving home for Europe to pursue a career in football was a 'viable livelihood strategy'. They were also well aware that there were risks involved. Both of these recurring themes were, surely, inconsistent with the self-reproach that the boys claimed they felt.

One 17-year-old Esson interviewed said: 'Everything turns around football and there isn't a single family in Guinea that doesn't have a son that wasn't pushed to play football, everyone thinks that if a boy is talented he can make it to a league in Europe and money will follow.' It was as Samuel, the agent and my guide in Accra, had said. Even middle-class families were taking their sons to football training.

So when an 'agent' came calling, promising a trial at Paris Saint-Germain or Marseille, it was hardly surprising that families acceded to his demands. 'During my time in Accra, I witnessed first-hand how young Ghanaian males' desire to use football as a means to earn an income and help their family financially, alongside their family's eagerness for them to do so, placed considerable pressure on players to do whatever was necessary to secure a trial abroad,' Esson wrote. That desire and pressure led to people taking a gamble. Esson consistently found that although boys had travelled in expectation of them attending a trial, rather than a hope, there was still an awareness that all might not go to plan. Jordan Anagblah, the former vice-president of the Ghana Football Association, vividly summed up the risks that families took when he described how the father of a boy he had coached in his academy revealed an approach had been made to take his son to Europe: 'There was a small boy in my team and the father came and told me, "Somebody is taking him to Belgium." Whether he is going to kill him he doesn't know, but because he has heard "football" and "Europe" he thinks his son will make money and be OK. "You don't know these people, you only met them now in Ghana when they came to watch him play and you say you are giving your boy out for adoption? Nonsense!" But it is his child, he says. The man wants to adopt his son. What can I do?'

It was clear from that example that often within families who are impoverished or desperate to improve their stock in life, risk did not quite have the same negative connotations to you or me. 'This is how the West African youth I encountered in Paris and

Accra understood football migration,' Esson wrote. 'If migrating through football was indeed a risk, it was a risk worth taking.'

In summary, it was possible boys had travelled to Europe as 'run of the mill' immigrants aware that a trial at Paris Saint-Germain or Marseille might not be waiting at the other end. The cynic in me could not fail to notice the grumble of another juggernaut. Could it be then, that those 'agents' who had so generously organised for them to go to Europe for such a small profit, or in some cases surely none at all, had them 'trafficked' for reasons other than football?

Stewart Hall has been a coach for 30 years, five of them in Africa. He has, he said, 'seen it all', including the 'online scam' where money was demanded for the chance of a lucrative career abroad. There was a difference, though. It wasn't boys who were the targets, it was the coaches. 'Someone, somewhere,' said Hall, 'had worked out that there were many, many coaches out of work. They needed jobs, they needed money.' Desperation. The 'online scam', whether targeting players or coaches, Hall said, had its roots in the oil industry.

'The oil industry has always had a history of bogus jobs,' he said, revealing that he had been educated about the trick by some of the oil-rich sponsors of a former club. 'People recruiting to Nigeria, or places like that, for jobs which didn't exist. They'd take you down the road of a job application, you'd send a copy of your passport, all sorts of information, and they'd get you on the hook by offering a very good contract. And all of a sudden right at the death when you're waiting for an air ticket they'd send a request for something to do with a visa or something. It would only be $400–500 and you'd think, "Surely it's not a scam, they can't be making much, lots of emails coming back and forth, they're going to a lot of trouble." But they had 100 people on the same hook from all over the world and that $500 is suddenly substantial. And then that's been replicated in the football scams.'

Hall had been an apprentice at Wolverhampton Wanderers but didn't make the grade. He took his coaching badges at the age of 25, managed Halesowen Town, spent eight years at Birmingham City's academy and then 'saw the world' with the FA's coaching education system. He began to coach for foreign clubs and national sides. He was youth and first-team coach for Tanzania and national coach for Saint Vincent and the Grenadines in the Caribbean. He also worked in South Africa, South Korea, Canada, India and Zanzibar.

It was not until he worked abroad that he was targeted. Three times. Hall was offered a 'bogus' job in Benin with a top division club, coaching the under-12s and under-20s with Nigeria, and the Togo national team role. For each of them he received an email out of the blue and was asked to begin an application process. He never had a face-to-face interview for any of them.

'The Benin one sticks out,' he said. 'They offered a fabulous job on an eight-month contract, which was the duration of the season, but the salary and win bonuses were fantastic. It was coaching AS Dragons – the top team in Benin. They took me all the way through the process, offered me the job and then said every foreigner coming in had to pay $500 for a safety certificate – that ensured you were registered with the police and that you're on their radar in terms of protection if there's any problems. I said, "You pay it and take it out of the first month's salary." They said that was impossible, "You have to pay yourself, to prove payment yourself." I refused. I was in work at the time so I wasn't desperate. I pulled out. At exactly the same time a friend had been offered a job in China. Same thing, same process. I told him, "If they ask you for money, pull out." They wanted $500 for the coach's association so he could be registered.'

Hall knew there was never any question he would have paid the money and then actually receive an air ticket, board a plane and fly to Benin, Nigeria or Togo only to be left stranded. 'It was all about getting the money out of me,' he said. 'What you're describing with the boys who actually go to these places doesn't make sense. There's more to it, of that I'm sure.'

Hall's explanation was stunning. 'The scouts or talent spotters go into the villages, small academies and they identify real talent when about 14 or 15. Before they have a club. So they give them football boots and a bit of kit. Then they introduce a person who is called "the groomer", and then he gets in with the family. He gives them some money, takes that player to an agent and that agent fixes that guy up with a club in Africa.

'He plays proper football, he's highly talented, does well, and the agent sees his passage through to somewhere outside of Africa. Now, it might be the Belgian league, or England. But it's harder to get into England. It might be Asia. But they get them out to the highest standard as possible. When they graduate to a senior team in that country, they then call in the favour. It's match-fixing. Spot-fixing, like they do in cricket. A red card in the 22nd minute. All these betting syndicates make money. "You give away a penalty in the 15th minute." It's quite specific. The money involved is phenomenal.

'Having worked in Africa for some time, to be honest, I don't know any African players who would say no. I honestly don't. I had an experience myself. I had a bribery scandal on my hands. My goalie and three of my back four were suspended for taking money to throw a game. I know those boys personally, worked very closely with them. They were and still are in a national squad, and I can't honestly look anyone in the eye and say, "They didn't do it." That's your problem. It's so easy. Corruption is endemic. It's part of the culture. They don't look at it the same way. To get those kids on a plane to Paris, Madrid or wherever, it's so, so easy.'

There was a silence on the other end of the line. Richard Hoskins had gone quiet.

'Hello?' I said.

'Oh, I'm still here . . . I was just waiting for you to finish the story. What happens next?'

'Nothing. That's the point. They go to a city in Europe and then they're just, well, left there.'

'Really?'

'Yes.'

'Extraordinary.'

Hoskins was a criminologist. He was best known for his work in trying to track down the killers of 'Adam', the six-year-old African boy whose severed torso was found floating in the Thames in 2001. It was known, grimly, as the 'torso in the Thames' murder and received widespread media coverage in the UK. The victim of a probable ritual killing, 'Adam' had been trafficked from Nigeria to Germany and then on to London. Hoskins was an expert in trafficking and African religion. He had been called as an expert witness in more than 100 criminal cases, most of them 'voodoo' or ritual killings.

'We know "Adam" was trafficked through Germany, we know he was handled there, stayed for a short time and came in through the Holland to Harwich route. He probably wasn't in London that long, maybe a matter of weeks. Why he was killed is still a mystery. The cases of kids I've been involved in who have been trafficked into Europe, often come through mainland Europe. There are always staging posts rather than direct.

'The people behind the trafficking of Adam would most likely be involved in other cases of trafficking. We are sure of that, actually. There would have been a person whose job it was to procure a boy. A trafficking gang. That gang would take girls to Italy for prostitution as well. That type of thing.'

'Would these gangs be using football as a lure to move children from one continent to another?'

'Anything is possible,' Hoskins said. 'The example you've just given about kids paying money and then being abandoned is interesting. Well, I say "interesting" but "odd" is a better word. Traffickers are not kind or generous people. They're dangerous, nasty people. They want something out of it and I would be surprised, very surprised, if there was not something more to it. Of course, I don't have any experience of this football activity, but in the criminal cases I've been involved with there is evidence that gangs operate on many fronts.'

One possible reason for the movement of boys could be a child benefit fraud which had swept Europe. It is an issue Hoskins was responsible for highlighting, claiming that the UK was the child abuse capital of the world with gangs trafficking kids from every corner of the globe to be abused. Hoskins explained the anatomy of the crime: 'A child is brought over and stays with relatives or friends. They will "adopt" or claim the child as their own. The child is registered for a school, triggering the benefit system, working tax credits and other payments. The child, though, might not ever actually attend a school. They're being worked in the underage sex industry. As soon as registration is complete, the gang moves the kid to another school and repeats the process. There just aren't the checks in place to stop it happening, and if any authority asks to see a child they have hundreds to choose from. They can lay their hands on fake birth certificates and passports anyway to convince people the child is real.'

This was a multiple-gain fraud. Money would flow straight to the criminal through repeated child benefit claims and from the child being worked in the sex industry. I asked Hoskins what he thought of Jay-Jay and his story, apprehensively nudging him about his passport being taken away in the hope that he would immediately say his story was legitimate.

'You know the score with passports,' he said. 'They are given the passport for the journey but then taken off them again. In the case of prostitution they're told they have to earn back loads of money to get it back. Jay-Jay's story seems plausible. Interesting to use football as a lure. Clever. You can say to a boy, "Come to Europe, you have a skill in football." But you can't say to a girl who you want to take to Thailand, "Your body is your skill." In the work I've done there is a lot of coercion, threats and rituals. So the child might be told, "If you don't earn this money we'll kill your family." They are terrified. They are put under spells, they are cut, made to drink pigeon blood . . . In football, there are no threats made, no rituals, no coercion?'

'Not that I'm aware of,' I said. 'But they could be keeping that to themselves . . .'

'Interesting,' said Hoskins. 'Interesting but horrible, of course. Did the boy seem fearful to you? Did he manage to break out?'

'Well, they let him go.'

'They let him go? That's unusual but, look, I don't know the specifics of the case and, as I said, anything is possible.'

There are, of course, plenty of other reasons why a child might be trafficked to Europe. Anti-Slavery International (ASI), which has worked at national and international level in an attempt to reduce trafficking, said that it was hard to believe that some of the stories of football trafficking abandonment were true. The ASI's Jakub Sobik said, 'It could be benefit fraud, as you say. But there is more than one reason. They might be forced to beg and sell drugs as well as being brought here for child benefit fraud.' The organisation had also reported there had been cases in France of victims being forced to claim social security benefits and giving the proceeds to the trafficking gangs. It brought us back to Jean-Claude Mbvoumin and Foot Solidaire. It was the charity's job, according to Jean-Claude, to act as the middleman between the boys and those social services in Paris.

It is worth reminding ourselves of the numbers. From 2005 to June 2014 it was estimated there had been more than 1,000 cases of football-related irregular migration in Paris, and around 7,000 in France. That meant there had been, on average, 777 cases a year in France. Or about 15 a week. It is also worth reminding ourselves where those numbers came from. Foot Solidaire.

Of course, Foot Solidaire have already been discredited in these pages. But their role is worth examining. They wouldn't be the first charity, or the last, to embellish a problem a little to justify their existence. Particularly a charity which had drifted in and out of existence through lack of funding.

For a moment, though, let's give Jean-Claude Mbvoumin and his maths credence. That's because Foot Solidaire had produced another set of startling statistics in 2014. It took some digging around to find them because they did not appear in the stories of the boys Foot Solidaire had offered to the media, but, according to Foot Solidaire, a massive 98 per cent of the football-related irregular migration cases in Paris concerned illegal immigrants.

If that number was to be believed, then it gave further weight to the argument that boys were complicit in their 'trafficking'. To be an illegal immigrant you have to have done one of three things: travelled on the sort of fishing trawler that was washed up on a beach in Tenerife in 2007; travelled on a fake visa/passport; or overstayed your visa. I wondered how many of the 98 per cent went to Jean-Claude when their visa had run out?

It was also true that many of the boys Jean-Claude had found had told him that they had worked on the black market. It was, he said, their only way of survival. Jean-Claude had never made a secret of the fact that the boys were working in illegal industries, drugs or crime. 'You know we have African solidarity,' he told me. 'They can work in the black market. People on the street talk. "Please help me." We are talking about a section of people who have illegally entered a country and have worked in crime.'

As Richard Hoskins and Anti-Slavery International said, there were many cases of people being forced to do things they did not want to do. But, if that is true, then it is also possible that there are boys who have travelled illegally to Europe under the guise of football with the intention of working in the black market to improve their lot in life.

At this point it should be made crystal clear that there were legitimate cases of football trafficking. Jay-Jay, for example, was hoodwinked in the most horrible of fashions. And there were boys who genuinely believed that they were going to make it at the trial they were promised. They turned up with their boots, they gave their all and when the club was not interested, the agent had told them to 'get lost'.

There is no gripe with them. Could it be, however, that those stories had been exploited? Exploited by the trafficking gangs themselves and the 'solidarity' in the African community. In each of those examples, everybody is a winner, bar the state, when a boy is told, 'Go to Foot Solidaire, they can help you.'

The 'abandoned' boy has the perfect cover. Remember how scammers stole the names of agents from the Fifa website? Anyone trying to check the validity of a boy's story would get nowhere. Sure, an investigator could contact the real agent and he or she would deny all knowledge. Puzzled, the investigator would dig further and discover the aforementioned anatomy. 'Ah, it's identity theft.' They may have even checked with the only charity in the world set up to deal with football's slaves. And Jean-Claude would readily attest authenticity. That gave a possible, and plausible, answer to another question which had grumbled away in the background. Why did Jean-Claude not hand over the names of each and every agent accused by his boys to Fifa, Interpol or the International Centre for Sport and Security or anyone who might help? Was it because it could have revealed the true nature of the 'problem'? Or was it because he knew it was a total waste of time?

Having digested the numbers, the contradictions and taken on board the views of Darragh McGee, James Esson, Stewart Hall, Dr Richard Hoskins and Anti-Slavery International – all highly qualified to pontificate and raise more questions – it was difficult not to have become sceptical. To query everything.

Indeed, was it possible that when Foot Solidaire first raised awareness of the issue back in 2000, they actually caused an explosion in the number of complainants? And was it possible that those complainants had tried to claim benefits from the state once they had proved their status as 'victims' or 'poor African boys'? It was not as far-fetched as it might seem. There was a precedent. 'You need to go to Belgium,' McGee told me. 'There's a guy you should meet.'

21

Searching for the Truth

'Did you hear that?' Jean-Marie Dedecker called out to his wife, Christine, in the kitchen, who had been preparing lunch at their home in the outskirts of Ostend. 'He said it took him two years to turn cynical.' He turned back to me. 'It took me five. I've met hundreds of boys. I just don't know the truth. I paid school fees for one, I paid for his mother to visit—'

Christine interjected: 'When the boy was married it continued, money for the wedding, money for the crib when they had a baby . . .'

'Ah, it was too much,' Dedecker said. 'It is the culture in Africa. When someone is doing well in the community they have to help others. I helped that boy. I did a lot for other boys, too.'

Dedecker is a liberal Belgian politician famous for speaking the truth. His book, *Telling It to You Straight*, about the political system in the country, was a bestseller. He had, though, made his name in sport. For five Summer Olympics he was head coach of Belgium's national judo team, demanding the highest standard of discipline and fitness from his judoka. For each second one of his charges was late for a training session, they had to do 100 press-ups. The 1996 Games were Dedecker's, and Belgium's, most successful. 'We had the Olympic champion, a silver and two bronzes. Belgium had six medals in total, four from judo,' he said. 'We were small but beautiful. I became quite famous after that.'

He was known for being hard but fair, a reputation befitting a burly stature which betrayed that he, too, had been a judoka in his youth. 'I was known as a direct man so when there was a problem in sports when I was in politics, people came to me to get it solved. They were desperate, those boys.'

'Those boys' were 16-year-old Omo Monday and his friend, Manasseh Ishiaku, 17. They were two of four Nigerians who, in 2001, had gone to Dedecker for help. They had been football trafficked from Nigeria to play for Roeselare FC, a Belgian first division club. Dedecker said he was 'stupefied' when he heard their story. 'They had been abandoned.' He wanted justice, the boys wanted justice. Dedecker set about conducting the first major investigation into the issue of football trafficking from Africa and South America to Europe. It was his crusade. He battled clubs, suffered death threats from the mafia, investigated scores of agents (Africans, Belgians, French, Mexicans, Peruvians, Brazilians, Americans, Chileans) and football managers, exposed embassy corruption and made changes to the law. It ended with a defeat in court and Dedecker a confirmed sceptic about the football trafficking business. 'I don't know what to believe now,' he said as we ate a traditional Belgian lunch of veal and potatoes.

'I know what I think,' Christine said. 'But you are not allowed to say such things. I think a lot of those boys were not telling the truth about why they were in Belgium.'

In the late 1990s and early 2000s, Belgium was bursting with African players and vied with France as the leading importer of talent from the continent. In 1997 there were 47 Africans playing in the top flight in Belgium, three fewer than in France. Clubs such as Beveren and Lokeren were largely made up of African players. The two teams had 'feeder clubs' in Africa. Beveren were known as the 'Black Pearls' and would eventually take to the field with an all-Africa starting XI. It was Beveren's arrangement with the ASEC Mimosas academy run by Jean-Marc Guillou, friend and former assistant to Arsène Wenger, which had led to the Football Association investigation into Arsenal.

During these years, Dedecker's nose for sporting controversy had sniffed out the exploitation of Africans. He had found 442 Nigerians who had been trafficked by agents linked to organised crime and lobbied lawmakers for change, succeeding in more than doubling the minimum wage for a foreign player – 'It was €29,620 and it went up to €69,479.' Dedecker believed that although that was too late to help Omo and Manasseh it did, eventually, prevent continued wide-scale exploitation.

'But the investigations, that was a policeman's work,' he said. 'Not a politician's. It was linked to the mafia, organised crime. The same people who were trafficking children for prostitution were trafficking children for football. The Turkish mafia were involved. I knew some of them were living in Brussels and I was told if I went to see them, I would be killed.' It is worth repeating this quote: 'The same people who were trafficking children for prostitution were trafficking children for football.'

Death threats were also made when Dedecker said he would go to Nigeria to explore the relationship between clubs, agents and the trafficking gangs. 'They sent me rat poison in the post,' he said. 'It just proved that I was right about the trafficking. It was a big noise at the time. It was on television, in all the newspapers.'

He had pages upon pages of evidence which detailed the movement of African children to Belgium. There were police reports, testimonies of boys, witness statements, admissions of guilt. He had lists of agents he had investigated. One had represented a former World Cup winner. The charge sheet for one, who remained active in the African academy system, ran to more than two pages. There were high-profile managers and coaches at big Belgian clubs.

We had spent the morning in Dedecker's office in Ostend as a squall raged outside, the granite sky and North Sea merging into one. 'I need to get my football file,' he had said. He put on his reading glasses, wetted his finger and leafed through the papers. 'Look here . . . these statements . . . same stories. The same names again and again,' he said. 'This guy. You recognise the name of this manager?' I did. 'This agent again . . . again. But this is the problem I found. Is it true, is it not true? Have these boys just taken the names of the agents? Some agents I couldn't find, so did they even exist? It just couldn't be proved that some of the boys were being accurate. They were telling lies so they could get help. Because of that a lot of cases could not go anywhere. It is as I said. What is the truth?'

So when Omo and Manasseh came to Dedecker, he had seen and heard similar stories. He was convinced, however, that he could build a case against Roeselare FC, the club that had brought them to Belgium. 'I just need to jog my memory here, it was a long time ago,' he said, as I asked him to tell me the boys' story. 'The boys, they knocked on the door of this office. Omo and Manasseh, and there were two others. Luka Tanku and Omerah Samuel. Tanku and Samuel disappeared to another part of Europe.'

In other words, as Darragh McGee had said, they had 'run'.

'Omo and Manasseh were playing football but they knew there was something wrong. They came here to become rich, they were very talented. Everybody here was collaborating against them.' Dedecker explained that the boys had not been paid. They were given an apartment to live in and money for food. 'They knew this wasn't right.'

His first action was to contact Solange Cluydts of Payoke, the Belgian anti-trafficking charity. 'I said, "Solange, I have a case of trafficking here that you need to hear for yourself." She came immediately.'

'So what happened next?'

Dedecker looked at me over the top of his spectacles, bemused at my impatience. 'I am just checking here, going through the files and I will tell you everything.' A few minutes later after some muttering in Flemish and more rifling through the football file, Dedecker cleared his throat. It was his way of saying, 'If you're sitting comfortably, the storyteller will begin.' Instead of turning the pages of a thriller, Dedecker told the story of Omo and Manasseh through the police reports, the witness statements and court papers. He would hand over each piece of evidence with a 'you see here?' and 'look at this page' as he went.

'Roeselare and a company called Football Soccer International set up an academy in Nigeria. The Nigerdock academy. They said it was just for football but it was trafficking of minors to come to play in Europe. The boys came from there. It doesn't exist now. Omo's and Manasseh's parents got 25,000 Nigerian Naira (about €150) each. The soccer academy bought them. The academy bought the air tickets. They [the boys] were brought to the airport in Lagos by the manager of the academy, who was a former minister of sport in Nigeria. He gave them €40, then they came to Lille and then to Belgium with the agent. They had left Nigeria on 8 July 2000. The boys signed a contract with the company [which had] the same shareholders as the academy. The company Football Soccer International made double contracts with Roeselare FC, one to satisfy the Belgian FA with the minimum conditions and one which was the real contract, so they didn't get anything.

'Is it a slave trade? Yes. When you are buying a human being for €150? It is proof. They had a slave contract. The "official" contract was for €1,000 per month, and they didn't get paid. They didn't get any of that money. Just food and lodgings. Even when they were sold, the players would get nothing. The academy took 70 per cent [of transfer fee profit] and the club 30 per cent. The player nothing. This is the contract. The official contract. They declared it. The agent was Bart de Bruyne. He said so. It's here. Here is his declaration.

'They were minors. They couldn't come as they were under 18, so what did they do? They changed their passports and I discovered they did that with the help of the Nigerian embassy here in Brussels. They weren't old enough to play football. They realised there was a problem with the passports so they had to go to the embassy with about €1,000 and the embassy changed the date of birth. They got the money from the club to go to the Nigeria embassy in Brussels to change the passports – that's De Bruyne's statement here . . . here is the proof in the club's accounts. The dates of birth were changed by hand at the Nigerian embassy. I will read this page from the police file: "DOB of bearer should read August 1, 1984 and not as erroneously written on ID page." Omo saw they had changed it. They made him two years older. After the passport incident and then not being paid, they came to me. They were afraid. They couldn't call home because in Nigeria you disappear for a lot less.'

With that evidence, Dedecker, and with the backing of Cluydts's charity, Payoke, four men were charged with human trafficking: Roger Havegeer, James Storme, Bart de Bruyne and Maurice Cooreman. They were each found not guilty. Havegeer was the president of Roeselare and Storme was a businessman who had helped to set up Football Soccer International (FSI). De Bruyne, the agent, and Cooreman, who Dedecker said was a scout, were also part of FSI and had set up the Nigerdock academy. The court said the accused did not make use of 'malicious manœuvres, force, threat or other means of coercion' and they did not manipulate the 'particular vulnerable position of the foreigner due to the unlawful or precarious administrative situation or state of minority'. Despite there being 'reasonable doubt' about passport fraud, the court said it was 'not unreasonable to pay for new passports'.

'I was very disappointed those guys went free,' Dedecker said. 'We had all the details, they changed the passports, the contracts, it was total abuse. The case was lost because the players declared they came to Europe. They wanted to come, so you can't speak about human trafficking when they come voluntarily. The parents were paid. The conditions were made. "It's your fault," the court said. They couldn't be slaves.'

Dedecker became disillusioned after the case. 'I was blamed by a lot of the clubs,' he said. 'Solange was disappointed also. Who was telling the truth and who wasn't?' Dedecker concentrated on politics but Omo and Manasseh were not 'abandoned' for a second time. He paid for Omo to attend a football academy in Belgium. 'With the help of Solange, Omo was in a special institute for minors, he went to school and he became a carpenter. I even paid for his studies myself. He's married, living in Ghent, playing football at a low level. He's not such a smart guy, very naïve. Manasseh went to Germany to play, had good contracts and lost everything, also I think because he's very naïve. Solange is the godmother of his child.'

Solange Cluydts had been reluctant to meet. She let out a sigh over the telephone. 'But this was a long time ago, no?' she said. 'It was all dealt with in the court and there was no crime.' I explained that I wanted to know the truth about the trafficking of young footballers, whether they were complicit, whether they knew what they were getting into. Another sigh. 'The football boys, you know, there is nothing in that story. Everyone knows that.'

Everyone didn't know that. I convinced Solange to talk to me, so a few weeks later we met at Payoke's poky office off a cobbled street in Antwerp. She was warm but seemed utterly bemused, almost to the point of amusement, that I had come from London to hear about Omo and Manasseh and Belgium's victims of football trafficking. In her eyes, Payoke dealt with cases of trafficking involving child prostitution and economic exploitation. 'Football?' she scoffed. 'It is not the same.'

Solange has been at Payoke for 11 years. Previously she had been the director of immigration at Zaventem airport and then worked for the Centre for Equal Opportunities and Opposition to Racism in Brussels. She was vastly experienced in the field. 'In Belgium, Payoke is the only organisation which can ask victims of trafficking to see their papers. When a victim is going to court against his exporter we have to give them legal advice, we give them social support, shelter for the first three months, and then afterwards we look for a private apartment for them. We are working with police and prosecutors. If the judge says, "Yes, for me this is a victim of trafficking," and the exploiters are punished with prison, on the basis of that judgement we can arrange it that people have a permit to stay in Belgium for ever.'

It was, however, fair to say that most of Payoke's cases had not generated the same media interest as Dedecker's 442 Nigerians or Omo and Manasseh. 'There was a lot of hype at that time. And Jean-Marie liked to be on TV.' The joke seemed to relax her and she began to talk of her memories of the case:

'Omo and Manasseh were staying with a woman who was doing their laundry, feeding them. For the first time I saw their passports and you could see someone had written by hand, changed the date and it had been stamped. When I was there the local Roeselare police came to get them and put them on a plane back home because the club knew what would happen if those two boys would talk. I said to the police, "On what basis are you going to take them? Hey, no way, *nooo* way." I said, "I'm taking those two to Brussels, to the federal police." I called a judge in Brussels who I knew very well, explained what was happening, and he said, "OK, take them in your car."

'Manasseh was very close with the family doing his laundry, I think the mother was in love with Manasseh! And Omo, he was younger. He didn't have a place to stay so I took him with me, he stayed a week, two weeks and then he started to look too much to my daughter so . . .' Solange laughed and clapped her hands, '. . . he has to go. So we put him in a shelter for minors, victims of traffickers. And he had another girlfriend, and there was, oh my god, there was always another one pregnant!'

A deal was done with Roeselare. Solange and Dedecker would not prosecute the club, which had undergone a change in ownership. Only the four individuals, including the old president, would face charges in return for Manasseh being given the contract he was supposed to have had.

'Omo was a tearaway and he went to school, but Manna was a football player and he became a good player. He went to Brugge and he went to Germany to play, so he was good. He earned a lot of money, so I didn't have to pay anything for him, like Jean-Marie did with Omo. Manna was a typical African. When they had money, they thought they could live like a king. They need Prada shoes, a sports car even if they had a car from the club. He spent all his money. And now he has a problem with his foot he can't play. I think he has a job in a factory. He has two children. I know his wife, Kellie, she is alone with the children. So now I'm paying, helping her out with the kids because they need shoes, clothes. I said to him, "You have to help Kellie a little bit for the children because it's not possible." He said, "Ya, searching for a job, it's not easy.'"

After the publicity surrounding Dedecker's investigations and the charges brought against the four men in the Omo and Manasseh case, Payoke's Antwerp office suddenly saw a spike in football trafficking cases. Normally they would have dealt with about 50 victims a year of 'ordinary' trafficking, like prostitution, but suddenly scores of boys began to arrive, claiming they had suffered the same fate as Omo and Manasseh. The reason for the surge in numbers was that a special permit to remain in the country could be issued for those trafficked for football. That was something widely reported in the newspapers and on television. Solange continued:

'So one day the director [of Payoke] called me and said, "Hey, Solange, I don't know what's happening but I have ten boys who are sitting here and they are complaining and saying they are football victims." I said, "OK, wait, I'm coming. I'm going to do the interviews of these boys."

'Immediately I understood they were seeking a permit to stay. They were not victims of trafficking. Those boys were like, "I'm a good football player, I'm gonna make it here." I checked it out with people at the administration of foreign affairs. Those boys, they were already here. Years and years in Belgium. There were boys who had come from Germany because they asked for political asylum there and when they didn't get it they came here. And of course they had read the newspaper stories here and said, "I can play football."'

'So there was an explosion in kids saying they were trafficked for football?' I asked.

'Listen, I know the football world. My father was a football player, my brother-in-law was a football player, and I was married to a football player. I know agents. Some of them are my friends. I know what's going on there. I know what's going on and it's big money, but on the other hand I know African people. I know Manasseh very well. I'm not going to say you don't have young people who were trafficked by agents. They went to Africa and if you find a good player, it's big money, eh? If he's really talented, that black pearl, I'm sure it happened. The problem is that when they're in Europe, even if there is not one club who is saying, "You are that pearl, come and play for us," they are not going back. They don't want to go back! They want to stay here! OK, they could trial at a club but if the club said, "No, you're not good enough," then they have to go back. Even if the agent said, "OK, you're not good enough, here's the ticket to go home," those boys throw that ticket in the garbage. And when there is that hype about football players brought to Belgium, and they can get the permit to stay, they are, "Hey, where do I have to be?"

'I was director of immigration at the airport. I have heard all the stories. They don't tell the truth. I remember one, he said, "The man took my passport, I've come from the street." We were in immigration at the airport. I asked him how had he got off the plane, gone through passport control and gone through the police without a passport. I said, "This is not possible. What did the policeman say?" "He opened the door and welcomed me to Belgium." Solange let out a laugh. 'Without a passport! You know, I had a field near the office at the airport and the African boys played football there. They had all asked for political asylum. "My life is in danger." It happened all the time.'

Jay-Jay's story. What did Solange make of that, then? I told her each detail.

'A story like that I believe,' she said.

'Yes? That's good.'

'You have the white man going to Africa not for football but to use young boys sexually. The white man, he knows that young boys like football shoes, and if he approaches a boy that boy will tell him, "My big dream is to play in Europe . . ." Of course that white man is going to arrange it for him and then he gets something he wants. No, it can be like that.'

So I asked what Solange thought of the example of a player paying money to an agent, being bought an airfare, passport and visa and then abandoned. She looked at me with that mixture of irritation and mirth. As if I hadn't been listening to what she had been saying for the last hour.

'It was stories like that we were told around this very table after the hype and publicity,' she said. 'That the boys paid someone and then they were standing there without a passport and nobody came, or they were in a hotel and no one came for them for the trial. I don't believe it. We checked it with the embassies. They have to go to ask for a visa. If it's somebody who is arranging the papers for all those who are arriving in Paris, the embassies have to know the name of that man. It's bullshit. It's impossible. I don't believe it.'

'Why not just take the money, you don't need to take the boy to Paris?' I asked.

'Of course. It's crazy. If you see what a ticket costs from Africa to Europe, and a passport. They don't earn money on those boys. The African wants a better life. It's bullshit.'

22

Amane's Story

I knew one boy who wanted to go home. 'My life can't continue like this,' Amane said. 'I have nothing here. In Africa things were easier for me.'

The Amane I had met in Geneva was no more. His eyes were tired and bloodshot, his face looked grey. That day his Atlético Madrid shirt had glistened under the lights from the television camera crews, now it was dull and faded. And there was no joking ('Willy Swing!'). No smiling.

'At home I didn't have anything to worry about, I had no problems,' he said. 'Here, there is always something. Nothing is happening with my football. I don't have the contacts to get a club, so it is useless. So I want to go home. Yeah, soon I will be going home.'

Home was the Ivory Coast, where he lived with his uncle. He had been born in Bamako, Mali, in 1994, but his parents had sent him away because they believed he would have better prospects further south. For four hours a day he cleaned shoes. He earned the equivalent of five pence per shoe. 'There were some customers who gave more. I washed the shoes, waxed them. I enjoyed it. I would put my money aside.'

It was his uncle who decided Amane should try his luck as a footballer in Europe. 'I liked football,' Amane said. 'I was an attacker. He thought I could make it as a footballer.' But it was not his dream. Amane would watch the European leagues on television for enjoyment, not for inspiration. 'Ronaldinho [the Brazilian] was my favourite player. I thought it would be good to play like him. But my uncle managed everything. It was his idea that I came [to Europe].'

Amane's uncle paid a human trafficker to take him to Spain when he was 16. He cannot remember how much money changed hands but it was likely to be around £1,500. 'I was smuggled in,' he said nonchalantly. 'It was complicated. I had no visa, no passport.' It had begun with a drive in the back of a van from the Ivory Coast to Morocco. He couldn't remember how long that part of the trip had taken, and he seemed irritated when I asked why. 'I was asleep,' he said. 'If I knew that when I came to Europe people would ask for all these things I would have written it down.' In Morocco he was put on a boat. Amane was one of the thousands of illegal immigrants who had risked their lives on the migrant boats which had set a perilous course for Europe.

'There were about 30 others on the boat. We waited in the ocean for one day until it was night so we wouldn't be spotted. Sometimes it can be longer than that, it depends on the type of boat you go on. Ours was quite small and we had a leak and we had to get the water out. We took turns getting the water out. It's traumatic when the water is coming in. Some people were going crazy. They couldn't cope. Maybe they thought we would sink. The wind was strong. I wanted to keep my head.'

I asked Amane whether he was scared. He laughed. 'The thing is I didn't realise that I was going by boat. No one told me. I was just following the instructions, what they told me to do. I didn't have time to be scared.' Those instructions included putting his birth certificate in his sock. 'So if you drown they can identify you.'

Amane did not know where his boat had docked but, according to the United Nations Office on Drugs and Crime, it was most likely to have been the Canary Islands. In 2010, the year he had been smuggled, there had been 2,246 'detected' illegal migrants entering the islands by sea. Amane was going to Bilbao to train at a soccer school. It had been arranged by an agent his uncle had contacted. He spent two months there before going to Paris.

He trained with four clubs, including Paris Saint-Germain, who told him that they couldn't sign him because he was a minor, but that he would be able to train with them if a parent or guardian could vouch for him. 'I said to them, "I have my agent," he said. 'So he came and *voilà*, I trained there for three weeks, maybe a month.' This was a different version to the story he had told the media at the conference in Geneva. I only discovered this after I had met him for a second time, when I contacted a journalist who had interviewed him. Back then he said the agent had driven him to the Paris Saint-Germain training ground, told him he would pick him up later, only to abandon him. It was another inconsistency, another contradiction. 'I haven't heard from my agent since after I left PSG,' he'd said.

He lived on the streets for a week in La Défense, the Paris business district, and was told about Foot Solidaire and Jean-Claude by another African he met. He was now attending school, had a flat and received €180 a month in benefits payable to minors who could prove they had been victims of trafficking. But not for much longer. 'I turn 21 in a few months and I will not get that money because I'm no longer a minor. That's why I'm going home.' His plan was to take a ferry from Spain to Morocco, a 35-minute journey, which costs around €50.

'If I knew it was going to be like this I would never have come,' Amane moaned.

'Like this?' I said. 'What's so bad?' Amane received money from the state, an apartment and he was sent to college.

'The way football is here.' That was his gripe. That he couldn't find a club, forge a career. He thought it made him a victim.

23

The Perfect Storm

Belgium's empty, monotonous landscape, with its flat, assuredly straight roads, encourages a motorist's mind to wander. On the long drive home from Antwerp I had much to dwell on. My investigation into the truth behind football trafficking had taken me on a journey full of twists and turns and, in many respects, I had ended up making a U-turn from my initial preconceptions. I had set out believing football trafficking to be an odious scheme operated by a scurrilous few. I imagined their victims to be, without exception, vulnerable, weak and unsuspecting. And Foot Solidaire, the only charity helping them, to be fighting an admirable, plucky fight. I had also assumed the sport's administrators were giving the problem due attention.

It turned out I had been wrong on all counts. The instigators and perpetrators could be found everywhere, infesting the bottom, middle and very top of the sport. They even included Foot Solidaire, whose founder Jean-Claude Mbvoumin had taken money from Shinji, while the self-interest of Fifa had criminally boosted the trade. It meant that trafficking was a far graver, grubbier problem than I could have envisaged when merely looking in from the outside. Once I became embroiled in it myself, by negotiating to buy kids or setting up fake clubs, it was clear corruption and exploitation were not only rife but at the very black heart of the sport.

There was a more dramatic, surprising and uncomfortable conclusion. To find it I had to peer behind the doleful look in the eyes of the boys. Discovering that the victims themselves were not always the easy prey I had been led to believe was as heart-stopping a moment as when Jay-Jay told me his tale. The evidence that there were boys complicit in their own trafficking, rendering their sob stories as sops, was compelling. Their claims in these pages have been dissected, analysed and questioned. The results reveal football trafficking to be a finely tuned business. Everyone knows their role: the agents intent on circumnavigating transfer rules; the criminal underworld providing documents for underage players; the desperate young dreamers – a product of football and social culture in West Africa; the administrators who look the other way; the clubs who want the next big star. They are all cajoled by football's obsession with money. Without it, no boy could go anywhere. It is the capacity for greed that has stamped their passport.

The jigsaw now complete, the picture before me was of a perfect storm. Circumstances and cash-hungry protagonists had combined to aggravate a situation drastically. The tempest had displaced boys thousands of miles from home. With a moral compass in its pocket, football would have been capable of saving some souls from the tumult. Sadly, there is nothing shocking about portraying football as a vast money-making machine. But that doesn't mean blame should not be apportioned for football's dirtiest secret. If a sport is cast in the image of its governing body, then Fifa must bear responsibility. They are, unquestionably, culpable for football's slave trade.

Fifa has been guilty of encouraging the trade of minors with a mixture of ill-advised regulations, a failure to thoroughly administer them, and a risible approach to example-setting. The myopic approach to Aspire and Qatar, their World Cup sweethearts, is a damning example of all three, as a culture of confusion, contradiction and corruption has come to permeate the game.

At the start of this story, confusion and contradiction had ruled at the bizarre UN conference in Geneva. It was called 'the Right Paths to Integration and Success for Young African Athletes', yet in attendance were Benfica, whose representative spoke of how they had benefited from African talent, and the Aspire Dreams academy programme, which had been actively moving minors from all over the world to Qatar and Senegal. Then there was Jean-Claude, with Shinji hanging on to his coat-tails. This was early evidence of football's one-eyed obsession, focusing solely on the prize. It was why Jake Marsh, the head of child protection for the International Centre for Sport and Security, believed it was people within football who were chiefly responsible for boys being left stranded and alone in foreign cities.

In time that troubling prediction proved correct. It also became apparent that trafficking and fighting the trafficking problem is central to preserving the status quo. The balance is retained. In order for those at the top of the tree – Fifa, the big European clubs – to keep their position it is vital that the have-nots and the hopefuls are scratching around below, supporting a grand edifice. Everyone is caught at their level, in their own world, hoping that their break, their chance, will come so they can be transported to the rung above. That energy, that desire, that desperation means that football becomes more and more greedy. This system was worth £155 million to international agents alone in 2014.

At the bottom of the chain are the aspirational young footballers. They are the willing fuel for the insatiable machine which Fifa and the super clubs keep well-oiled. The good times must keep on rolling. So the scouts, the agents, the underworld fixers, the clubs all have their role to play. And round and round we go. Football's trafficking problem is not unlike the anatomy of street drugs. The 'high' is sought by all concerned: the addicts at the bottom, the pushers in the middle, the all-powerful overlords at the top, and the politicians demanding more money to try to beat it all.

There is a production line of talent for people like Forsythe, Lois, Hamid and Imari to trade. It is made up of the Sulleys, the Bens, the Didiers and the Amanes. Dreamers one and all, they want a better life. They want their fix. They had wanted to get out of Burkina Faso, Cameroon and Ivory Coast respectively. To play football on the pitches of Europe which were turfed in gold. To earn big money. To live the good life.

It didn't work out that way. Each of them had a tale of woe, some more distressing than others. Amane aside, they all had something else in common, though: they didn't want to go home. Sulley, Ben and Didier had been unequivocal about that over lunch that afternoon. Life was easier in Paris. Sulley was on his third country while Didier had been all over the world in his search. This rather exploded the notion of the Lost Boy, or the 'poor African boy', who had been exploited and could not return to his family because he was ashamed. That, don't forget, had been the mantra of almost every boy Foot Solidaire and Jean-Claude had offered up to the media down the years.

There was also the awkward realisation, when dining with Sulley, Ben and Didier, that they were not prepared to work hard to earn a football contract, or do their time at clubs they considered beneath them. They expected to go straight in at the top. My sympathy had vanished almost as quickly as dessert. I had no reason to doubt each of their stories but the subsequent visit to Belgium to see Jean-Marie Dedecker and Solange Cluydts gave a whole new perspective on football trafficking.

Between them the Belgians had grown tired of the 'poor African boy' yarn, and there was more than a hint that illegal immigrants had used genuine examples of football trafficking to try to get money from the state. It is an uncomfortable thought, and one that few would have had the courage to air. The notion that there was complicity on behalf of the boys was taboo, also. James Esson, the academic, whose research led him to believe that boys knew there was an element of risk to the journey they were taking, and Darragh McGee's assertion that boys 'run', did not toe the politically correct line. The nonsensical 'con', where players had paid money to an agent who then bought them airfares, visas and passports before disappearing in the city of their destination, was rubbished by every expert I spoke to.

It was why all was not as it seemed at the outset. One couldn't be sure that the vast number of claims of football trafficking – 7,000 in France alone from 2005 to 2014 – were genuine, not least because the majority had said they had fallen prey to a scheme which didn't make sense. It was also convenient that the 'agent' who trafficked them couldn't be traced because of the plethora of examples of identity fraud from Fifa's published list of licensed agents.

What we can be sure of is that when the chairman of a European club – Roeselare FC – and his cohorts were taken to court by Dedecker and Cluydts for the treatment of Omo Monday and Manasseh Ishiaku in 2001 in Belgium, football trafficking was not considered a crime. The pair had been complicit. They had agreed to go to Europe. So there was a legal precedent for claiming that football trafficking didn't actually exist. There were no victims. It didn't matter if an agent had abandoned a player before a trial or after a trial. The player had agreed to go. And there was, of course, the nagging doubt that so-called football trafficking victims were merely illegal immigrants adopting a story for benefits.

There is no intent with that analysis to offer an excuse for football. Just because the supply was there didn't mean there had to be a demand. Football was more than happy to take advantage. The agents and scouts like Hamid and Imari, the academy managers like Lois, and the 'big shots' like Forsythe all took their lead from the clubs. And we have learnt the lengths to which clubs would go to for even the smallest of advantages. Bottom feeders Cheltenham and Premier League wannabees Brentford held Article 19 in such low regard that they offered it for sale at pocket-money prices. At the other end of the spectrum there were clubs like Arsenal, whose manager, Arsène Wenger, had criticised the term 'child slavery' when applied to football. Arsenal's relationship with Beveren and ASEC Mimosas, the academy in Ivory Coast, had been investigated although no charges were brought. Chelsea had paid the parents of Gaël Kakuta for his signature. Then there was Barcelona and the Aspire Academy, who had both shown exactly what they thought of rules protecting minors.

All this was confirmation of the existence of the machine. At every level, aspiration is more important than the ethical and legal. It is not dissimilar to the footballer diving to be awarded a penalty. In football, you cheat to get ahead. With each passing echelon the aspiration has become grander and the hunger for more money and success harder to sate. The Hamids, the Lois's, the Cheltenhams, the Forsythes, the Barcelonas, the Qataris . . . they all wanted a slice.

Generally, the excuse given for those wanting to have their cake and eat it was the same. Education. At each step of the trafficking problem, a conman, a scout, academy or club could be found claiming that the boy would be receiving a level of education that would have not been available had he stayed at home. In Old Fadama, the traffickers made false promises to kids' families that they would take them to school. Instead they might end up at Lake Volta, risking their lives untangling fishing nets. Christopher Forsythe used education as an excuse to move players through his charity. 'We get to help the kids,' he said. 'We get the player.' Barcelona's La Masia is focused more on education than football, they have said. Aspire Dreams have claimed that their programme is almost completely humanitarian. There is no exemption under Article 19 for the education of players. FC Midtjylland found that out when they were the first club to be sanctioned.

It is the job of Fifa to ensure that aspirations do not run so wild that children are exploited. In that, they have failed. In fact, they have been guilty of making it far easier. However well intentioned their Training Compensation Scheme is, it has, in effect, monetised children, made them commodities. And as soon as a 14-year-old from Old Fadama, the Accra slum, became worth something, it was inevitable that trade in under-18 footballers would become an industry. The solidarity payments, the explosion of football in Africa – which can be linked to individual country success (Cameroon in the 1990 World Cup or the big-money transfer of Ghana's Michael Essien to Chelsea) – the 'fantasy of exile', the illegal academies, widespread poverty and migratory culture . . . all are ensuring the problem cannot be solved.

Article 19 should have prevented this. It didn't because Fifa, focused on keeping the status quo, gave the clubs a get-out. The exemption clause which stated a player's parents had to be moving to the country for non-footballing reasons effectively made the rule worthless. Any club could comfortably sidestep the rule. It was a trifling inconvenience. Look at the time and trouble agents would take to move a kid – fake passports, bridge transfers, ghost clubs.

Fifa was damned further by the statistics provided by its own Transfer Matching System unit, which proved that the exemption was not worth the paper it was written on. Huge percentages of transfers involving minors were rubber stamped for that reason. Mark Goddard, the head of the TMS, said that exemptions should be rare. But why the need for an exemption? If Fifa was serious about a curb, then it could do away with it totally. It should be forbidden to transfer a minor. No ifs, no buts. There is no other conclusion to draw.

The organisation's attitude to the problem is best summed up by the regulation of agents. Or lack of it. In the spring of 2015, agents were essentially deregulated. Previously a prospective agent had to complete a multiple-choice exam – including questions about immigration law and registration rules – with a requirement of more than 95 per cent of questions answered correctly to pass. Now the only necessary qualification is the ability to pay a £500 registration fee. Today, effectively, anyone can become an agent, or an 'intermediary' as they will officially be known. Consider the implications of that in the example of John Hawkins and Scout Network. There is no regulation of scouts, either. In just a few days, posing as a scout, I was able to price up the cost of buying a kid and the required paperwork to move him out of the country.

The reasoning behind the deregulation is stupefying. There have been such a vast number of complaints against agents – Fifa said that only 30 per cent of transfers were conducted by those with licences – that football's governing body has claimed it no longer has the resources to supervise all transfer activity. So they've scrapped any regulation. To borrow Goddard's analogy about speeding motorists, it's akin to a police force, upon discovering everyone is breaking the speed limit, deciding not to apply the law because it can't cope with the workload. A raft of agents have claimed that the move puts young players at the risk of exploitation. The Association of Football Agents (AFA) reacted by considering plans to regulate itself. Mel Stein, chairman of the AFA, said, 'It's going to create anarchy and everybody is going to be sorry about it. I can see the bloke who knows a parent or a footballer's dad saying, "I'll represent you," and then undercutting everyone.'

It is the under-18 footballer who is at most risk from this change. Unlike in England, where the Football Association has banned agents from striking deals with youngsters before they turn 16, there is no such ruling with Fifa. There is a fear that in countries where national associations are corrupt or have little power, agents will be able to bind players to contracts which, as soon as they pass 18 (the age when rules allow an agent to start being paid by the player), demand backdated money or huge, unfair sums.

'It will be a return to the "wild west" before regulation, and I'll tell you why,' Stein said. 'They're saying you can't make a charge for a professional player unless he's 18. What will happen is they won't charge anything, they'll go to the club and say, "You give us a scouting agreement for £1 million a year," and that will push it underground.'

This fiddling is consistent with Fifa's desertion of child footballers. It is a charge Fifa rejects. 'The protection of children is of major importance,' a spokesman said. 'We are convinced that all these measures [Article 19] have a positive impact on the situation of minor players.' It was reiterated that the organisation closely monitors the international transfers of under-18s and is 'ready to investigate' any 'potential' breaches.

Back in 2003 Sepp Blatter appeared to adopt a similarly hard line, using the highly emotive term 'rape' in describing European clubs' search for talent. He criticised Aspire in 2007 as a 'good example of the exploitation of dreams'. But these were shown to be empty words when, a year later, he visited Doha and changed his mind. The same year he trivialised football's slave trade when he compared Manchester United's attempts to retain Cristiano Ronaldo as 'modern slavery'. Worse followed when he washed his hands of the plight of slave workers who were building Qatar's 2022 World Cup stadia.

Such ignorance by the head of the beautiful game supplies further ugly confirmation, if any were needed, of the arrogance and selfishness that allows a modern-day slave trade to thrive. In that regard, football is stuck stubbornly in the grim past. The plantation fields have been replaced by football fields. The boys are cheap. They can be sold for profit. That's all that matters. That's all that has ever mattered.

24

The End

It was a beautiful day at Oxford United's training ground. The sky was blue, the wind gentle, and there were signs that spring had arrived. This was not a beginning, however. It was an end. The football season was drawing its last breath. When I first met Jay-Jay, the previous summer, hope had been healthy and hearty in the chests of football managers, players and supporters all over the country, at every level. For a minority, like the two Chelsea supporters who kicked a ball impishly outside Jay-Jay's kitchen window, and Diego Costa, the striker to whom they paid homage with his shirt on their backs, dreams had been realised. Almost everyone else's had disappeared long ago, leaving them through a disaffected and disappointed sigh followed by the words, 'Oh well, there's always next year.' And then there were those involved in a chest-tightening battle for survival. Oxford United were one such club. Their Football League status, and by dint their very existence due to debts in the millions and counting, was in jeopardy.

Inside the clubhouse Michael Appleton, the Oxford manager, was taking his coaches through a Powerpoint presentation. A young player had been dispatched to the local supermarket to buy some biscuits. A gaggle of players milled around. 'We gonna talk about your shagging then?' said one. 'Top shagger, me,' was the reply. An apprentice, a young dreamer, swept up the mud. Another mopped floors.

Outside, sitting on a picnic-style table, was Luke Werhun, Oxford's head of football operations, and Chris Allen, the youth team coach. They were talking about Jay-Jay. Allen, 42, had been a winger as a player, making his name with Oxford before a big-money transfer to then Premier League Nottingham Forest. He had pace to burn but was, like all wingers, enigmatic – incisive one day and invisible the next. 'You used to get into the penalty box and fall over,' I joked with him. Allen sniggered. 'Yeah, yeah, I did, didn't I? Got a lot of pens.' Allen, despite a gentle demeanour, was a hard man. He would have to be to have earned a living from the game for more than 20 years. He had been critical of the modern youth footballer, questioning their mental toughness, in the local paper, the *Oxford Mail*, reckoning it all came too easy. 'I don't know if it's because they get so much handed to them now, they're not prepared for the rigours,' he said. 'Whereas when I was their age we didn't have a great deal and we had to go and fight and scrap for everything.' Allen has been credited with helping to transform the club's youth system since he returned in 2010. The most difficult aspect of the job is telling a young player that he isn't good enough. That his time is up. 'We have 30-odd boys, and maybe we might offer just one of them a contract at the end of a season.' That's a lot of awkward conversations.

'Listen,' Werhun said. 'What do you think is best for Chris to say to Jay-Jay? To be honest, he's nowhere near good enough. Should we tell him straight?'

'Yeah, I think that would be best,' I said. 'He knows that these few days were all about getting an assessment for his future. We've talked about it. No one has told him before that he's not good enough and that's part of the problem. He needs to move on.'

Jay-Jay emerged from the changing room. He shook my hand, smiled and sat down.

'Enjoy it, Jay-Jay?' Allen said.

'Yes, yes, thank you. It was good.'

Allen took a deep breath.

Oxford's assistance with the Scout Network project had made them an obvious choice for Jay-Jay's trial. However, Simon Lenagan, who had provided an official letter stating that 'John Hawkins' was genuine, was no longer a director. The Lenagan family had sold Oxford to a consortium. The new chief executive was Mark Ashton, an engaging and effervescent Brummie. With Ashton at the helm, Oxford had, coincidentally, become the perfect club to advise Jay-Jay. Ashton knew all about the perils of football trafficking and kids like him. Just like him, in fact. When he was the chief executive of Watford, they had signed Al Bangura, an 18-year-old from Sierra Leone. His story was eerily similar to Jay-Jay's. Bangura had been granted asylum in the UK because of death threats if he returned home. How he got there was extraordinary.

Bangura had grown up in Freetown in a powerful family. His father was a leader of the Poro secret society, a disturbing force in Sierra Leone, Guinea, Liberia and the Ivory Coast. An all-male 'tribe', it used violence, intimidation, abduction and murder to maintain law in rural areas and to benefit from trade and political corruption. Boys were initiated at puberty in a process involving scarification, which often led to death, and they were taught witch-craft. When Bangura's father died, custom dictated he replace him. He refused. He was cursed and threatened with death. 'I didn't like it all,' Bangura understated. 'So I fled to Guinea.'

On the streets of Guinea's capital, where he was sleeping rough, he was befriended by a Frenchman. 'He pretended be a friend but turned out to be the devil incarnate,' Bangura has said. The Frenchman trafficked Bangura, who was 15 at the time, for sex. First to Paris, then London. 'He wanted to get me into prostitution and the homosexual business but I refused. From France he brought me to the UK and again wanted me to do the same thing, so I escaped and approached the Home Office to seek asylum.' It could have been Jay-Jay talking.

That was where the parallel finished. Bangura quickly launched a career in professional football. He had begun by training alone in a park and then joined Chertsey Town, where he was scouted by Watford. He went on to win promotion to the Premier League, earned a six-figure salary and played 16 times in the top flight. In another coincidence, his agent was Eby Emenike. His career had declined, however, and he ended up in non-league football at Forest Green Rovers. The government had tried to deport him and, at an asylum and immigration tribunal, Bangura had been accused of lying about being sex trafficked. But after support from Ashton, Aidy Boothroyd, then Watford manager, MPs and the pop star Elton John (a well-known Watford fan), Bangura was allowed to stay.

'It sounds just like what happened to Al,' Ashton told me on the phone as I explained Jay-Jay's situation. 'It's so, so sad. We'll do anything we can so, absolutely, let's get him in for a trial to help him out.'

The help that Jay-Jay needed was an honest appraisal of whether he had a future in football. He had not received any feedback about his strengths or weaknesses from trials at Cambridge, Wimbledon, Brentford or Cheltenham. Despite confidence in his ability – over-confidence one might say given the way he criticised teammates for being 'lazy' – never had he been told at what level could he expect to play. He was in desperate need of guidance. As he said when we last met, he didn't know whether he should be pursuing his 'dream' or concentrating on becoming a mechanic or electrician.

'I'll get it sorted,' Ashton had said. 'What you're telling me about him paying for trials and then not being told where he's going wrong is very unfair on so many levels. We'll get him in, Chris [Allen] can have a good look at him and we can advise him the best route forward.' I warned Ashton not to expect the next Pelé. 'If I'm being honest with you, Mark, he's really not very good, which makes his story even more upsetting. I took him to Cheltenham for a trial and it was embarrassing how bad he was. But he needs a bit of a reality check because I'm worried he's wasting his time. He needs to move on with his life.'

Oxford liaised with Jay-Jay's social worker, Ahmed. A three-day assessment was arranged. It was a trial in all but name. Jay-Jay was told that he would be assessed by the coaches, who could then tell him how best to pursue a career and at what level. It was not a trial to earn a professional contract. Social services paid for Jay-Jay's train tickets and accommodation. Oxford agreed to pick him up from his hotel and take him back in the evening.

I attended his first day and stood on the touchline with Ahmed and Luke Werhun. Jay-Jay had been grouped with Oxford's under-18s, so at 20 he was over-age. He had improved markedly since the trial at Cheltenham. His control and shooting accuracy was sharper. 'I tell you what, he's OK, isn't he?' said Werhun. 'I was expecting him to be really bad after what you'd said.'

Ahmed, the social worker, admitted 'he wasn't into football' but was grateful to Oxford for helping Jay-Jay find his true calling. It was time, he said, for him to consider that he might not have what it takes to become a professional. 'He's a great boy,' Ahmed said. 'He's what we call "gold standard" because he's well-behaved, he attends college, he's showing signs of progression in education and language skills. But he can't keep going to the trials, spending money, getting nowhere. He needs to think about a career. I've said to him before, "How great would it be if you could learn a trade?" But he always brings it back to football.'

'So,' Allen had begun, 'we love your energy, your enthusiasm, your work rate. We thought, "Really good stuff." But what you need to do is improve your technical ability, dealing with the ball, getting decent contact with your shots. So at the moment you're quite a way off professional standard. But if you work really, really hard, then who knows?'

Jay-Jay didn't say anything. He stared at the ground. He bit off a piece of dead skin on his bottom lip and chewed it.

'Perfect on work rate, energy, keep that,' Allen continued. 'But practise, practise, practise on controlling the ball, dealing with the ball and getting shots off and then you can focus on tactics. Try to get your technical game up. You're not ready to play professionally at this level. Maybe go down, three or four levels below. What do you reckon?'

Jay-Jay shrugged his shoulders. 'It's good about the technical things but the coach can give that for the player.'

'Ed said that you've not been playing regularly for one team,' Allen said. 'I think you've got to pick a team and play for them the whole season.'

'Sometimes I change teams because I want to progress quickly and I don't think the team is very good.' This was Jay-Jay, once again, appearing to blame others for his shortcomings.

I thought it was time for a dose of reality. I asked Allen whether he thought it would be best for Jay-Jay to play part-time football with one club and look to learn a trade or a skill.

'Absolutely,' he replied. 'Then you're getting an income, learning a trade as well as playing a good standard of football that suits your ability. That is a great route. You can grasp it but you need to knuckle down and work hard. You hear the stories all the time of players in non-league getting contracts from pro clubs. It happens. Be settled. It's not great going from one club to the other. Find one that suits your ability and try to do something outside football, because they only train twice a week. Learn a new skill outside of football. What do you think?'

'I think I love football,' Jay-Jay said. His voice was quiet and he had brought up his hands in a cross to cover his chest. He leant forward slightly. 'I want to play football. Since I came to England I don't improve my skill, if you don't do training you don't learn.'

Jay-Jay didn't appear to have taken in what Allen had said. He could still play football, he could still train. It just wouldn't be with a professional team. A veteran of such conversations with youngsters, Allen perhaps recognised that he needed to be tougher.

'Are you going to walk into a pro club and get a contract?' Allen said. 'That's not going to happen. I know what you're thinking. You want to be in a full-time environment where you can practise all the time. But you can also supplement practice with five-a-side leagues, less players, more touches of the ball. That again improves your control. That's another idea. So have a Saturday team and play five-a-side leagues. There's plenty of those in London. But I think, professionally, you're not there yet, Jay-Jay. If you keep going for that now it'll be a waste of your time. You're not there yet. I know you enjoy the full-time aspect and enjoy playing with lads at a decent level but you need to find your level. You'll go to another club and they'll say the same, and then to another and they'll say the same.'

'I think what we're worried about, Jay-Jay,' I said, 'is the trials you keep paying for. We're just trying to save you money and time. Best thing is to pick a team, learn a trade. Knuckle down and do it that way.'

It was too much. Jay-Jay pulled at the skin between thumb and forefinger alternately on each hand. He looked like a school kid who had been severely scolded by the headmaster. I was transported back to that day when I first met him. The awkward silence. The uncomfortable realisation that there was a person suffering in front of your eyes and you didn't know what to say. Pools of tears had formed in Jay-Jay's eyes.

'Keep playing, Jay-Jay,' Allen implored. 'That's what you've got to do, keep playing. Be the best player in your team. But you've got to be realistic, that's what's causing the problem at the minute.'

But Jay-Jay had stopped listening. He began to sob and he pulled at his hands with increasing anxiety. The tears came like a river. They fell down his pockmarked face. 'When I think about my life . . . it's getting difficult. I was doing well at home at my football and when I come here it has gone wrong for me.'

The sobs had grown louder. He held his head in his hands. He didn't want to see any more, he didn't want to hear. Allen, Werhun and I looked at each other. It wasn't said, but we were all thinking the same: 'Christ, I didn't expect this.' I had not learnt from my previous meetings with Jay-Jay. His pain was never far from the surface.

But then why wouldn't he react like that? Since his arrival in England, in such awful circumstances, football had been the light at the end of a gloomy tunnel. It had gone out. He had been left alone in the dark, where memories lurked of people wanting to kill and abuse him. It had been an unreal life, so one couldn't be surprised that he could not recognise realism when it hit. To him, it was not an impossible dream that he could walk into a professional club and earn a contract. Being told that he would have to graft in amateur football and play five-a-side was not how they tell you it's going to be in West Africa. The scouts, the agents, the child abusers have grander promises than that. The stars that the likes of Jay-Jay watched on television back home didn't have to roll up their sleeves in park football. They didn't first have to learn how to be a car mechanic. They drove the car. An expensive one with a trophy girlfriend in the passenger seat.

There followed a period of desperate appeasement by the three of us, all stunned by the outpouring of emotion.

'You can still make it,' Allen whispered to him, placing a comforting hand on his shoulder.

'Jay-Jay, if you play non-league football and you do well you will be scouted,' Werhun said.

'It's just hard work, Jay-Jay,' I said. 'You're not afraid of that, are you?' No answer. He bit his hand so hard pink teeth marks were left on his skin. His face was stained with silver streaks where the tears had dried. 'Shall we go to McDonald's?' I said. 'Like we did after Cheltenham.' He shook his head.

'Hey,' said Allen, shaking him on the shoulder, perhaps deciding enough was enough. 'Pick yourself up now. Be Strong. You're a big, strong boy. It's not the end.'

It probably was the end. After sitting and staring straight down for a further five minutes, and further attempts to raise him from the doldrums by Allen, Jay-Jay looked broken as he walked off to collect his bag. Werhun puffed out his cheeks. Allen raised his eyebrows.

'That was tough,' Werhun said.

'Yeah,' I said. 'Wasn't expecting that. But no one's ever been straight with him before. Cruel to be kind, I guess.'

I didn't believe that, actually. I regretted it. Jay-Jay, patently, had not been robust enough for rejection. Who was I to decide that he needed to move on with his life? He had been happier that way. I had made him miserable in the belief that, in the long run, it would be to his benefit. There was no guarantee. Maybe I would be proved right, but I couldn't be there to help him through the difficult days or weeks which would follow. He was on his own, without friends or family. He was lost. I had not thought of that. I could go home and talk to my wife about what had happened. Jay-Jay would go back to his dank ground-floor flat with mould on the ceiling and cracks in the wall. Alone and utterly bereft. And he would cry. Because he wasn't a footballer. Because he missed his family. Because he had been abused. That's what the tears were really about. He had been abused. I felt sick. Once again I cursed myself for being just a sports writer. I should have shown more empathy, more understanding. I should have listened more to what he had to say. Asked more questions, tried to counsel him. In the void where compassion should have been, I tried to fill it with bravado about how the football industry worked and what I thought would be best for him. He was railroaded into the 'trial' with Oxford because I said he needed to 'move on'. I didn't ask whether he wanted to 'move on'. Well, I did, and he said he did. But, hell, Jay-Jay might not have even understood the question. Just like he didn't understand, clearly, that the trial at Oxford wasn't actually a trial. I had ploughed on, unthinking. Hadn't I behaved much like the rogue agents? The player had done what I had wanted him to do. What I had told him to do. And to hell with the consequences. When the player failed the trial, I had abandoned him. Washed my hands of him. Out of my life.

I felt guilt, too, for doubting his story, questioning him when I spoke to Richard Hoskins, the criminologist, and Solange Cluydts, the anti-trafficking charity worker in Belgium. Despite both experts saying they believed him, a little bit of faith in Jay-Jay had died, not helped by his arrogant attitude to trials. Perhaps that's why I had disregarded his feelings and pressed on regardless with the three days at Oxford.

In the car to Oxford station, Jay-Jay looked solemnly ahead in silence. Just like he had when I had driven him to Cheltenham at the start of the season. I kept asking if he was OK, whether he was sure he didn't want to go to McDonald's. Yes, that had been the best I could do. Before leaving him to catch his train back to London I told him I was sorry. That I wouldn't have organised the trial had I known he would have reacted like that. In a final bid for conciliation I told him that he should call me at any time if he needed help. Perhaps I could go to watch him play soon? But maybe that's what all the agents say.

'Football is my dream,' he said. 'I am confused now. It is not coming true?' Jay-Jay let out a heavy and hurt sigh, as if he had released hope into the spring air. 'Thank you for trying to help me, friend.' Then he turned and walked away.

Glossary and Cast of Characters

Accra:
Capital city of Ghana, where I visited to understand the social and football culture and work undercover for Scout Network.

Phaedra Al-Majid:
'Fifa whistleblower' who revealed that Qatar had paid Fifa members to vote for them to host the 2022 World Cup. Heavily criticised the Aspire Dreams programme.

Amane:
Trafficked from Ivory Coast to Europe via a migrant boat at the age of 16. Poster boy for Foot Solidaire.

Anti-Slavery International:
Charity which doubted that players would be trafficked for football purposes only.

Arsenal:
Found to have invested in Beveren, the Belgian club which fielded players from the Ivory Coast academy, ASEC Mimosas.

Article 19:
Fifa's law to protect under-18s, written in 2003. No player under the age of 18 should be subject to an international transfer. There were three exceptions to the rule: the player's parent(s) moves to the country for

reasons not linked to football; the transfer takes place within the territory of the European Union or European Economic Area; the player lives no further than 50 kilometres from a national border and the club with which the player wishes to be registered in the neighbouring association is also within 50 kilometres of that border.

ASEC Mimosas:

Academy in Ivory Coast which produced players including Yaya and Kolo Touré. Were a feeder club for Beveren, a Belgium club. BBC *Newsnight* revealed Arsenal had invested in Beveren in 2001. It also found Arsène Wenger was an investor in ASEC. Arsenal bought Kolo Touré from Beveren.

Aspire Academy:

Futuristic Olympic sports and football academy in Doha, Qatar. Funded by the Al-Thani royal family. Hosted Aspire Dreams scholars.

Aspire Football Dreams:

Qatar's talent-scouting project which targeted 13-year-olds all over the world for scholarships in Doha and Senegal.

Charlie Baffour:

London-based Fifa-licensed agent who met with Simon Lenagan and me in London to discuss taking underage players to Oxford United.

Barcelona:

Handed a 14-month transfer ban by Fifa for signing six players from overseas under the age of 18 to their La Masia academy, a breach of Article 19.

Craig Bellamy:

Former Wales international striker who set up an academy in Ivory Coast.

Ben:

Footballer who at 16 paid an unscrupulous agent €3,000 to take him from Cameroon to Paris for trials at clubs. He was told to wait at a hotel. The agent did not return.

Beveren:
Belgian club which fielded an all-African XI in the early 2000s, largely thanks to an agreement with ASEC Mimosas.

Sepp Blatter:
Former president of Fifa, football's governing body, laid the blame firmly at the feet of Europe's clubs for football's trafficking problem. He said they were 'neo-colonialists who don't give a damn about heritage and culture but engage in social and economic rape by robbing the developing world of its best players'. He called the recruitment of children from Africa 'unhealthy if not despicable'. Criticised the Aspire Academy in Qatar for much the same but performed a U-turn after visiting Doha in 2008.

Andreas Bleicher:
Head of the Aspire Dreams project.

Erin Bowser:
Works for the Ghana office of the International Organisation for Migration, the anti-trafficking charity headed by William Swing. Revealed some of the methods of the traffickers.

Brentford:
English Championship club which charged footballers for trials, including underage players from outside the EU, despite work-permit rules and Article 19 preventing them being signed on the professional contract that was on offer.

Chelsea:
Banned by Fifa for signing players for two transfer windows for inducing Gaël Kakuta, a 16-year-old from RC Lens, to break his contract with the French club.

Cheltenham Town:
English League Two club which charged footballers for trials, including underage players from outside the EU, despite work-permit rules and Article 19 preventing them being signed on the professional contract that was on offer.

Solange Cluydts:
Works for Payoke, the charity which investigated the cases of Omo Monday and Manasseh Ishiaku. Former director of immigration at Zaventem airport and had worked for the Centre for Equal Opportunities and Opposition to Racism in Brussels.

Dr Paul Darby:
Senior lecturer in sport and exercise at the University of Ulster who researched exhaustively African football labour migration and denounced the Aspire Dreams project.

Jean-Marie Dedecker:
Former Belgian politician who investigated football trafficking and was responsible for the rise in the minimum wage for foreign players in the country. Took the case of Omo Monday and Manasseh Ishiaku to court.

Didier:
Footballer from Cameroon who went to the Aspire Academy in Doha at 13. Was 'sold' to an agent in Argentina who beat and racially abused him and told his mother to fake her death certificate so he could sign for a club.

Eby Emenike:
London-based Fifa-licensed agent. Revealed the anatomy of child football trafficking. Was agent to Al Bangura, the former Watford player who was sex trafficked from Guinea.

Michael Essien:
Former Liberty Professionals player who, when he signed for Chelsea, inspired a generation of young Ghanaian footballers and their families.

James Esson:
Lecturer in human geography at Loughborough University who has written extensively on football slavery.

Old Fadama:
Largest Accra slum, which the locals call Sodom and Gomorrah.

Farook:
11-year-old from Old Fadama, Accra, who works in one of largest digital waste dumps in the world.

Feyenoord Fetteh:
One of the first football academies in West Africa. Launched in 1999, it was a joint partnership between Feyenoord, the Dutch club, the Ghanaian Sports Ministry and tribal chiefs. Was subsumed by the West African Football Academy, or Wafa for short. Such academies gave rise to charge of 'neo-colonialism'.

Fieldoo:
Football social networking site which connects players with scouts and agents. Used by Som Kalou, my fake footballer, to find Hamid.

FifPro:
Worldwide players' union.

Foot Solidaire:
Charity set up to counter football trafficking by the former Cameroon international, Jean-Claude Mbvoumin. Reported that there were 7,000 cases in France alone in nine years from 2005.

FootballCV:
English company who charged footballers for trials, including underage players from outside the EU, despite work-permit rules and Article 19 preventing triallists being signed.

Christopher Forsythe:
Agent banned by Ghana FA for his role in a match-fixing sting. Revealed anatomy of trade in kids to 'John'.

Frank:
19-year-old footballer from Ghana who Lois had adopted and took to Larnaca. Was still in Larnaca after his visa had expired.

Gabriel:
Ghanaian footballer who had been trafficked to Cyprus and had ended up working without pay as a hotel caretaker.

George:
21-year-old footballer from Ghana who Lois had taken to Larnaca.

Mark Goddard:
Manager of the Fifa Transfer Matching System.

Jean-Marc Guillou:
Close friend of Arsène Wenger, the Arsenal manager. Ran the academy at ASEC Mimosas.

Ralph Gyambrah:
Business partner of Christopher Forsythe.

Asamoah Gyan:
Former Liberty Professionals player and star of the Ghana national team.

Stewart Hall:
Football coach for 30 years who has worked all over the world and extensively in Africa. Suggested traffickers could be moving players for match-fixing purposes.

Hamid:
Agent from Lanrnaca, Cyprus, who told Som Kalou to pay him €1,000 for a visa. Arranged a trial match with 21 Africans for Scout Network and discussed ways to circumnavigate Article 19.

John Hawkins:
Founder of Scout Network. My cover name when speaking to agents and scouts.

Richard Hoskins:
Criminologist and expert in trafficking and African religion. Doubted that players would be trafficked for football purposes only.

Imari:
In partnership with Hamid. In 2002 he was detained in Cyprus, with two teammates, following arrest by immigration officials. Claimed to have been trafficked from Russia.

International Centre for Sport and Security (ICSS):
A sort of self-proclaimed police force for world sport, funded by the Qatari royal family. Tried to counter match-fixing and trafficking of minors.

International Transfer Certificate (ITC):
For a player to move abroad he must have an ITC. It is ratified by Fifa's Transfer Matching System and released by the association of the selling club.

Manasseh Ishiaku:
17-year-old Nigerian footballer who said he was trafficked in 2001 by Roeselare FC, a Belgian first division club.

Jamestown:
Accra slum more famous for producing boxers, but Samuel (agent and my guide) claimed would soon produce a raft of football stars due to the desperation and large number of academies.

Jay-Jay:
Sex trafficked at 17 from Guinea to London under the false promise of career in football. I took him to trials at Cheltenham Town and Oxford United.

Joseph Kaltim:
16-year-old Nigerian footballer who was sent a false trial invitation letter from Queens Park Rangers. Was the inspiration for Som Kalou.

KAS Eupen:
Belgian second division club effectively bought by the Aspire Academy in 2012.

Lake Volta:
Ghana reservoir, largest in the world. Children as young as four are sold to fishermen, often under the guise of football, who use them to untangle nets from trees below the water line.

George Lamperty:
Coach of Liberty Professionals.

Larnaca:
City in Cyprus where I posed as John Hawkins for Scout Network to uncover the 'cell' of Hamid, Mohamed Opong Imari and Lois.

Simon Lenagan:
Former director at Oxford United. Provided me with a letter from the club to convince agents that Scout Network was a bona fide operation.

Liberty Professionals:
Ghanaian Premier League team with no interest in winning matches, only in producing young talent to sell to Europe. Have produced Michael Essien, Asamoah Gyan and Sulley Muntari.

Lois:
Academy manager in Accra. Claimed she had sent seven underage players to Europe. Boasted about using the influence of her sister at Ghanaian embassies to get visas. Advised Scout Network about the illegal 'bridge transfer'. Said she adopted boys to make it easier to move players.

David Mallinger:
Founder and director of FootballCV. Director at Corby Town and Kettering Town.

Manchester City:
Admitted involvement with Right to Dream Academy, Ghana, and refused to deny they part-funded the operation. By 2013 City had signed six Right to Dream graduates.

Jake Marsh:
Head of child protection at the International Centre for Sport and Security. Revealed the anatomy of child football trafficking.

Mathieu:
Volunteer with Foot Solidaire.

Jean-Claude Mbvoumin:
Founder of Foot Solidaire, the anti-trafficking charity. Former Cameroon international.

Darragh McGee:
Lived in Accra and had worked as a football coach at academies in the city, including Feyenoord Fetteh. He is an academic, a faculty member of the school for health at the University of Bath, and has authored a paper on child trafficking in sport.

'Mehdi':
Formerly part of the Aspire Dreams management group. Criticised the project for the attempted naturalisation of players.

FC Midtjylland:
Danish club which, in 2007, became one of the first to fall foul of Article 19 when they were found to have imported 17-year-olds from a feeder club in Nigeria.

Roger Milla:
Former Cameroon striker and star of the 1990 World Cup who had been a 'roving ambassador' for Foot Solidaire.

Bora Milutinović:
Serbian coach and former manager of the USA, Mexican and Nigerian national sides (among others), and ambassador for the Aspire Academy, Qatar. Boasted that from 2007 to 2013, 3.7 million children had been screened by the Aspire Football Dreams programme.

Miyu Mitake-Leroy:
Japanese translator hired to help me interview Shinji.

Omo Monday:
16-year-old Nigerian footballer who said he was trafficked in 2001 by Roeselare FC, a Belgian first division club.

Sulley Muntari:
Former Liberty Professionals player and star of the Ghana national team.

James Murphy:
Organised the trials for Cheltenham Town. Said they accepted players from Africa, Australia, New Zealand and Canada.

Cardinal Vincent Nichols:
Archbishop of Westminster who, in 2014 at an anti-trafficking conference in London, demanded more information about football's slave trade.

Oxford United:
League Two club which provided a letter of authenticity to Scout Network. Also staged a three-day trial for Jay-Jay.

Payoke:
Belgian anti-trafficking charity who Solange Cluydts works for.

Player passport:
Records details of each club or academy a player has played for, and for how long, so monies due under Fifa's Training Compensation Scheme can be worked out.

Right to Dream Academy:
Based in Ghana, run by Tom Vernon, a former coach at Manchester United. Manchester City would not deny that they part-funded the academy.

Roadside academy:
Known as 'neighbourhood teams' and operated on an informal basis, the roadside academy phenomenon is hugely prevalent in West Africa. Academy managers hope to find the next Michael Essien to sell to a European scout or Ghanaian professional team. Would waive rights to the Training Compensation Scheme because they are not affiliated to national associations. At the bottom of the three-tier football system in West Africa.

Roeselare FC:
Belgian first division club involved with Omo Monday and Manasseh Ishiaku, although Roger Havegeer, the president, was found not guilty of human trafficking.

Samuel:
Agent with small stakes in lower division clubs in Ghana. My guide in Accra.

Schengen:
Visa which allows the holder to move freely between 26 European countries, although not the UK and Ireland. They cost about €150. Tino, the Accra underworld figure, charged €7,000 to secure a Schengen.

Scout Network:
Fake talent-search company set up to help expose the methods used by agents to move under-18 footballers from country to country.

Shinji:
21-year-old Japanese footballer present at Football Solidaire/UN conference in the company of Jean-Claude Mbvoumin.

Slave contract:
Player contract heavily in favour of the club and the agent. It might include a meagre salary, or in some cases no wage at all. Often expenses or the rent for an apartment are all that is offered.

Graham Starmer:
Managing director of FootballCV and vice-chairman of Corby Town.

Sulley:
Footballer from Burkina Faso who went to Portugal at 16 only for his agent to ditch him when he couldn't find him a club. Had travelled to Paris in search of a team and was destitute.

William Swing:
Director general of the International Organisation for Migration who spoke at the Geneva conference at the UN organised by Foot Solidaire.

Al Thani family:
Royal family of Qatar. Have invested heavily in sport and football, including in the Aspire Academy, Barcelona and Paris Saint-Germain. Bankrolled Qatar's World Cup bid.

Tino:
Accra underworld figure capable of illegally obtaining passports, birth certificates and visas for the purpose of football trafficking.

Transfer Matching System (TMS):
Launched in 2010, the TMS regulates the international transfer market, ensuring data from both the selling club and buying club match. Designed to prevent fraud, money laundering and trafficking of underage players.

Unicef:
World's largest children's charity, which benefited from a sponsorship deal with Barcelona. Refused to condemn the club for breach of Article 19.

West African Football Academy:
One of the largest academies in West Africa. Incorporated the Feyenoord Fetteh academy and Red Bull academy.

Work-permit regulations:
In the UK a club can only sign a non-EU passport holder if he is an international from a country ranked within Fifa's top 70 and has played in 75 per cent of his country's international matches in the preceding two years. In 2015 the English FA introduced new rules to make it harder to sign non-EU players, including restricting imports to only the top 50 ranked countries.

Bibliography and Sources

Foot Solidaire:
'Fifa "abandons" child trafficking campaign', *Guardian*, 4 February 2010
'Qatar finalists', *When Saturday Comes*, March 2008
'Premier League foreign players by club and country 1992–93 to 2014–15', MyFootballFacts.com

Scout Network:
'Mpong escapes death threat after refusing dodgy deal in Turkey', Ghanasoccernet.com, 31 July 2012
'Agent denies Mpong death threat story', Modernghana.com, 15 August 2012
'All set for Sunderland–Kotoko clash', Sunderland AFC Facebook page, 12 July 2013

Drawing the Sting:
'What is a bridge transfer?' Lawinsport.com, 30 April 2014
'Argentinian and Uruguayan clubs sanctioned for bridge transfers', Fifa.com, 5 March 2014

'I Have Integrity':
'World Cup turning moments: Cameroon stun Argentina in 1990', *Guardian*, 12 February 2014
'Fifa "abandons" child trafficking campaign', *Guardian*, 4 February 2010

England Exploits:

The Nowhere Men: the Unknown Story of Football's True Talent Spotters, Michael Calvin, Century, 2013

'Open trials', Brentfordfc.co.uk, 23 August 2014

Slave Trade:

'Modern slavery, child trafficking, and the rise of West African football academies', James Esson, opendemocracy.net, 15 January 2015

'Study on the transfer system in Europe 2011–2014', European Club Association

'Making football dreams come true', BBC Sport, 17 October 2014

'Football academies and the migration of African football labor to Europe', Paul Darby, Gerard Akindes and Matthew Kirwin, *Journal of Sport and Social Issues*, May 2007

'Arsenal face Fifa investigation', BBC *Newsnight*, 1 June 2006

'FA inquiry: *Newsnight* statement', BBC, 23 June 2006

Out of Africa:

Sport and Migration: Borders, Boundaries and Crossings, edited by Joseph Maguire and Mark Falcous, Routledge, 2010

'The scandal of Africa's trafficked players', *Guardian*, 6 January 2008

'Europe's ethical dilemma over migrants', BBC News, 3 January 2015

'Fighters exploit trafficking routes to get into Europe', *The Times*, 4 February 2015

The Forsythe Saga:

'Football match-fixing deal casts cloud over World Cup', *Daily Telegraph*, 23 June 2014

'Football match-fixing: the key figures', *Daily Telegraph*, 23 June 2014

'We Don't Care Who You Are':

'Fifa's new transfer system will cut through "jungle"', *Daily Telegraph*, 24 February 2010

'Barcelona transfer ban: *La Liga* giants cannot sign players until 2016 after CAS reject appeal', *Independent*, 30 December 2014

'Thousands of children have been traded already', *Sport Executive* magazine, February 2015

'Danish football club reported to FIFA for trafficking of young players',
  Playthegame.org, 23 February 2007
'Chelsea hit by transfer ban for stealing young French star', *Daily Mail*,
  6 September 2009

Aspire:
'Fifa whistleblower Phaedra Al-Majid fears for her safety', BBC Sport,
  20 November 2014
'Qatar's bid for soccer respect', *New York Times*, 14 July 2014
'Qatari soccer empire buys a foothold in Europe', *New York Times*, 15
  July 2014
'FIFA whistleblower Phaedra Al-Majid: I will have to look over my
  shoulder for rest of my life after revelations over World Cup bids . . .
  I have already had FBI agents at my door', *Daily Mail*, 20 November
  2014
'Qatar handball team coach faces questions over foreign players', BBC
  News, 29 January 2015
'Qatar finalists', *When Saturday Comes*, March 2008
'Fifa Chief Sepp Blatter expresses support for Aspire's vision and
  mission', Albawaba.com, 14 February 2008
'Aspire Africa Football Dreams – largest football talent search in history
  launched in Qatar', PR Newswire, 19 April 2007
'Sepp Blatter: Qatar World Cup workers' welfare is not Fifa's respon-
  sibility', *Guardian*, 2 December 2014
'How Qatar became a world force', *Guardian*, 18 November 2013
'World Cup chief asked for favours from Qatar', *Daily Telegraph*, 7 July
  2015
'Thailand FA chief handed suspended jail term', Associated Press,
  23 July 2015
'Fifa boss's secret World Cup deal with Qataris', *Sunday Times*, 12 April
  2015

'Please Help Me':
'The dark side of football transfers', *Daily Telegraph*, 31 December
  2014

Lost Boys:
'Wave of violence hits Guinea', christiantoday.co.uk, 1 August 2013

Run:

'Trafficking for forced criminal activities and begging in Europe', Anti-Slavery International, September 2014

'Better off at home? Rethinking responses to trafficked West African footballers in Europe', James Esson, *Journal of Ethnic and Migration Studies*, 2014

Searching for the Truth:

'The muscle drain of African players to Europe: trade or trafficking?', Jonas Scherrens, 2006–07

'The lost continent', *When Saturday Comes*, August 1997

Amane's Story:

United Nations Office of Drugs and Crime, Smuggling of Migrants from West Africa to Europe, 2008–2011

The Perfect Storm:

'Football agent rule changes "could leave young players exploited"', BBC Sport, 1 April 2015

'Football agents want to regulate themselves and warn against Fifa's "irresponsible" plans, *Daily Mirror*, 16 November 2013

'Football agents fear "Wild West"', *Guardian*, 13 March 2015

The End:

'Fear of forced initiation into the Poro secret society in Freetown', Country of Origin Research and Information (CORI), refworld.org, 6 March 2009

'Watford manager backs player at asylum tribunal', *Guardian*, 26 November 2007

'Bangoura looks to football future', BBC Sport, 5 April 2006

'A sudden jolt of violence and a bloody corpse', *Independent*, 30 May 2010

Acknowledgements

Thanks to all the interviewees who gave up their time. Special praise to Simon Lenagan for his door-opening letter, Mark Ashton and his staff at Oxford United for taking Jay-Jay on trial and Darragh McGee's help. Also thanks to Vic Brewer, Celeste Hicks, Sule Lansah, Lars Andersson, Marie-Louise Albers, Steve Eder, Brian Blickenstaff, Eleanor Drywood, Hans Vendeweghe, Celia Clements and Miyu Mitake-Leroy. Charlotte Atyeo and Ian Preece were supportive and diligent respectively. Immeasurable gratitude to F for patience, wisdom and gratis editing.